HEALTHFUL
HERBS

from
Back to Eden

HEALTHFUL HERBS

from
Back to Eden

Jethro Kloss

THUNDER BAY
P·R·E·S·S

San Diego, California

Thunder Bay Press

THUNDER BAY
P·R·E·S·S

An imprint of the Advantage Publishers Group
10350 Barnes Canyon Road, San Diego, CA 92121
www.thunderbaybooks.com

"Thunder Bay" is a registered trademark of Baker & Taylor. All rights reserved.

Text © Jethro Kloss 1988 (Revised and Expanded Second Edition published by
Back to Eden books, Loma Linda, California), published in 1999 as *Back To Eden*,
Revised and Expanded Second Edition by Lotus Press, Twin Lakes, Wisconsin.

Design and layout © 2008 by Ivy Press Limited

This 2008 edition published by Baker & Taylor
by arrangement with the Ivy Press.

This book was conceived, designed, and produced by Ixos, an imprint of

Ivy Press
The Old Candlemakers
West Street, Lewes,
East Sussex BN7 2NZ, U.K.
www.ivy-group.co.uk

Creative Director Peter Bridgewater
Publisher David Alexander
Editorial Director Caroline Earle
Art Director Clare Harris
Senior Editor Lorraine Turner
Design Michael Morey
Picture Research Joanna Clinch, Katie Greenwood, Sarah Skeate

This book contains the opinions and ideas of its authors. It is intended to provide
helpful and informative material on the subjects addressed in this book. It is sold with
the understanding that the author and publisher are not engaged in rendering medical,
health, or any other kind of personal professional services in the book. The reader should
consult his or her medical, health, or other competent professional before adopting any
of the suggestions in this book or drawing inferences from it. The authors and publisher
disclaim all responsibility for any liability, loss, or risk, personal or otherwise, which is
incurred as a consequence, directly or indirectly, of the use and application of any of the
contents of this book.

ISBN-13: 978-1-59223-870-5
ISBN-10: 1-59223-870-X

Library of Congress Cataloging-in-Publication data available upon request.

Printed and bound in Thailand.

1 2 3 4 5 12 11 10 09 08

Contents

Jethro Kloss

Jethro Kloss and the Rediscovery of Natural Medicine

Jethro Kloss ranks among the greatest herbalists of all time. Born in 1863, on a large Wisconsin farm as the ninth child of pioneering parents, his rural upbringing gave him a knowledge and understanding of "natural" medicine— the practical application of homemade, largely herbal remedies, and good diet to promote healthy living.

Kloss devoted himself to the promotion of healthy lifestyles, and his vocation culminated in 1939 with the publication of his great work, *Back to Eden.* This best-selling book is a digest of over half a century's experience of developing what the 21st century might call "alternative" remedies, but which, in much of 19th-century America, were the only medicine. Kloss himself put it simply: "This book contains inexpensive remedies for the prevention of disease and sickness: treatments that are the result of my own practical experience." As he also pointed out, this experience was part of a tradition stretching back through the centuries, to Elizabethan herbalists such as Culpeper and even the earliest recorded physicians of Ancient Greece.

At the age of 20, Kloss moved away from Wisconsin, and began a career that took him to many parts of the United States of America, working in a variety of different medical institutions, before opening his own small hospital, or sanitorium, assisted by his wife, at St. Peter, Minnesota, in 1907.

In *Back to Eden*, Kloss cites many case studies from his early experiences as a natural healer. In an age and place when scientific medicine was expensive, and quack doctors and remedies were still a common trap for the unwary, Kloss's basic, common-sense approach with its emphasis on rigorous hygiene and methods of supporting the body's own self-healing mechanisms were a godsend to many of the ordinary people whom he assisted. At the same time, Kloss also drew on the long traditions of herbal medicines to encourage his patients to use the natural remedies that were gradually being lost to an increasingly urban population in the United States. In the original *Back to Eden*, Kloss writes: "The use of herbs in the written record actually dates back for several thousands of years BC. The Chinese, Sumerians, and Egyptians used plants for medicinal purposes. A Chinese book on herbs, dated around 2700 BC, lists over 300 plants with their medicinal uses."

Natural remedies

None of this is to say that Kloss was unsympathetic to modern medicine. He recognized the limits of his own methods—for instance, he warned acute appendicitis sufferers: "You should seek competent medical help immediately. Any significant delay may result in dangerous complications." But Kloss also realized that there was much that could be done with natural remedies, both to prevent illness, and to treat illnesses when modern medical treatments were not available.

The world has changed beyond recognition since Jethro Kloss first practised his natural medicine, yet many of his methods remain as valuable today as they were on the Wisconsin farmstead of his youth in the 1860s and 1870s.

Herbal remedies can still be used to alleviate many everyday ailments, and, when so many people lead hectic, demanding, and stressful lives, Kloss's advice on staying healthy is as necessary as ever. *Healthful Herbs* distills the wisdom recorded in *Back to Eden* and makes it accessible for yet another new generation in the 21st century.

THE KLOSS ETHOS

For Jethro Kloss, promoting healthy living was not only a humanitarian endeavor but also a practical application of his religious beliefs. A Christian and licensed minister, his work rests on the conviction that "Miraculous things are found in the Bible and in Nature . . . Our Heavenly Father sees the world's untold suffering and wretchedness. He has made provision that if we use these things He has provided they will surely bring relief. Read about the wonderful properties that are in trees, herbs, flowers, and roots, and leaves of the trees, which the Holy Book says are for our medicine."

Using Herbs

The Remedial Properties of Herbs

The great remedial properties of herbs and the juices of fruits and vegetables have been recognized and appreciated from time immemorial. Only since the 16th century have people been looking for, and depending on, medicines artificially prepared from chemicals. People have been diverted from the true healing remedies by misleading advertising. Chemical poisons are now very convenient to obtain and are quick-acting. People were deceived for a time, but at last they are seeing the effects of drugs and their evil aftereffects, and are looking for something better.

When the Saxon invaders entered Great Britain they took with them much knowledge concerning herbal healing. It is well-known that they made frequent use of the dandelion, comfrey, nettle, burdock, and other common wayside herbs in treating the sick. A knowledge was planted that grew until it has become customary to have an "herb garden" in England. What a blessing it

Even the most common plants can make effective herbal medicine.

would be to the homes in this land if our children were taught the value of raspberry leaves, thyme, sage, peppermint, yarrow, and dozens of other wayside herbs. More than half the sickness and deaths in early life would be unknown, and chronic sufferers would be a curiosity. Only those who know the value of herbal remedies can appreciate the wonderful effects that a knowledge of the herbs we tread underfoot daily would produce.

With all our boasted knowledge, we have to admit that the North American Indians and the natives of other countries, though unskilled in letters and without any knowledge of anatomy, physiology, or chemistry, use simple herbs to prevent and cure many diseases that baffle the best efforts of the medical doctors.

Herbal healing was the first system of healing that the world knew. My parents, originally from Germany, brought with them much knowledge of these simple herbs, as told elsewhere in this book. I gathered many of them as a small child, and was taught their use.

Why use herbs? They are Nature's remedies and have been placed here by an all-wise Creator. There is an herb for every disease. Herbs were mentioned in the Bible from the beginning of creation.

The Bible on herbs

When God created this world and planted a garden in Eden, He placed the tree of life in its center (Genesis 2: 8,9). This tree corresponds to the tree of life. "The angel also showed me the

A diet rich in unprocessed foods is the most beneficial to health.

river of the water of life, sparkling like crystal, and coming from the throne of God and of the Lamb and flowing down the middle of the city's street. On each side of the river was the tree of life, which bears fruit twelve times a year, once each month; and its leaves are for the healing of the nations" (Revelation 22:1, 2 *Good News Bible*).

On the third day of creation He also made all kinds of plants for food. "Then He commanded, 'Let the earth produce all kinds of plants, those that bear grain and those that bear fruit—and it was done. So the earth produced all kinds of plants, and God was pleased with what he saw" (Genesis 1:11,12, *Good News Bible*). After He had created human beings, God told them what He had made for them to eat. "And God said, Behold, I have given you every herb bearing seed, which is upon the face of all the earth, and every tree, in which is the fruit of a tree yielding seed; to you it shall be for meat (food)" (Genesis 1:29).

After man was driven from the Garden of Eden and no longer had access to the tree of life, God added herbs to man's diet. He also advises us to partake of them to keep from getting sick. "Thorns also and thistles shall it bring forth to thee; and thou shalt eat the herb of the field" (Genesis 3:18). Herbs are one of God's remedial agents for afflicted humanity. His plan was that everyone should raise herbs in his garden, and also gather those that grow wild and use them when needed.

Some of the first things Moses taught the Israelites after they left Egypt was to live on simple nourishing food and to use herbs for their medicine. David, in the Psalms, wrote that the grass was caused to grow for the cattle, and herbs for the service of man (Psalms 104:14).

The Prophet Ezekiel said that the fruit of the tree was for man's meat (food), and the leaves for man's healing (Ezekiel 47:12). The great Apostle Paul said, "Don't you realize that you yourselves are the temple of God, and that God's Spirit lives in you? God will destroy anyone who defiles his temple, for his temple is holy—that is exactly what you are!" (1 Corinthians 3:17, *Phillips*.) Solomon, the wisest man that ever lived, said, "Better is a dinner of herbs where love is than a fatted ox and hatred with it" (Proverbs 15:17, *R.S.V.*).

Addendum We quote from the *FDA Consumer*, October 1983, as follows. "If you gather your own herbs to brew a cup of tea, *be absolutely 100 percent* certain that the herb you pick is the herb you seek...There are half a million known plant species. Less than one percent are poisonous. But it takes only one error." This is good advice.

Gathering & Preserving Herbs

It must be understood that both wide experience and knowledge of herbs are needed to successfully gather and preserve them. It is a study of a lifetime. Lack of knowledge in the gathering and preserving of herbs may render them of little or no medicinal value. Knowledge of the soil is also necessary. Plants grown in virgin soil will contain far greater medicinal value than those that are grown on poor, nutritionally depleted soil. The same plants grown in different localities will show a great difference in the amount of curative properties they contain. There is a difference between cultivated plants and those growing in their natural wild state. For instance, the dandelion growing wild has rare medicinal properties that are almost entirely lost when the plant is cultivated. Wild herbs are more effective for use in medicines than those grown in the garden.

Gather herbs only in dry weather, preferably when the plant is in full bloom or the seeds are getting ripe.

Barks The barks should be taken when the sap is rising in the spring. Shave off the rough outer part; then peel the inner part from the trunk of the tree. To dry, put in the sun for a short time (if desired), then complete the drying in the shade. Be sure the pieces of bark are thoroughly dry. If there is any moisture left in them when they are put away, they will mold.

Bark should be dried thoroughly before it is stored.

Hang flowering stems upside down in a shady, airy place until they are completely dry.

Roots Dig up the roots either in the spring when the sap is rising or in the late autumn, after the sap has gone down. Slice and dry the roots in the shade, tie them up in small bundles, and put them in the attic or some place where they are sure to keep dry.

Flowers, seeds, and leaves Flowers, seeds, and leaves should be gathered when they are in their prime, gathering only the perfect ones. These should also be dried in the shade. When thoroughly dry, put them in heavy brown paper bags. Do not preserve herbs in glass because sometimes the glass sweats.

If any moisture comes in contact with the herbs they will become moldy. When barks, roots, or other herbs are thoroughly dried and kept dry, they will retain their medicinal value for years.

Bark, roots, flowers, seeds, or leaves may all be dried for a short time in the sun, but always complete the drying process in the shade. Too much exposure to the sun tends to lessen the medicinal value. They may be dried entirely in the shade in an airy place. The only thing gained by putting them in the sun for a short time is to hasten the drying process.

General Directions for the Preparation & Use of Herbs

Herbal preparations should be made fresh every day: the only exceptions are the herbal salves, liniments, and ointments and also those preparations that are made with alcohol, such as tinctures.

Eating a good, diversified diet, getting regular rest and outdoor exercise, and following the other rules for good health given in this book will all be a great help in assisting the herbs to do their work of restoring the normal healthy balance in the system. Don't forget that herbs do not usually give rapid results as drugs do. BECAUSE OF THEIR MILDER ACTION, HERBS MUST BE TAKEN OVER A PERIOD OF WEEKS OR EVEN MONTHS, DEPENDING ON THE CONDITION BEING TREATED, IN ORDER TO PRODUCE A LASTING, BENEFICIAL EFFECT. In general, the longer the disease has been in the body, the longer it will take the herbs to have a noticeable effect.

It is also important to remember that when herbal preparations are used for children, weak or debilitated persons, or the elderly, the doses given in this book must be adjusted downward to one-third to two-thirds of the average adult dose.

While the proper use of herbs can be of very great importance in the maintenance or recovery of one's health, the careless or excessive use of certain herbs can result in a real health hazard. There is a common saying that if a little is good, more is even better. This must be interpreted with great care when it is applied to taking medicine, even natural products such as herbs.

A more accurate paraphrase of this saying might be: if taking three capsules of a certain herb makes you feel better, then taking six capsules will not necessarily make you feel twice as good, nor will it help you to recover your health twice as fast. In fact, taking more than the recommended dose may result in serious health consequences, for plants may contain chemicals, as well as other substances, that can prove dangerous if they are not recognized and treated with proper respect.

Each and every herb, such as this wormwood, has very specific applications.

Camomile has been used as a medicinal herb for more than a thousand years.

Types of Herbal Preparations

Infusion An infusion is usually made just like a tea. Boiling water is poured onto a certain amount of the herb, usually the leaves or flowers, in a cup or other suitable container. This is covered with a saucer or other cover and allowed to steep, in order to give the ingredients in the herb time to pass into the water. The aromatic and volatile ingredients, vitamins, and essences are removed by the infusion. The average amount of herb used is ½ to 1 ounce in a pint of water or 1 teaspoon of the herb in 1 cup of water. After the boiling water has been poured on the plants, let them set, covered, for about 10 to 20 minutes. Never allow an infusion to boil. After the water has cooled sufficiently, strain carefully into a cup or other container and drink when it is cool or lukewarm. Some honey may be added if desired, to improve the taste. Take the infusion while it is still hot for colds, influenza, coughs, or to produce sweating.

Herbal teas, decoctions, and infusions should be strained before drinking.

Most infusions are taken in small doses, regularly spaced during the day, using a total of about one to three cups, depending on the condition and the herb used.

When the twigs, stems, or other larger parts of the plant are used, they should be cut into small pieces and let steep for a longer period of time.

Always use glass, porcelain, or enamel cooking utensils.

Decoction A decoction is made by simmering the plant part in water, in a nonmetal container, for 3 to 5 minutes or even up to 30 minutes if the material is very hard. Keep the container covered. Use either 1 teaspoon of the powdered herb or 1 tablespoon of the cut herb to a cup of water. If you are planning to simmer the decoction for 30 minutes, always start with about 30 percent more liquid to allow for evaporation. For example, if you would usually use 1 ounce of the herb to a pint of water, start with 1½ pints instead, so that there will be about 1 pint left after 30 minutes. Strain carefully before using. Directions for taking are the same as for infusions. This method is used for extracting the active ingredients from the tougher parts of the plant, such as roots, bark, and seeds. Roots must be simmered one-half hour or more in order to extract their medicinal value. Simmer only; DO NOT BOIL HARD.

When you gather the roots and bark yourself, cut or crush them fine. If you raise or gather herbs and barks, use good judgment in making teas; if you find them too strong, add more water.

The roots, twigs, berries, seeds, or bark of a plant are "decocted" to release their active ingredients.

Herbal extracts can be kept in reserve as a part of the family medicine chest.

Tincture A tincture is a very concentrated extract of an herb in liquid form. Tinctures are useful when it is unpleasant to take the herb in another form because of its bad taste or if it must be taken over a long period of time. Tinctures are also used to rub on the skin as a liniment. Tinctures are usually made from potent herbs that are not commonly used as teas.

Extract An extract is a highly concentrated liquid form of an herb, about ten times as potent as a tincture. It is made by a variety of means such as high pressure, evaporation by heat, or cold percolation. Extracts are a popular and convenient way of taking and storing herbs and they are faster acting than teas, capsules, or powdered herbs.

Herbal extracts are readily obtained at most herb shops. The usual dose is from six to eight drops. This amount is about equal to 1 teaspoon of the tincture.

Teas There are some general rules that should be followed when making herb teas. The usual amount of herb used is 1 teaspoon of the dried herb or 3 teaspoons of the freshly crushed herb to one cup of boiling water. Pour the cup of boiling water over the herb and let set (steep) for 5 to 10 minutes. To make the tea stronger, use more of the herb; do not steep for a longer time as this will tend to make the tea bitter. Milk or cream added to the tea will cover up the natural flavor of the herb.

In warm weather, herb tea must be made fresh every day to prevent souring. It can be kept longer in a refrigerator, but not for more than one week.

How much to take? Good judgment must be exercised in the amount of herbs taken, usually four cups a day—one cup an hour before each meal, and one cup upon retiring. Each person has a different constitution; therefore, if good results are not obtained by taking as directed, increase or decrease as may be best. For instance, if the herbs are not laxative enough, increase the dose; if too laxative, decrease the dose. The bowels should move one or two times a day if three meals are eaten.

Most herb teas now come already prepared in tea bags, either as a single herb or in various combinations. Some feel that the bag filters out the delicate flavor of the herb. You may wish to try both methods to see which one you prefer. When using a tea bag, it should be placed in a cup and boiling water added. Cover and let steep for 3 to 5 minutes. Never use aluminum pans.

For example, golden seal may be taken in three ways, as follows:

1 Take one-fourth to one-half teaspoonful golden seal dissolved in one-fourth glass of water. Follow by drinking one glass of water. Take one to four doses a day. One No. 00 capsule equals one-fourth to one-half teaspoonful of powder. This varies somewhat according to the size of the powder grains, with the finer powders being less potent.

2 Steep a heaping teaspoonful of golden seal in a pint of boiling water for 20 minutes, stir thoroughly, let settle, and pour off the clear liquid. Take 8 tablespoonfuls a day, taking 2 tablespoonfuls 15 minutes before each meal and the remainder upon retiring. You may double the above amount and take even more with benefit. For some, taking this amount of golden seal only every other week or two weeks out of three, is more beneficial than using it constantly.

3 Take in gelatin capsules and drink one or more glasses of water with the capsules. Gelatin capsules may be purchased at most retail or wholesale drug stores. I make most use of No. 1, No. 0, and No. 00 sizes, but there are smaller sizes. As a rule, take two of the No. 00 size for a dose, more or less according to need.

If you have chiefly used herbs for culinary purposes, you may be surprised by the range of medicinal uses they offer.

When fresh herbs are not available, the dried variety can work as well.

Granulated or finely cut herbs Steep a heaping teaspoonful of herbs in a cup of boiling water for 20 minutes, strain, and take one cup one hour before each meal and one cup on retiring. You may take more or less as the case requires. If too strong, use less herbs per cup.

Powdered herbs The powdered herbs may be mixed in hot or cold water. The herbs take effect quicker if taken in hot water. Use one-half teaspoonful of the herb to one-fourth glass of water. Follow by drinking one glass of water, either hot or cold. This is about the same as taking one No. 00 capsule.

Capsules Most herbs may be purchased in either powdered or capsule form. The average dose is two capsules two or three times a day. Whichever form you decide to use, capsules or powder, follow the directions as given on the container. A No. 0 capsule contains about 10 grains of the herb, while a No. 00 capsule holds approximately 15 grains. Notice that a No. 00 capsule does not contain twice as much material as a No. 0 capsule, but holds roughly half again as much.

Herbs for sensitive patients and children Persons who have very sensitive stomachs, stomach ulcers, etc., may at times become nauseated and sick after taking some of the best old-fashioned herbs. If this happens, do not become alarmed. It is not the herbs that are at fault, but the sensitive condition of the stomach.

In cases where the stomach is extremely sensitive, start by taking teaspoonful doses of tea often—say, every 15 minutes—and increase the amount until it becomes possible to take the required amount.

Powdered herbs may be mixed with foods such as mashed potatoes, mashed vegetables of any kind, or ground-up sweet fruits such as figs or dates.

To the herb tea you can add a little honey or malt sugar, especially for children, to make it more palatable. Do not use refined sugar or sugar substitutes.

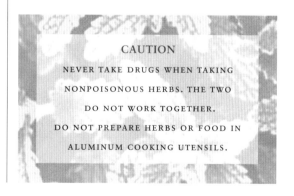

CAUTION

NEVER TAKE DRUGS WHEN TAKING NONPOISONOUS HERBS. THE TWO DO NOT WORK TOGETHER. DO NOT PREPARE HERBS OR FOOD IN ALUMINUM COOKING UTENSILS.

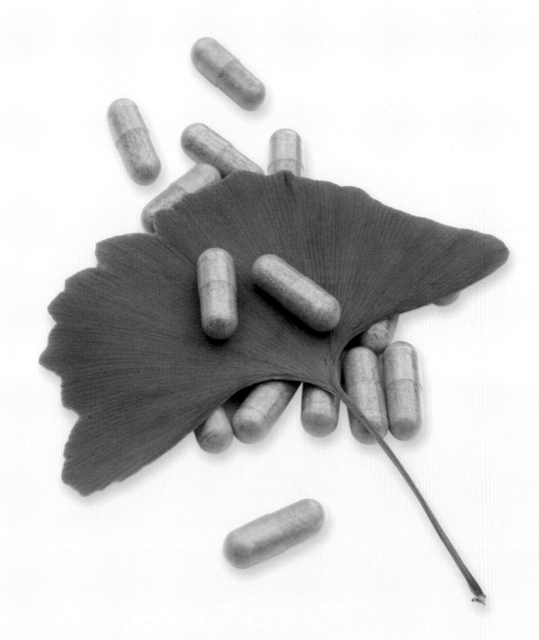

Herbs are especially easy to take in simple capsule form.

How to Make Syrups & Salves

A simple syrup Dissolve three pounds of brown sugar in a pint of boiling water and boil until it is thick. To this you may add any medicinal substance.

Malt honey, bees' honey, or Karo syrup may also be used in making syrups. To make an herb syrup, you simply add the cut herbs (or if using granulated herbs, sift them first so there will not be any dust or sediment). Boil to a syrupy consistency and stir thoroughly; then strain through a double cheesecloth, and bottle.

Lemon syrup Boil 1 pint of lemon juice for 10 minutes, strain, add 3 pounds of brown sugar, and boil a few minutes longer.

Wild cherry syrup

2 ounces wild cherry bark

2 ounces cubeb berries

2 ounces mullein

2 ounces skunk cabbage

2 ounces lobelia herb

4 pounds brown sugar

juice of 4 lemons

Place the first five ingredients in a large kettle. Add 4 quarts of boiling water, simmer for 10 minutes, let stand until nearly cold, then strain through a double cheesecloth. Put in a large porcelain cooking pan and add 4 pounds of brown sugar. Boil this down to a medium thick syrup—it must

Soothing herbal syrups are of particular efficacy in treating coughs and colds.

Wild cherry syrup is made using the bark of the tree, simmered to extract its goodness.

be thick enough so it will not sour. Add the juice of four lemons and let boil 2 or 3 minutes longer. Strain again. When cool, it is ready for use or for bottling.

Herbal salves

Use fresh leaves, flowers, roots, barks, or the dried granulated or powdered herbs. If you gather the herbs yourself and use them fresh, be sure to cut them up fine.

Use 1 pound of herbs to 1½ pounds of cocoa fat, or any pure vegetable oil, and 4 ounces of beeswax. It is necessary to use a little more beeswax in the warmer climates, as this is the ingredient that keeps the salve firm.

Mix the above together, cover, and place in the hot sun or in an oven with the fire turned low for three or four hours. Strain through a fine sieve or cloth. When it is cold, it will be firm and ready for use. It can be used, however, before it is cold.

How to Make Poultices

The following herbs are especially useful for making poultices: balm, flaxseed, gum arabic, hyssop, marshmallow, mustard, slippery elm, virgin's bower, wintergreen, chickweed, poke root, cayenne pepper, flaxseed meal, smartweed and charcoal, red sage, burdock, lobelia, and comfrey.

To make herb poultices it is best to have the herbs in a ground or granulated form. When using the herbs in powdered form, mix with just enough water to make a thick paste. When using them granulated, mix with water, cornmeal, and flaxseed meal to make a thick paste. Apply the paste in a layer about one-quarter inch thick onto a piece of muslin or linen cloth large enough to cover the area completely. Cover this with a piece of plastic. This can readily be found in today's kitchen, such as in a plastic trash bag. The plastic should be several inches larger than the poultice and held in place with pins or some kind of cloth binder. Leave it on for one to eight hours. Wash the skin thoroughly after removing. If fresh green leaves are used, beat them well, steep, and apply to the affected parts. Once a poultice has been used, do not warm it over. Do not allow a poultice to become cold. Have a second poultice ready immediately upon removing the first one.

A wide range of different herbs can be applied as poultices, but they must first be reduced to their granulated form.

Poultices are excellent for enlarged glands of any kind, such as neck, breast, groin, prostate, etc. They are also excellent for eruptions, boils, carbuncles, and abscesses. Occasionally the use of a poultice will increase the amount of pus in a sore. If this should occur, stop the use of the poultice. Be careful when using a mustard poultice as it may cause blistering of the skin. They are also good to relieve pain and congestion, to reduce any instances of inflammation and swelling, and to relax tense muscles.

An excellent thing to do first in any case where poultices are to be used, is to bathe the affected part thoroughly with mugwort tea. If this is not available, then cleanse the area with hydrogen peroxide before applying the poultice. It must be remembered that many herbs are used for poultices, so study these herbs and use those best suited or those recommended for that condition.

Types of Poultice

Slippery elm poultice This has no superior in the line of poultices, used either alone or combined with other herbs. Stir ground slippery elm bark in water or any strong herb tea, to the consistency of a thick paste. It is excellent for inflamed sores.

Lobelia and slippery elm poultice Mix one-third part lobelia with two-thirds part slippery elm. Is excellent for blood poisoning, boils, and abscesses. Also use it for rheumatism.

Charcoal and hops poultice This poultice will relieve gallstone pain quickly.

The Native Americans used poke root both for skin conditions and as an effective emetic.

Charcoal and smartweed poultice Excellent for inflammation of the bowels or inflammation in other parts of the body. When using for old and inflamed ulcers and sores, add powdered echinacea, golden seal, myrrh, or a small amount of all three. They all have powerful healing properties and are also disinfectant.

Poke root and cornmeal poultice Very excellent for caked and inflamed breasts. Also good for blood poisoning.

Burdock leaf poultice A burdock leaf poultice is very cooling and drying. It is good to use on old skin ulcers and sores. A poultice made of the root, adding a teaspoonful of salt, eases the pain of a wound caused by the bite of a dog.

Nettles, used in a poultice, can be effective in the treatment of tumors.

Plantain poultice This is excellent in rabid dog bites and to prevent blood poisoning.

A poultice made of any of the following herbs is very good for dissolving tumors: origanum, nettle, wintergreen, fenugreek, and mullein.

To bring a boil to a head quickly, apply poultices at a temperature of 100°F and repeat as often as necessary to keep the temperature above body heat. When a soothing effect is desired, as in painful wounds or bee stings, apply a poultice agreeably warm, and renew sufficiently often to prevent souring or becoming dry.

When applying poultices, the aim is to have the warmth and moisture retained as long as possible.

Yeast poultice In making a yeast poultice, dilute ordinary cake or powdered yeast with enough liquid to make a stiff batter. It can be diluted with strong infusions of the desired herb tea and cornmeal to make a stiff batter. In sluggish conditions, such as gangrene, old sores, etc., mix either myrrh, charcoal, ginger, or golden seal with the batter before applying.

To decrease or stop discharges from ulcers, add witch hazel or wild cherry bark tea. When there is much inflammation and tenseness, then sprinkle lobelia over the poultice, either the herb or crushed seeds.

Potato poultice Scrape or grate a raw Irish potato and apply to any feverish part, such as a carbuncle or boil. It has a very soothing and cooling effect and will draw the infection to a head.

Bayberry poultice This poultice is used in the treatment of foul ulcers, old sores, and cancerous sores.

White pond lily poultice This poultice, either used alone or combined with slippery elm or linseed, is one of the best for old sores, inflamed tumors, and similar ailments.

Sage poultice Excellent for sore breasts or for any local inflammation.

Charcoal and slippery elm poultice Use equal parts of each to make the poultice and use for gangrenous sores.

Slippery elm and yeast poultice Make a regular slippery elm poultice. Mix a yeast cake with warm water and add to the slippery elm. The poultice will bring boils and abscesses to a head and keep gangrene from setting in.

Hyssop poultice A small handful of this herb (used fresh), boiled in water for a few minutes, then drained and applied, will remove discoloration from bruises, or from a black eye. If you use the dried herbs, steep in boiling water.

Comfrey, ragwort, and wood sage poultice Use equal parts of these three herbs and steep in boiling water. Apply poultice to external cancers and tumors. It is most beneficial and will give excellent results.

Bread and milk poultice A poultice of bread and milk, with a little lobelia added, is very soothing and will bring boils to a head.

Bran poultice Use enough hot water to make a paste of the bran and apply as hot as can be borne. Use for inflammations of any kind, sprains, or bruises. When there is great pain, mix equal parts of lady's slipper and lobelia with the bran. Cover the poultice with several thicknesses of flannel or oiled silk to retain the heat. This is an unusually excellent poultice.

Carrot poultice Boil carrots until soft, or they can be used raw. Mash to a pulp, add some vegetable oil to keep them from hardening, spread on a cloth, and apply. Excellent for offensive sores.

Garden carrots, grated raw, and applied as a poultice, will cleanse old sores and ulcers. Follow with an application of healing lotion or a wash of golden seal and myrrh solution.

Onion poultice Make in the same way as carrot poultice. Very stimulating to indolent sores, and for boils that are slow to heal.

Lobelia poultice Mix 1 ounce of powdered lobelia and 1 ounce of powdered slippery elm; excellent for wounds, fistulas, boils, felons, erysipelas, insect bites and stings.

Elderberry poultice Use elderberry leaves, bruised or steamed to wilt them; add a little pure olive oil. This makes an excellent poultice for inflammation and for piles and hemorrhoids. Apply as warm as can be borne for an hour or more to relieve pain.

Lobelia, also known as "Indian tobacco," can be used on wounds.

How to Make Herbal Liniment

Good for all pains, painful swellings, bruises, boils, skin eruptions of any kind, and pimples. Apply herbal liniment every few minutes for an hour or two. It will stop a sty from developing on the eye in a short time if used freely. BE CAREFUL NOT TO GET IT INTO THE EYE.

Herbal liniment is also very useful for headaches. Apply to the temples, the back of the neck, and the forehead. It is very effective for rheumatism. For toothache, apply in the cavity and all around on the gums and on the outside of the jaw if necessary. It will take the swelling and soreness away. It is excellent for pyorrhea and sores in the mouth.

Saturate a piece of cotton and thoroughly wash the mouth with liniment; or take a mouthful, rinse the mouth with it and spit it out. It is very good for pain located in any part of the body. It is also useful for the control of athlete's foot. Apply frequently, saturating the affected parts thoroughly.

To make HERBAL LINIMENT, combine 2 ounces powdered myrrh, 1 ounce powdered golden seal, ½ ounce cayenne pepper and 1 quart rubbing alcohol (70 percent). Mix together and let stand seven days; shake well every day, decant off, and bottle in corked bottles. If you do not have golden seal, make the liniment without it.

Liniment can be applied to the temples or the back of the neck to help relieve a stress headache.

How to Make Herbal Laxative

Fennel seed is used to soothe the stomach and to help prevent excess gas.

Rhubarb root is particularly effective as a laxative.

To make HERBAL LAXATIVE, combine equal parts of buckthorn bark, rhubarb root, cascara sagrada bark, calamus root, and fennel seed. Mix thoroughly. These herbs are nonpoisonous, are soothing to the stomach and will help to prevent gas and fermentation.

Dose One-fourth teaspoonful in one-fourth glass of water. Follow with a glass of hot water. Take after each meal if the digestion is slow, or you can take a half-teaspoonful in the same manner upon retiring. Increase or decrease the amount taken to suit your personal need, but take enough so that you have a good elimination every day or at least so the bowels stay open. Children should be given proportionately less according to age.

This laxative should be made of the powdered herbs as it can then be used in the gelatin capsules. Two No. 00 capsules are the usual dose for an adult. If making a tea of granulated herbs, steep a teaspoonful to a cup of boiling water for 30 minutes and drink.

If you do not have on hand or cannot obtain all the herbs used in the above laxative, any one of the following three will bring good results when used singly in the same dose as given in the preceding paragraph: buckthorn bark, rhubarb root, or cascara bark.

Other herbs that act as a laxative are: horehound, hyssop, mandrake, mullein, peach leaves, psylla, sage, senna, wahoo, blue flag, wild Oregon grape, fringe, and aloes.

How to Make a Nervine & Tonic

Combine equal parts of gentian root, skullcap, burnet root, wood betony, and spearmint. This will prove a blessing to anyone who takes it. It is soothing and relaxing, quiets the nerves, has many good qualities, and is perfectly harmless.

Take one-half teaspoonful of the powdered herbs, combined and mixed in one-half glass of cold water, followed by a glass of hot water, one hour before each meal, and upon retiring. This tonic can be put in gelatin capsules. Two No. 00 capsules would contain the required amount for one dose. More can be taken with benefit.

How to make composition powder

Composition powder is a fine remedy for colds, flu, hoarseness, colic, cramps, sluggish circulation, and the beginning of fevers. It should be kept in every home, and used when the need arises. It is safe and effective.

In fevers and colds, give a cup of composition tea every hour until the patient perspires freely. This will clear the body of the cold, and bring the fever down.

To make COMPOSITION POWDER, combine the following herbs:

4 ounces bayberry

2 ounces ginger

1 ounce white pine

1 dram cloves

1 dram cayenne

Use all herbs in powdered form. Mix and put through a fine sieve twice. Steep one teaspoonful in a covered cup of boiling water for 15 minutes.

Fragrant and mild, spearmint is an excellent tonic for the digestive system.

Drink the clear liquid that is poured off from the sediment.

How to make antispasmodic tincture

Antispasmodic tincture may be used either internally or externally. It is very effective for cramps in the bowels when taken internally. Take eight to fifteen drops, according to age, in one-half glass of hot water in cases of snake bites, mad dog bites, or any dangerous illness. Increase the dose to one teaspoonful every two or three hours; children less according to age. It is a mild stimulant without any harmful reaction as it is nonpoisonous. It is very effective for pyorrhea and sores in the mouth, and is an excellent remedy for tonsillitis, diphtheria, or any other throat trouble. As a gargle, use one-half teaspoonful to a glass of water. Gargle with this solution until the throat is perfectly clear.

Repeat as often as necessary. It will cut all the mucus and kill the germs. It is also a very good voice tonic.

Apply externally to any kind of swelling or muscle cramps: it is very beneficial in rheumatism and lumbago.

It is an excellent remedy for lockjaw. Put it into the mouth, getting it behind the teeth so that it will get on the tongue. It will invariably unlock the jaw in a few minutes. For small children, when it is hard to get it behind the teeth, bathe the neck and jaws frequently with it until relief is obtained.

To make ANTISPASMODIC TINCTURE, combine the following herbs:

1 ounce lobelia seed, granulated

1 ounce skullcap, granulated

1 ounce skunk cabbage, granulated

1 ounce gum myrrh, granulated

1 ounce black cohosh, granulated

½ ounce cayenne, powdered

1 pint boiling water

1 pint apple (cider) vinegar

Steep the herbs in the pint of water just below the boiling point for one-half hour, strain, add the apple vinegar, and bottle for use.

A tonic will work best if a glass of hot water is taken after it.

Emetics

Emetics have been used from time immemorial. Hippocrates called them "upward purges." When Rome was the chief city of the earth, the fashionable had their palaces built with a special room in which to take "upward purges."

A pennyroyal emetic can help to cleanse the stomach and alleviate nausea.

Such rooms were called "vomitories." In these vomitories there was a marble rail, where, after they had eaten a feast, the Romans would go and lean over and have a slave tickle their throats, after drinking some warm water or decoction. Then they would go back and finish their feast.

An emetic is given when it is necessary to empty the stomach or cleanse it. In nausea, when there is a lot of undigested food, it must be cleaned out. When a person has been bitten by a rabid dog, or poisonous snake, or poisons of any kind have been taken internally, an emetic is one of the remedies. It is also good to take a high enema, and rid the body of as much poison as possible in that way. Poisonous materials in the stomach are much more easily thrown out by emetics than any other means, but anyone who is weak or subject to hemorrhages of the stomach should not take emetics. The stomach, in those cases, should be cleaned out by fasting, mild herb laxatives, and enemas used to cleanse the rest of the system.

How to take an emetic Drink five or six cups of lukewarm water. If vomiting does not occur freely, touch the back of the throat far down. This will bring up the contents of the stomach. In some cases it may be necessary to drink more. This should be repeated until the stomach is entirely cleansed and the water comes back clear. The addition of a teaspoonful of salt is very helpful.

Herb emetics are very beneficial. Use a tea made of boneset, pennyroyal, or Canada snakeroot. Other herbs that are good for emetics and antiemetics are: bayberry bark, buckbean, lobelia

A pipette is necessary to measure tiny doses of herbal extracts.

Some herbs that act as stimulants are: cayenne, elder, prickly ash, peppermint, ginger, cloves, red sage, raspberry, nettle, pennyroyal, rue, shepherd's purse, valerian.

The following herbs can be used in place of quinine: fit root, golden seal, magnolia, white poplar (bark), yarrow, willow (excellent), Peruvian bark, skullcap, gentian root, dogwood blossoms, peach, sage, vervain, wahoo, wood betony, willow bark, and red pepper (these act quickly; they are a tonic and stimulating without any harmful reaction), boneset, turnips (grated, skin and all). Any of these can be given in tablespoonful doses whenever a dose of quinine is indicated. Use instead, because they are better than quinine.

(large doses: small doses will stop spasmodic vomiting), mint (antiemetic), mustard, myrica, peach leaves (antiemetic), peppermint (antiemetic), giant Solomon seal (antiemetic), spearmint (antiemetic), white willow, colombo (antiemetic), ragwort (emetic).

A cup of peppermint, spearmint, or catnip tea taken after an emetic has a soothing and settling effect on the stomach. Golden seal taken afterwards is very healing and destroys mucus and fermentation in the stomach.

After taking the emetic, followed by an herb tea to settle and soothe the stomach, take a tonic herb, such as wild cherry bark, skullcap, valerian, or calamus root. Make the tea according to directions given earlier in this chapter. Take one-half cupful every two hours.

Herbal tea, taken after an emetic, works well to soothe the stomach.

Tonic Herbs

A tonic is an agent that is used to give strength to the system. The remedies that are given in this book all work toward the strengthening of the body and are not like any of the patent medicines or drugs generally given for that purpose.

One of the best things to do to tone up the body is to accustom it to a cold shower or a cold towel rub in the morning, followed by a vigorous dry towel rub. A fruit diet to begin with is advisable, as this makes it easier to rid the system of poisons. These tonics may be taken with great benefit by anyone who is not overflowing with health and vitality.

It is always good, of course, to take tonic herbs when convalescing from any disease or ailment. If the millions working in offices and those having taxing brain work knew what these things would do for them with no harmful aftereffects, the herb

A cold shower each morning is an excellent way to tone up your system.

TONIC HERBS

agrimony	gentian root	red clover
angelica	ginger root	blossoms
apple tree bark	ginseng	red raspberry
balmony	golden seal	leaves
bayberry	ground ivy	sage
bitterroot	heal-all	sanicle
boneset	hops	sassafras
broom	horehound	self-heal
camomile	hyssop	skullcap
capsicum	lavender	sweet flag
celery	magnolia	turkey corn
centaury	marjoram	valerian
colombo	meadow sweet	vervain
comfrey	mistletoe	white oak bark
coriander	mugwort	white pond lily
cudweed	myrrh	white willow
dandelion	Oregon grape	wild cherry
elder root	poke root	bark
elecampane	poplar bark	wood betony
fireweed	prickly ash	yarrow
fringe tree	quassia	yellow dock

Skullcap acts as a mild sedative on the system.

business would increase a hundredfold. To overtaxed mothers and overtaxed nurses with too many household duties and peevish sick children, they would prove an untold blessing that no pen could fully describe. No one can overestimate the benefits, both general and specific, to be derived from using the simple treatments given in this book.

Be sure to study the following list of herbs. You will be surprised to discover all the valuable properties these herbs have.

Specific nerve tonics Golden seal is a pure tonic to the nervous system. It acts as a tonic and powerful cleanser to all of the mucous membranes in the body. In my estimation, there is no herb that can take the place of golden seal.

White willow, called Nature's aspirin, is a very effective tonic.

Skullcap is one of the finest nerve tonics; used alone, it gives excellent results.

Valerian, taken cold several times during the day, acts powerfully on the nerves.

Mistletoe is good for nerves.

Equal parts of wood betony, agrimony, and self-heal are good for nervous tremors.

Tonic for lungs One teaspoonful of each of the following: comfrey, black horehound, cudweed, ground ivy, elecampane, ginger root, and one-half teaspoonful of cayenne: take as directed for use of herbs on pages 14–15.

Tonics for general debility and loss of appetite
Centaury, dandelion, ground ivy, meadow sweet, mugwort, wood betony, self-heal, agrimony, capsicum, balmony, poplar bark, black horehound, broom sanicle, yarrow, and sage. Boneset by itself can act as a specific tonic whenever one is needed. Take as directed on pages 14–15, "General Directions for the Use of Herbs."

A good general diet of fresh foods will support your general health.

Herbs Used to Treat Disease

Achillea millefolium

Yarrow

Common Names

Milfoil, noble yarrow, nosebleed, millefolium, ladies' mantle, thousand leaf, old man's pepper, thousand seal, soldier's woundwort.

Part Used

Entire plant.

Medicinal Properties

Astringent, tonic, alterative, diuretic, vulnerary, diaphoretic.

Excellent for hemorrhages and bleeding from the lungs. If taken freely at the beginning of a cold, with other simple remedies, it will break it up in twenty-four hours. A fine remedy in all kinds of fevers when taken hot. It will open the pores to release toxins, raise the temperature, and increase the circulation. An ointment of yarrow will cure old wounds, ulcers, and fistulas. Good for dyspepsia and hemorrhages from the lungs and bowels.

Where there is a bad condition of piles or hemorrhoids, take a cleansing enema and a yarrow enema each day. Good for expelling gas from the stomach and intestines. Very useful in diabetes and Bright's disease. For fevers, drink hot yarrow tea. Drink three cups a day an hour before meals, and one upon retiring. It must be given warm to be effective.

Acorus calamus

Calamus

Common Names Sweet flag, grass myrtle, sweet grass, sweet root, sweet cane, sweet rush, sweet sedge, myrtle flag, sweet myrtle, sea serge.

Part Used Root.

Medicinal Properties Carminative, aromatic, tonic, vulnerary.

Excellent for use in intermittent fevers. It is a valuable stomach remedy and is good for that purpose when mixed with other herbs. It is also helpful in preventing griping caused by other herbs. It stimulates the appetite, is good for dyspepsia, prevents fermentation and hyperacidity, and keeps the stomach fluids sweet. If the dried root is chewed, it will cause nausea in those who smoke, thereby helping to destroy the taste for tobacco. The tea is excellent when applied externally to sores, burns, and ulcers. Valuable in the treatment of scrofula. Take one capsule a day for only one week at a time without a break.

CAUTION
Calamus may have some toxic effects when taken internally. It is good when used externally.

Aletris farinosa

Star Grass

Common Names
Ague grass,
bitter grass,
blazing star,
colic root,
mealy starwort, star root, true unicorn root.

Part Used Rootstock (rhizome).

Medicinal Properties Tonic, stomachic.

Be sure to use only the dried rootstock. The fresh rootstock is toxic and should never be used. Star grass is an excellent female tonic and is used in painful menstruation. It is also useful in digestive trouble, colic, and gas.

Small doses only should be used. Boil a teaspoonful of the dried rootstock in a cup of water; let cool and drink no more than a cup a day, taking only a small mouthful at a time. Fifteen to thirty drops of the tincture in hot water can be taken daily for menstrual problems.

Aloe socotrina

Aloes

Common Names
Bombay aloes,
Turkey aloes, mocha
aloes, Zanzibar
aloes, Barbados aloes,
and Curacao aloes.

Part Used Leaves.

Medicinal Properties Cathartic, stomachic, aromatic, emmenagogue, emollient, vulnerary.

Aloes is one of the most healing agencies we have among the herbs. It is used in many cathartics since it is one of the best herbs to clean out the colon in connection with other herbs in the following mixture: 1 ounce powdered buckthorn bark, 1 ounce powdered rhubarb root, 1 ounce powdered mandrake root, ¼ ounce powdered socotrina aloes, 1 ounce powdered calamus root. Start with one-fourth teaspoonful, then increase or decrease the dose as needed. Do not take it during pregnancy or while nursing.

This is one of the finest body cleansers and brings most gratifying results. It does not gripe and is very healing and soothing to the stomach and the rest of the body. Aloes may be used alone for any kind of sore, cut, burn, or wound on the outside of the body, and is a very excellent remedy for piles or hemorrhoids.

Althaea officinalis
Marshmallow

Common Names Althea,
sweet weed, wymote,
mortification root, mallards,
Schloss tea.

Part Used Root, leaves.

Medicinal Properties Diuretic,
demulcent, mucilaginous,
emollient.

As a poultice it is excellent for
sore or inflamed parts since it is
very soothing and lubricating.
For lung troubles, hoarseness, cough,
bronchitis, diarrhea, or dysentery, put a
teaspoonful in a cup of water, simmer for
10 minutes, let stand until cool. Drink one
to two cupfuls a day, a large mouthful at
a time.

For irritation of the vagina, use as a douche,
and also take internally. One to two capsules
a day is an average dose. The tea is also good
to bathe sore, inflamed eyes. Very soothing and
healing to any inflamed condition of the bowels.
Valuable in pneumonia, strangury (slow and
painful discharge of the urine), gravel, and all
kidney diseases. The root is sometimes used to
increase milk in nursing mothers.

Anethum graveolens
Dill

Common Names
Garden dill, dilly, dill seed,
dill fruit.

Part Used Seed.

Medicinal Properties
Stomachic, aromatic,
stimulant, carminative,
diaphoretic.

Dill tea is an
excellent old-
fashioned remedy for upset stomach and
dyspepsia. It helps prevent gas and fermentation
in the intestines. It stimulates the appetite.

It is very quieting to the nerves and useful
in swellings and pains. It also helps to stop
hiccoughs. The seeds may be chewed in cases
of bad breath.

Dill seeds have been used to flavor other
foods. The leaves and seeds have been used
in preparing pickles, but pickles should never
be introduced into the stomach.

Angelica atropurpurea
Angelica

Common Names

Dead nettle, purple angelica, masterwort, high angelica, archangel, American angelica.

Part Used

Root, seed, herb.

Medicinal Properties

Stimulant, carminative, emmenagogue, tonic, aromatic, diuretic.

Angelica is a good tonic and a remedy for stomach pain, sour stomach, heartburn, gas, and cramps. It is also good for flu, colds, and fevers. Tea made from this herb when dropped into the eyes helps dimness of sight, and, dropped into the ears, it helps deafness. It should be taken hot to break up a cold quickly. For a general tonic, one to three cupfuls should be taken every day.

Angelica is a most effective remedy in epidemics and is used to strengthen the heart. Excellent in diseases of the lungs and chest. Eases stoppage of urination, good for suppressed menstruation, and helps expel the afterbirth. Good in sluggish liver and spleen. A tea made of angelica when dropped into old ulcers will cleanse and heal them. An infusion is made by taking 1 ounce of the dried herb to 1 pint of boiling water and drinking wine-glassful doses frequently. *Do not take angelica if you are pregnant or have severe diabetes.*

Anthemis nobilis
Camomile

Common Names Roman camomile, garden camomile, low camomile, ground apple, whig plant.

Part Used Flowers.

Medicinal Properties Stimulant, bitter, tonic, aromatic, emmenagogue, anodyne, antispasmodic, stomachic.

An old well-known home remedy that grows freely everywhere. Was supposedly dedicated to the sun by the Egyptians because of its curative value in the treatment of ague. An excellent general tonic that increases the appetite and is good for dyspepsia and a weak stomach. Used in various parts of the world as a table tea. Good to regulate monthly periods. Splendid for kidneys, spleen, colds, bronchitis, bladder troubles, to expel worms, for ague, dropsy, and jaundice.

The tea makes an excellent wash for sore and weak eyes and for other open sores and wounds. Use as a poultice for pains and swellings.

Intermittent and typhoid fever can be broken up in the early stages with this herb. Good in hysteria and nervous diseases. Made and used as a poultice, it will prevent gangrene. Combine with bittersweet as an ointment for bruises, sprains, calluses, or corns. *Do not use during pregnancy.* Take one capsule twice daily.

Apium graveolens

Celery

Common Names

Smallage, garden celery.

Part Used Root, seed.

Medicinal Properties

Diuretic, stimulant, aromatic.

Excellent for use in incontinence of urine, dropsy, and liver troubles. Produces perspiration and is a splendid tonic. Good in rheumatism, neuralgia, and nervousness. Is much used as a table relish and the ground seed for flavoring soups.

Apocynum androsaemifolium

Bitterroot

Common Names Dogsbane, milkweed, honey bloom, milk ipecac, flytrap, wandering milkweed, catchfly, bitter dogsbane, western wallflower, wild cotton.

Part Used Root.

Medicinal Properties Emetic, diuretic, sudorific, cathartic, stimulant, expectorant.

This is a very good remedy for intermittent fever, typhoid fever, and other fevers. Has an excellent effect on the liver, kidneys, and bowels. Increases the secretion of bile. Excellent for poor digestion. Bitterroot has been known to cure dropsy when everything else has failed. Expels worms. Is very useful in syphilis, and to rid the system of other impurities. Especially valuable in gall-stones. Good in rheumatism, neuralgia, diseases of the joints and mucous membranes. Wonderful for diabetes.

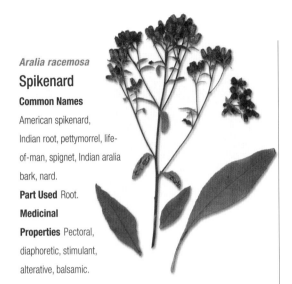

Aralia racemosa
Spikenard
Common Names
American spikenard, Indian root, pettymorrel, life-of-man, spignet, Indian aralia bark, nard.
Part Used Root.
Medicinal Properties Pectoral, diaphoretic, stimulant, alterative, balsamic.

One of the old-fashioned remedies. It makes childbirth easier and shortens the length of labor. Take the tea for some time before labor. It is an excellent blood purifier. For use in treating venereal diseases, combine spikenard with the following: equal parts of dandelion, burdock, and yellow dock. Flavor with one of the following by using an equal part: catnip, peppermint, wintergreen, or sassafras.

Good in all skin diseases, pimples, or eruptions. Very useful in coughs, colds, and all chest infections. As an infusion use ½ ounce of the herb in a pint of boiling water. Take in wineglass doses.

Arctostaphylos uva-ursi
Uva-ursi
Common Names Bearberry, upland cranberry, universe vine, mountain cranberry, mountain box, wild cranberry, bear's grape, kinnpikinnick, mealberry, sagackhomi, red bearberry, arberry.
Part Used Leaves.
Medicinal Properties Diuretic, astringent, tonic, mucilaginous.

Very useful in diabetes, Bright's disease, and all kidney and bladder troubles. Good when there is mucous discharge from the bladder with pus and blood. Excellent remedy for dysentery, piles, hemorrhoids, excessive menstruation, and for spleen, liver, and pancreas problems. Excellent in gonorrhea, ulceration in the mouth of the womb, and other female troubles.

Take internally and use also as a douche. Steep a heaping teaspoonful in a pint of boiling water for 30 minutes and drink one-half cupful every four hours. Also comes in capsules; one to two daily. When combined with an equal amount of buchu, uva-ursi makes an excellent treatment for kidney and bladder troubles.

Arctium lappa

Burdock

Common Names Grass burdock, clotbur, bardana, burr seed, hardock, hareburr, hurr-burr, turkey burr seed, beggar's buttons, thorny burr, lappa, cocklebur.

Part Used Roots, leaves, seeds.

Medicinal Properties Roots—diuretic, depilatory, alterative. Leaves—maturating. Seeds—alterative, diuretic, tonic.

The root is one of the best blood purifiers for syphilis and other diseases of the blood. It cleanses and eliminates impurities from the blood very rapidly. Burdock tea taken freely will heal all kinds of skin diseases, boils, and carbuncles. Increases the flow of urine. Excellent for gout, rheumatism, scrofula, canker sores, sciatica, gonorrhea, and leprosy. Wring a hot fomentation out of the tea and use on swellings. It is good to apply externally as a salve for skin eruptions, burns, wounds, swellings, and hemorrhoids. Excellent to reduce flesh.

Burdock root can be obtained either as a powder or in capsules. Take one capsule twice daily; or for powder, use half a teaspoonful twice daily in a glass of water. Make a decoction of the seeds or root, using 1 ounce of the herb to 1½ pints of boiling water. Take a wineglassful three or four times a day.

Artemisia absinthium

Wormwood

Common Names Absinthium, green ginger, absinthe, old woman.

Part Used Entire plant.

Medicinal Properties Aromatic, tonic, antiseptic, febrifuge.

Good for bilious and liver troubles, jaundice, and intermittent fevers. Excellent appetizer. Will expel worms. Good in chronic diarrhea and leukorrhea. Good in poor digestion or lack of appetite.

CAUTION

Follow the directions carefully and do not take larger doses, as wormwood can be poisonous.

ADDENDUM

Wormwood is the principal herb used in absinthe, a bitter, aromatic, alcoholic drink that was very popular in Italy, France, and Switzerland during the 19th century. Because of the addictive nature of wormwood, however, and the frequent side effects when absinthe was used to excess—dizziness, seizures, stupor, delirium, hallucinations, and even death—it has now been banned in nearly every country of the world.

Artemisia vulgaris
Mugwort

Common Names Common mugwort, sailor's tobacco, felon herb.

Part Used Entire plant.

Medicinal Properties Emmenagogue, laxative, diaphoretic.

Splendid for female complaints when combined with marigold flower and some of the herbs recommended on page 184 under menstruation. Take a heaping teaspoonful to a cup of boiling water. Steep 20 minutes, and drink one to three cups a day as needed. The leaves and flowers are full of virtue.

Mugwort is very useful in overcoming inflammatory swellings, gravel and stones in the kidneys and bladder, to increase the flow of urine, and for fevers and gout. After using a poultice of chickweed or slippery elm, thoroughly bathe the affected part for some time with the hot tea, made by steeping a tablespoonful of mugwort to a pint of boiling water for 20 minutes. Bruises, whitlows (felons), abscesses, carbuncles, and sometimes even tumors will yield to this treatment if it is continued. Good for rheumatism and gout. Acute pain in the bowels and stomach can quickly be relieved by drinking the warm infusion and applying hot fomentations.

Asclepias tuberosa
Pleurisy Root

Common Names Butterfly weed, wind root, Canada root, silkweed, orange swallow wort, tuber root, white root, flux root, asclepias.

Part Used Root.

Medicinal Properties Expectorant, carminative, tonic, diuretic, diaphoretic, relaxant, antispasmodic.

This herb is very valuable in pleurisy. It eases the pain, which helps to make breathing easier. It is excellent for breaking up colds as well as for asthma, and all bronchial and pulmonary complaints. Very useful in scarlet fever, rheumatic fever, bilious fever, typhus, all burning fevers, and measles. Good for suppressed menstruation and acute dysentery.

TREATMENT OF PLEURISY

Steep a teaspoonful of powdered pleurisy root in a cup of boiling water for 45 minutes, strain, and take two tablespoonfuls every two hours—more often if necessary. Apply a cold compress to the affected part, covering well with a flannel. Give a high enema of pleurisy root. Using a tablespoonful to a quart of boiling water, let steep, and use at about 112°F. It also acts as a tonic for the kidneys.

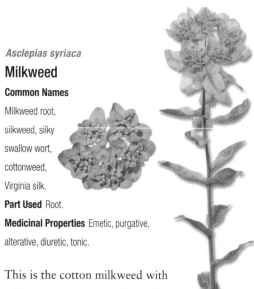

Asclepias syriaca

Milkweed

Common Names

Milkweed root, silkweed, silky swallow wort, cottonweed, Virginia silk.

Part Used Root.

Medicinal Properties Emetic, purgative, alterative, diuretic, tonic.

This is the cotton milkweed with which almost everyone is familiar. A splendid remedy for female complaints, bowel, and kidney troubles. It increases the flow of urine and is therefore good for dropsy. Also good for asthma, stomach troubles, and scrofulous conditions of the bladder.

It is often used in place of lobelia. It is a very effective remedy for gallstones. Take equal parts of milkweed and marshmallow, steep a teaspoonful in a cup of boiling water; take three cups daily and one hot upon retiring. Children less according to age. Fomentations applied to the liver after the liver has been thoroughly massaged are very effective. The boiled roots taste similar to asparagus. Caution should be exercised in using milkweed since it may be poisonous, especially when used in large doses and particularly in children. Follow the directions carefully and take no more than is necessary.

Balsamodendron myrrha

Myrrh

Common Names Gum myrrh tree.

Part Used Powdered gum, resin.

Medicinal Properties Antiseptic, stimulant, tonic, expectorant, vulnerary, emmenagogue.

Valuable as a tonic and stimulant for bronchial and lung diseases. Excellent for pyorrhea, as it is antiseptic and very healing.

For use as a gargle and mouthwash, steep a teaspoonful of myrrh and one of boric acid in a pint of boiling water. Let stand for one-half hour, pour off the clear liquid and use. Cures halitosis (bad breath) when taken internally.

It is also an excellent remedy for ulcers, piles, hemorrhoids, and for bathing bedsores or any sores on the body. Made into an ointment with equal parts of golden seal, it is an excellent injection for piles and hemorrhoids; or the tea can be used for these conditions as a wash. After thoroughly washing sores, ulcers, etc., with the tea, sprinkle a little of the powder on the sore.

Charcoal moistened with this tea and applied to old ulcers and sores is healing. Is also effective for gangrene. This is also an excellent remedy for diphtheria, ulcerated throat, and sores in the mouth. Use for cough, asthma, tuberculosis, and all chest affections, as it diminishes the mucus discharge.

Barosma betulina

Buchu

Common Names Bookoo, bucku, short-leaved buchu, buku, buchu, bucco, round buchu.

Part Used Leaves (use the short-leaved buchu).

Medicinal Properties Diuretic, tonic, stimulant, diaphoretic.

One of the best remedies for the urinary organs. Take one capsule three times a day. It is very soothing and is a most excellent remedy when there is pain while urinating, stoppage of the urine, inflammation of the bladder, or dropsy. When used specifically for this purpose, give a cold, strong tea. DO NOT BOIL BUCHU LEAVES. When given warm, it produces perspiration, helps to reduce swelling of the prostate gland and soothes irritation of the lining membrane of the urethra. Useful in diabetes in the first stages and also for leukorrhea.

When it is combined with equal parts of uva-ursi, it is a wonderful help for urinary problems. Take one capsule three times a day with a glass of water. Infusion: 1 ounce of the leaves in 1 pint of boiling water. Take one wineglassful three or four times a day.

Berberis aquifolium

Wild Oregon Grape

Common Names Oregon grape, holly-leaved barberry, mahonia, California barberry, mountain grape.

Part Used Root.

Medicinal Properties Tonic, alterative.

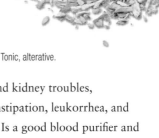

Useful in liver and kidney troubles, rheumatism, constipation, leukorrhea, and uterine diseases. Is a good blood purifier and useful in chronic skin diseases such as eczema. The medicinal uses of this plant are nearly identical to Barberry (*Berberis vulgaris*).

Berberis vulgaris

Barberry

Common Names Berberidis, European barberry, jaundice berry, pepperidge bush, sowberry.

Part Used Root, root-bark, berries.

Medicinal Properties Tonic, purgative, hepatic, antiseptic.

The berries can be taken as a drink for fever or diarrhea. The fresh juice is also good as a mouthwash or gargle. The root-bark is excellent for all liver problems; it acts as a mild purgative, and helps to regulate the digestive processes.

Betonica officinalis

Wood Betony

Common Names Lousewort, betony, bishop's wort.

Part Used Leaves.

Medicinal Properties Aperient, stomachic, nervine, tonic, aromatic, antiscorbutic.

Excellent for the stomach. Mildly stimulating to the heart. Unsurpassed for headache, neuralgia, pains in the head or face, heartburn, indigestion, cramps in the stomach, jaundice, palsy, convulsions, gout, colic, pains, all bilious and nervous complaints, dropsy, colds, la grippe, tuberculosis, worms, delirium, poisonous snake and insect bites. Opens obstructions of the liver and spleen. More effective than quinine. Today this herb is not commonly used as a medicine. The formula is two parts wood betony, one part skullcap, one part calamus root. Use as an infusion, one to two teaspoonfuls to a cup of water. Take one or two cups a day.

Borago officinalis

Borage

Common Names Burrage, bugloss, common bugloss.

Part Used Leaves, flowers.

Medicinal Properties Pectoral, tonic, febrifuge, aperient, demulcent.

It is excellent to bathe sore inflamed eyes with the tea. Taken internally, the tea cleanses the blood and is effective for fevers, yellow jaundice, to expel poisons of all kinds due to snake bites, insect stings, etc. Strengthens the heart and is good for cough, itch, ringworms, tetters, scabs, sores, and ulcers. Use as a gargle for ulcers in the mouth and throat, and to loosen phlegm. Steep three teaspoonfuls of the herb in one cup of hot water and take three tablespoonfuls two times a day for one week at a time.

Calaminta officinalis

Calamint

Common Names Mountain mint, basil thyme, common calamint.

Part Used Herb.

Medicinal Properties Expectorant, diaphoretic.

Calamint is a wonderful herb to use in attacks of asthma or bronchitis. It is also good when applied to joints affected by arthritis.

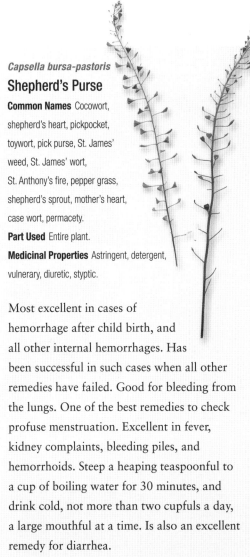

Capsella bursa-pastoris

Shepherd's Purse

Common Names Cocowort, shepherd's heart, pickpocket, toywort, pick purse, St. James' weed, St. James' wort, St. Anthony's fire, pepper grass, shepherd's sprout, mother's heart, case wort, permacety.

Part Used Entire plant.

Medicinal Properties Astringent, detergent, vulnerary, diuretic, styptic.

Most excellent in cases of hemorrhage after child birth, and all other internal hemorrhages. Has been successful in such cases when all other remedies have failed. Good for bleeding from the lungs. One of the best remedies to check profuse menstruation. Excellent in fever, kidney complaints, bleeding piles, and hemorrhoids. Steep a heaping teaspoonful to a cup of boiling water for 30 minutes, and drink cold, not more than two cupfuls a day, a large mouthful at a time. Is also an excellent remedy for diarrhea.

Nearly every wheat field is full of this herb. It grows over the entire United States. When you chew the green grass, it has a very pleasant peppery taste.

Cassia marilandica

Senna

Common Names American senna, locust plant, wild senna.

Part Used Leaves.

Medicinal Properties Laxative, vermifuge, diuretic.

Senna is a valuable, effective laxative. It sometimes causes griping; therefore it should be combined with an aromatic herb. Some of the many common aromatic herbs are goldenrod, mint, rosemary, anise, balm, allspice, buchu, coriander, lavender, and pennyroyal. Excellent for worms, biliousness, halitosis (bad breath), and bad taste in the mouth. Most effective for worms when combined with other herbs that are also indicated for worms. Steep 2 ounces in a pint of boiling water with 1 teaspoon of ginger for 30 to 60 minutes, strain, and drink a wineglassful, more or less according to needs.

Cayenne

Common Names Cayenne pepper, red pepper, capsicum, Spanish pepper, bird pepper, pod pepper, chillies, African pepper, chili pepper, African red pepper, cockspur pepper, American red pepper, garden pepper.

Part Used Fruit.

Medicinal Properties Stimulant, tonic, sialagogue, alterative, rubefacient, carminative, digestive.

Red pepper is one of the most wonderful herb medicines we have. It can be put in an open wound, either in a fresh wound or an old ulcer, and it is very healing instead of irritating. It causes no harm and has no unhealthy reaction.

It is effective when used as a poultice for rheumatism, inflammation, and pleurisy, and is also helpful if taken internally for these. For sores and wounds it also makes a good poultice. It is a stimulant when taken internally as well as being an antispasmodic. Good for kidneys, spleen, and pancreas. Wonderful for lockjaw.

It is one part of a most wonderful liniment, called KLOSS'S LINIMENT, which may be made as follows:

2 ounces gum myrrh

1 ounce golden seal

½ ounce African red pepper (cayenne pepper)

Put this either into a quart of rubbing alcohol, or a mixture of a pint of raspberry vinegar and a pint of water. Add the alcohol or vinegar to the powder. Let it stand for a week or ten days, shaking every day. It is very healing to wounds, bruises, sprains, scalds, burns, and sunburns, and should be applied freely.

It is good in all forms of low diseases. The key to success in medicine is stimulation, and capsicum is the great stimulant. It is excellent in yellow fever, black vomit, putrefaction or decay, given frequently in small doses. It is good, also, in asthmatical asphyxia combined with lobelia. It is good in profound shock.

For local application it is, or should be, the base of all stimulating liniments. It is not injurious to the skin, as is turpentine or acetic acid. It is an agent that is seldom used alone.

A CAPSICUM TINCTURE may be made as follows: Take two ounces of cayenne and macerate for ten to fourteen days in one quart of alcohol. Strain and bottle. Keep in a warm place while macerating during cold weather.

A splendid STIMULATING LINIMENT is made as follows:

tincture of cayenne	1 quart
Castille soap	2 ounces
oil of hemlock spruce	½ ounce
oil of origanum	½ ounce
oil of cedar	½ ounce
oil of peppermint	½ ounce

Shave or scrape the soap very fine, and dissolve in one pint of water. Stir the oils into the tincture and mix with the soapy solution. A little additional oil of peppermint will greatly increase its efficacy. In a four-ounce bottle put 1 ounce of lobelia compound (without gum myrrh) and fill the bottle up with the stimulating liniment. Shake this well, and after application cover the affected part with a piece of warmed flannel.

The following paragraphs are quoted from *The Medicine of Nature*, by R. Swinburne Clymer, pages 69–71, 79–80, 143, 150.

Capsicum (red pepper) is the most pronounced, natural, and ideal stimulant known in the entire materia medica. It cannot be equaled by any known agent when a powerful and prolonged stimulant is needed, as in congestive chills, heart failure, and other conditions calling for quick action. The entire circulation is affected by this agent and there is no reaction. In this it stands alone as ideal.

In congested, ulcerated, or infectious sore throat it is an excellent agent, but should be combined with myrrh to relieve the morbidity.

Capsicum is antiseptic and therefore a most valuable agent as a gargle in ordinary sore throat or in diptheria.

In all diseases prostrating in their nature, whether pneumonia, pleurisy, or typhoid fever, capsicum is invaluable in the prescription as the toning agent which helps the system to throw off the disease and re-establish equilibrium.

Capsicum plasters are valuable in pneumonia, pleurisy and other acute congestions. Combine with lobelia and bran or hops. One hour is the maximum time to keep them applied.

As the common red pepper of table use, capsicum is well-known to almost all people. None know better its virtue than the habitual drinker who considers it his best friend and never fails to use plenty of it in his hot soups when sobering up and soothing his cold and sore stomach after a prolonged spree. In the onset of chills and colds it is the sovereign remedy.

Capsicum increases the power of all other agents, helps the digestion when taken with meals, and arouses all the secreting organs.

Carum carvi

Caraway

Common Names

Caraway seed, caraway fruit.

Part Used Seeds.

Medicinal Properties

Carminative, aromatic, stomachic, emmenagogue.

It is very useful for colic in infants when taken in hot water or milk. It should be taken hot for colds and female troubles.

It is very good for the prevention of fermentation in the stomach and aids digestion. It strengthens and gives tone to the stomach, and helps to expel gas from the bowels. It is often used to flavor other herbs and to prevent griping. Use as a poultice for bruises.

Caulophyllum thalictroides

Blue Cohosh

Common Names

Blueberry, squaw root, papoose root, blue ginseng, yellow ginseng.

Part Used Root.

Medicinal Properties

Stimulant, sudorific, parturient, emmenagogue.

Used to regulate menstrual flow and for suppressed menstruation. It makes childbirth easier and brings on labor pains. Good for chronic uterine trouble, leukorrhea, rheumatism, neuralgia, vaginitis (inflammation of the vagina), dropsy, cramps, colic, hysteria, palpitation of the heart, high blood pressure, and diabetes. Good for hiccough, whooping cough, spasms, and epilepsy.

Blue cohosh contains minerals that help to alkalinize the blood and urine. This herb can be quite irritating to mucous surfaces and therefore should be used with some caution.

CAUTION

It should not be used during pregnancy and should be taken for only one week at a time, one to three capsules daily.

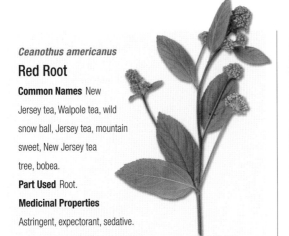

Ceanothus americanus

Red Root

Common Names New Jersey tea, Walpole tea, wild snow ball, Jersey tea, mountain sweet, New Jersey tea tree, bobea.

Part Used Root.

Medicinal Properties Astringent, expectorant, sedative.

This is one of the most wonderful remedies for any spleen trouble. It is also good in dysentery, asthma, chronic bronchitis, whooping cough, and tuberculosis, and as a wash for a sore mouth. If tonsils are sore, make a swab and work around good and then gargle. Excellent for hemorrhoids. Inject the strong tea often.

It is effective in spasms, also is very effective in syphilis and gonorrhea. When combined with fringe tree and golden seal, it is good for sick headache, acute indigestion, and nausea due to poor activity of the liver. Use one teaspoonful of the granulated red root to a pint of boiling water. Steep for 20 or 30 minutes. Drink one cupful of this tea before each meal and before going to bed. If the powdered herb is used, take half a teaspoonful in a cup of hot or cold water, an hour before each meal and before going to bed.

Red root is also an excellent remedy in diabetes and is commonly used in asthma, bronchitis, and other lung infections.

Chelidonium majus

Celandine

Common Names Greater celandine, garden celandine, tetterwort, jewel weed, quick-in-hand, slippers, snap weed, pale touch-me-not, slipper weed, balsam weed, weathercock, touch-me-not.

Part Used Herb.

Medicinal Properties Alterative, antispasmodic, caustic, diuretic, purgative.

The fresh juice mixed with vinegar may be applied for removal of warts and corns. It may also be made into an ointment to be used on various skin diseases, such as ringworm, eczema, etc. When taken internally as an infusion, is good for diseases of the stomach, gallbladder, and liver. Also may be useful in asthma. Take one or two capsules daily.

Do not confuse this herb with small or lesser celandine, commonly known as pilewort.

CAUTION
Do not give this herb to children.

Chelone glabra

Balmony

Common Names Snake head, turtle bloom, turtle head, fishmouth, shell flower, bitter herb.

Part Used Leaves.

Medicinal Properties Tonic, antibilious, stimulant, detergent, anthelmintic.

Specific tonic for enfeebled stomach and indigestion, general debility, biliousness, jaundice, constipation, dyspepsia, and torpid (sluggish) liver. An excellent remedy for worms in children. Increases the gastric and salivary secretions, and stimulates the appetite. Good for sores and eczema. This herb may be difficult to obtain. An infusion of 1 ounce of the herb in 1 pint of water can be used freely, a wineglassful at a time.

Chimaphila umbellata

Pipsissewa

Common Names Prince's pine, ground holly, false wintergreen, rheumatism weed, bitter wintergreen, king's cure.

Part Used Entire plant, leaves.

Medicinal Properties Diuretic, tonic, alterative, astringent, diaphoretic.

A good herb to use in kidney diseases and infections.

One of the great advantages of this herb is its almost total lack of irritating side effects. It has been reported to dissolve small stones in the bladder. A poultice may be made from the leaves and applied to the skin for ulcers, sores, bruises, blisters, etc.

Make an infusion of 1 ounce of the herb in 1 pint of boiling water; drink cold one or two cupfuls a day, a swallow at a time. Use 5 to 15 drops of the tincture. Follow the directions as given on the bottle.

Chrysanthemum parthenium

Feverfew

Common Names

Featherfew, featherfoil, febrifuge plant.

Part Used The herb.

Medicinal Properties

Aperient, carminative, purgative, tonic, emmenagogue.

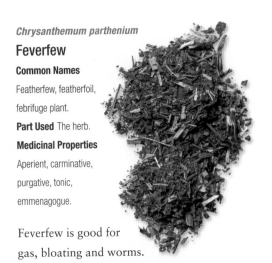

Feverfew is good for gas, bloating and worms. It promotes the onset of the menstrual period. Is good to treat hysteria and alcoholism with delirium tremens. The flowers act as a purgative. As an infusion, use 1 ounce of the herb to a pint of boiling water and take frequently, a teaspoonful at a time. Take 10 to 30 drops of the tincture in a glass of water every four hours as needed.

Cichorium intybus

Chicory

Common Names

Succory, wild chicory, garden endive, garden chicory, endive.

Part Used Root.

Medicinal Properties

Tonic, laxative, diuretic.

While chicory root is very well-known for its combination with coffee, its value for various remedies is not well-known.

Chicory is effective in disorders of the kidneys, liver, urinary organs, stomach, and spleen. It is good for jaundice. It is also good for settling an upset condition in the stomach, expelling the morbid matter and toning up the system. The leaves of the common garden endive (*Cichorium endive*) are commonly used in salads. It is available in most grocery stores.

Cimicifuga racemosa

Black Cohosh

Common Names Black snakeroot, bugwort, bugbane, squawroot, rattleroot, rattleweed, rattlesnake's root, richweed.

Part Used Root.

Medicinal Properties Emmenagogue, nervine, alterative, expectorant, diaphoretic, astringent, antispasmodic.

A powerful remedy in hysteria, St. Vitus's dance (or chorea), epilepsy, convulsions, and all spasmodic afflictions. Good for pelvic disturbances, female complaint (menstrual cramps), all uterine troubles, and relieves pain in childbirth. Dependable herb to bring on menstrual flow that has been retarded by cold or exposure. Splendid for dropsy, rheumatism, spinal meningitis, asthma, delirium tremens, poisonous snake bites, and poisonous insect bites. A wonderful remedy for high blood pressure and for equalizing the circulation.

By making it into a syrup, black cohosh is effective in coughs, whooping cough, and in liver and kidney troubles. This herb should not be used during pregnancy. Because of its potency it should not be used constantly over a long period of time without a break. One to three capsules a day is the average dose.

Cinnamomum zeylanicum

Cinnamon

Part Used Bark, oil obtained from bark and leaves.

Medicinal Properties Aromatic, astringent, stimulant, carminative.

The wonderful cinnamon tree contains many remarkable properties, besides its delicious flavor. The powdered bark is stimulating and prevents gas and sour stomach. It warms up the stomach, expels gas from the stomach and bowels, and is somewhat laxative.

Cinnamon is somewhat astringent and therefore is good in diarrhea as well as for nausea and vomiting. It is sometimes combined with other herbs to prevent griping and to give them a better flavor. Take a rounded teaspoonful of cinnamon to a cup of boiling water, stir it and drink while hot. Drink a small portion at a time, four or five times a day, or drink a cup as needed for griping and pain in the bowels. Use ¼ teaspoon to a cup of other herbs to flavor them. Put it in with the herbs when you make the tea.

Clematis virginiana

Virgin's Bower

Common Names

Common virgin's bower, traveler's joy.

Part Used

Leaves, flowers.

Medicinal Properties

Stimulant, diuretic, sudorific, vesicant.

Will relieve severe headaches. Combine with other herbs in poultices for cancer, ulcers, and bedsores. Combine with other herbs in ointments for cancer, itching, and ulcers. For internal use, steep a heaping teaspoonful in a cup of boiling water for 30 minutes, strain, take a tablespoonful four to six times a day.

Cocculus palmatus

Colombo

Common Names

Calumba, calumbo, columbo root, columba, foreign columbo, kalumb, calumba root.

Part Used Root.

Medicinal Properties

Antiemetic, tonic, febrifuge.

One of the best and purest tonics to strengthen and tone up the entire system. Useful in intermittent and remittent fevers.

Will keep the system pure and toned up in debilitating and hot swampy climates. Excellent to allay vomiting during pregnancy and can be used with good effect before and after pregnancy. Can be used for colon trouble such as cholera, chronic diarrhea, and dysentery, no matter how longstanding the disease. A splendid remedy in dyspepsia and improves the appetite. Good for rheumatism and pulmonary consumption.

Convallaria majalis

Lily of the Valley

Common Names May lily, May bells, convallaria, conval lily.

Part Used Entire plant.

Medicinal Properties Diuretic, cardiac, tonic, laxative, mucilaginous.

Very quieting to the heart and good for the heart generally. Useful in epilepsy, dizziness, and convulsions of all kinds.

Good for palsy and apoplexy. Strengthens the brain and makes the thoughts clearer. Extremely useful in dropsy. Large doses may cause nausea vomiting and diarrhea.

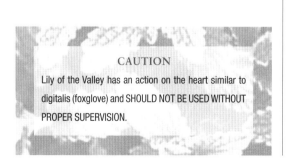

CAUTION

Lily of the Valley has an action on the heart similar to digitalis (foxglove) and SHOULD NOT BE USED WITHOUT PROPER SUPERVISION.

Coptis trifolia

Gold Thread

Common Names Yellow root, mouth root, canker root.

Part Used Root.

Medicinal Properties Tonic.

Excellent for digestion. A well-tried remedy for ulcers and canker sores in the mouth and for sore throat when used as a gargle. Has also been used in ulcers of the stomach, as well as inflammation of the stomach and in dyspepsia.

Effective in destroying the desire for strong drinks. Especially beneficial and effective when used in combination with golden seal in ulcers and cancerous afflictions of the stomach.

Corallorhiza odontorhiza

Coral

Common Names

Crawley, crawley root, coral root, chicken's toes, turkey claw, fever root, scaly dragon's claw.

Part Used Root.

Medicinal Properties Febrifuge, sudorific, sedative, diaphoretic.

A most powerful and effective remedy in skin diseases of all kinds, scrofula, scurvy, boils, tumors, fevers, acute erysipelas, cramps, pleurisy, night sweats, and is highly recommended for cancer. Very useful for enlarged veins. Dip a cloth in the tea and apply to boils and tumors. Will produce profuse perspiration without exciting the system. Especially good in low grade fever. Valuable in typhus and inflammatory diseases. Excellent combined with blue cohosh for scanty or painful menstruation. It is available in tincture form. Follow the instructions on the label.

Coriandrum sativum

Coriander

Common Names

Coriander seed.

Part Used Seed.

Medicinal Properties Aromatic, stomachic, cordial, pungent, carminative.

Coriander is a good stomach tonic and very strengthening to the heart. Will allay griping caused by other laxatives and expel wind from the bowels. Good for flavoring other unpleasant-tasting herbs. You may take one or two capsules daily or 5 to 15 drops of the fluid extract in water.

Crataegus oxyacantha

Hawthorn

Common Names English hawthorn, May bush, May tree, quick-set, thorn-apple tree, whitethorn, haw.

Part Used Flowers, dried berries.

Medicinal Properties Antispasmodic, sedative, tonic.

This herb is very good when treating either high or low blood pressure by strengthening the action of the heart. Helps many blood pressure problems. The tea is good for nervous tension and sleeplessness. Make an infusion by steeping one teaspoonful of the flowers in one-half cup of water.

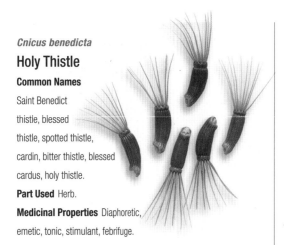

Cnicus benedicta

Holy Thistle

Common Names

Saint Benedict thistle, blessed thistle, spotted thistle, cardin, bitter thistle, blessed cardus, holy thistle.

Part Used Herb.

Medicinal Properties Diaphoretic, emetic, tonic, stimulant, febrifuge.

This plant is such a good blood purifier that drinking a cup of thistle tea twice a day will cure chronic headaches.

About 2 ounces of the dried plant simmered in a quart of water for two hours makes a tea satisfactory for most purposes. This tea is best taken at bedtime as a preventive of disease and it will cause profuse perspiration. The tea can be used for stomach and digestive problems, as well as for gas in the intestines, constipation, and liver troubles.

Caution should be used not to make the tea too strong as it may cause vomiting. It is very good combined with any of the dock roots (red dock, yellow dock, or burdock).

It is very effective for dropsy, strengthens the heart, and is good for the liver, lungs, and kidneys. It is also a good tonic for girls entering womanhood. It is claimed that the warm tea given to mothers will produce a good supply of milk.

Crocus sativus

Saffron

Common Names

Dyer's saffron, saffron seed, American saffron, thistle saffron, false saffron, bastard saffron, parrot's corn, safflower.

Part Used Flower, seed.

Medicinal Properties Laxative, emmenagogue, condiment, carminative, sudorific, diuretic, diaphoretic. Seed: aromatic, laxative, diuretic.

Saffron is one of the old-fashioned remedies. One of the most reliable in measles, all skin diseases, and scarlet fever. Will produce profuse perspiration when taken hot; therefore, it is very useful in colds and la grippe, also in regulating and increasing the menstrual flow, especially when checked by cold. It is available as a tincture, but is quite expensive. Take 5 to 15 drops in water.

As a culinary herb, it is used for flavor and as a food coloring.

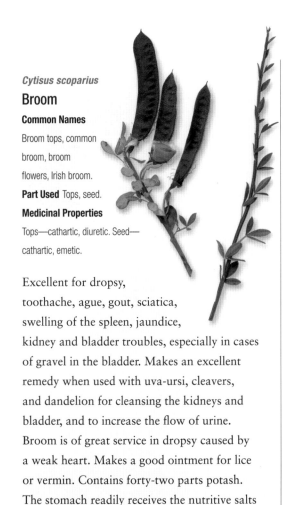

Cytisus scoparius

Broom

Common Names

Broom tops, common broom, broom flowers, Irish broom.

Part Used Tops, seed.

Medicinal Properties

Tops—cathartic, diuretic. Seed—cathartic, emetic.

Excellent for dropsy, toothache, ague, gout, sciatica, swelling of the spleen, jaundice, kidney and bladder troubles, especially in cases of gravel in the bladder. Makes an excellent remedy when used with uva-ursi, cleavers, and dandelion for cleansing the kidneys and bladder, and to increase the flow of urine. Broom is of great service in dropsy caused by a weak heart. Makes a good ointment for lice or vermin. Contains forty-two parts potash. The stomach readily receives the nutritive salts found in the plant, since they are natural.

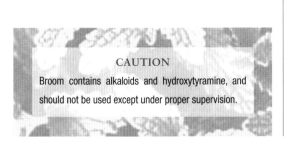

CAUTION
Broom contains alkaloids and hydroxytyramine, and should not be used except under proper supervision.

Daucus carota

Carrot

Common Names

Garden carrot, bee's nest plant, bird's nest root, wild carrot.

Part Used Root, seed.

Medicinal Properties

Anthelmintic, carminative, diuretic, stimulant.

If carrots were used more extensively as a vegetable, they would prove of great benefit to mankind. Patients are often put on a carrot diet for a short period of time for cancer, liver, kidney, and bladder troubles. Carrots are very useful in dropsy, gravel in the bladder, painful urination, to increase the menstrual flow, and in expelling worms from the bowels. Grated carrots make an excellent poultice for ulcers, abscesses, carbuncles, scrofulous and cancerous sores, and bad wounds.

The seeds of carrots, ground to powder and taken as a tea, relieve colic and increase the flow of urine. The powder may also be placed in capsules and one or two taken daily with a glass of water.

Carrot blossoms, used as a tea, are a most effective remedy for dropsy and will very often effect a cure when all other means have failed.

Dicentra canadensis

Turkey Corn

Common Names Wild turkey pea, staggerweed, dielytra, turkey pea, squirrel corn, choice dielytra.

Part Used Root.

Medicinal Properties Tonic, alterative, diuretic, antisyphilitic.

An excellent remedy in syphilis, scrofula, and all skin diseases. For boils, it is most effective when used in combination with hot baths and salt glows. An excellent tonic in all enfeebled conditions. One of the most valuable alteratives in the herbal kingdom. Take as a tea like other herbs.

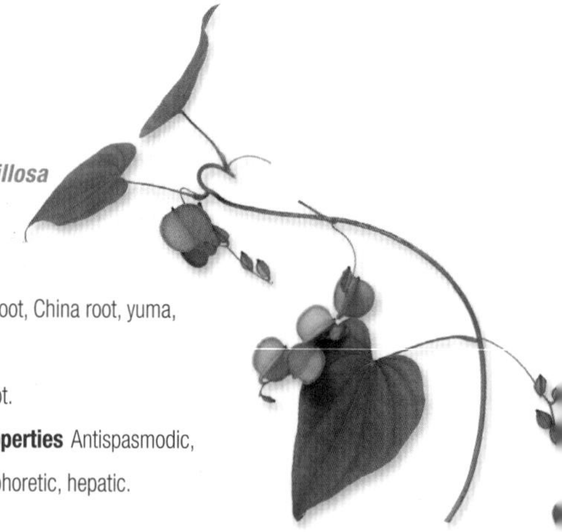

Dioscorea villosa

Wild Yam

Common Names Colic root, China root, yuma, devil's bones.

Part Used Root.

Medicinal Properties Antispasmodic, antibilious, diaphoretic, hepatic.

Very relaxing and soothing to the nerves. Useful in all cases of nervous excitement. Will expel gas from the stomach and bowels. Good in cholera. Useful in neuralgia of any part. Excellent for pains in the urinary tract. One of the best herbs for general pain during pregnancy. Take during the whole period of pregnancy. Will allay nausea in small frequent doses, but may cause vomiting if taken in large amounts. Combined with ginger, it will greatly help in preventing miscarriage. Use a teaspoonful of wild yam and one-fourth teaspoonful of ginger. Also good to combine with squaw vine for use during pregnancy.

Valuable in ailments of the liver, spasms, and rheumatic pains. Steep a heaping teaspoonful in a cup of boiling water for 30 minutes. Drink one to three cupfuls a day cold, a large swallow at a time.

Erechtites hieracifolia

Fireweed

Common Names Pilewort, various leaved fleabane.

Part Used Entire plant.

Medicinal Properties Astringent, tonic, emetic, alterative.

Is strongly astringent and therefore most excellent in diseases of the mucous membranes, colon troubles, cholera, and dysentery. Will quickly relieve pain in these conditions. Is almost a specific for piles.

Very effective in children for summer diarrhea. It gives prompt relief when taken very hot. Excellent remedy for fevers and as a tonic and blood purifier. Take for only one week at a time. Take the capsules with a swallow of milk. Steep a heaping teaspoonful in a cup of boiling water for 30 minutes. When cool, drink one to two cups a day, taking just one swallow at a time.

Echinacea angustifolia

Echinacea

Common Names Sampson root, purple cone flower, black Sampson, red sunflower.

Part Used Root.

Medicinal Properties Alterative, antiseptic, tonic, depurative, maturating, febrifuge.

An excellent blood cleanser. Used for blood poisoning, fevers, carbuncles, acne, eczema, boils, peritonitis, syphilitic conditions, bites and stings of poisonous insects or snakes, erysipelas, gangrenous conditions, diphtheria, tonsillitis, sores, infections, wounds.

Use as a gargle for sore throat. Combined with myrrh, it is an excellent remedy for all of these purposes. It acts powerfully to cleanse the morbid matter from the stomach and to expel poisons, toxins, pus, or abscess formations. Combined with myrrh, it is also excellent for typhoid and other fevers. In severe cases use two capsules four times a day or 10 to 25 drops of the tincture every two hours in water.

Erigeron canadense

Fleabane

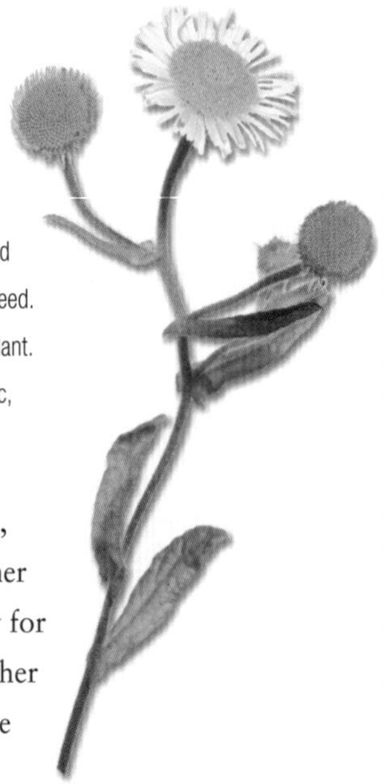

Common Names Canada fleabane, horse tail, cow's tail, horseweed, pride weed, colt's tail, mare's tail, scabious, blood staunch, butter weed, bitter weed.

Part Used Leaves or entire plant.

Medicinal Properties Styptic, astringent, diuretic, tonic.

Excellent for cholera, dysentery, and summer complaint, especially for children, when all other remedies fail. In these afflictions, use as an enema. Steep a teaspoonful in a quart of boiling water for 20 minutes; use hot, about 112° to 115°F. This is an excellent remedy for all colon troubles. It can be improved by using equal parts of white oak bark, wild alum root, and catnip. Taken internally, it is very reliable for bladder troubles, burning urine, and hemorrhages from the bowels and uterus. Good for tuberculosis.

Eriodictyon glutinosum

Yerba Santa

Common Names Consumptive's weed, gum plant, bear's weed, mountain balm, tar weed.

Part Used Leaves.

Medicinal Properties Tonic, expectorant, aromatic.

This is a well-tried and much used remedy in laryngitis, chronic bronchitis, asthma, and various catarrhal lung ailments. Effective when there is excessive discharge from the nose. Good in rheumatism. Can be applied as a poultice for sores, insect bites, sprains, and bruises.

Erythraea centaurium

Centaury

Common Names

Century, centory, feverwort, bitter herb, common centaury, lesser centaury.

Part Used Herb.

Medicinal Properties Tonic, stomachic, aromatic, cholagogue, diaphoretic, digestive, febrifuge, emetic.

This is an herb that may be used for nearly any problem. It is also good as a tonic for those who are unable to get sufficient exercise in the open air. It is used extensively for gas, colic, bloating, heartburn, dyspepsia, and constipation and aids the proper assimilation and digestion of food. If taken in too concentrated an infusion, it will produce vomiting. Lotions containing centaury have been used on the skin to remove different kinds of blemishes.

Use two teaspoonfuls of the herb to a cup of boiling water: let steep for 20 to 30 minutes, cool, and take a cupful every day, one swallow at a time.

Eucalyptus globulus

Eucalyptus Globulus

Common Names

Bluegum tree.

Part Used Leaves, bark.

Medicinal Properties

Antiseptic, stimulant, expectorant, antispasmodic.

The wonderful eucalyptus tree, from which eucalyptus oil is made, has a wide range of uses. The leaves and bark are very useful in fevers, acute and chronic bronchitis in its various forms, asthma, and similar ailments. The oil made from the leaves may be inhaled for asthma, diphtheria, or sore throat. The antiseptic properties make it useful for use on wounds and ulcers. When used in this way, 1 ounce should be added to a pint of warm water. The oil may also be applied externally to the neck and chest for cough, croup, and sore throat.

Euonymus atropurpureus

Wahoo

Common Names

Whahow, wauhoo, Indian root, Indian arrow, Indian arrow wood, burning bush, bitter ash, arrow wood, spindle tree, strawberry tree, pegwood.

Part Used Bark, bark of the root.

Medicinal Properties

Tonic, laxative, expectorant, diuretic, alterative.

A splendid laxative. Excellent in chest and lung infections. Useful in fevers, malaria, dyspepsia, liver disorders, pancreas and spleen troubles. Good remedy for dropsy. Steep a small teaspoonful in a cup of boiling water for 30 minutes. Take two or three cups a day, an hour before meals. Better than quinine.

CAUTION

Using too much wahoo bark may result in a severe purgative action. Be careful not to use too much and use only under proper supervision.

Eupatorium purpureum

Queen Of The Meadow

Common Names Grave root, kidney root, joe-pye weed, purple boneset, trumpet weed.

Part Used Root, whole herb.

Medicinal Properties

Diuretic, stimulant, tonic, astringent, relaxant.

This is a good remedy for gravel in the bladder, chronic urinary and kidney disorders, dropsy, neuralgia, and all such ailments. Excellent for rheumatism. Very soothing and will relax the nerves. Increases the flow of urine. Wonderful remedy when combined with uva-ursi, marshmallow, blue cohosh, and lily root for female troubles, bladder and kidney infections, diabetes, and Bright's disease. As a tincture, take 5 to 15 drops in a cup of water.

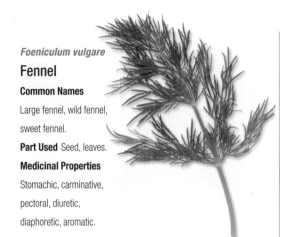

Foeniculum vulgare

Fennel

Common Names

Large fennel, wild fennel, sweet fennel.

Part Used Seed, leaves.

Medicinal Properties

Stomachic, carminative, pectoral, diuretic, diaphoretic, aromatic.

Fennel is an old reliable household remedy and is also used as a culinary herb. It is good for flavoring foods and other medicines. The tea makes an excellent eye wash. Fennel is one of the thoroughly tried remedies for gas, acid stomach, gout, cramps, colic, and spasms. Ground fennel sprinkled on food will prevent gas in the stomach and bowels. It is an excellent remedy for colic in small children. For this use, the herb should be steeped and given in small doses every half hour until the infant or child is relieved. Fennel seed ground and made into a tea is good for snake bites, insect bites, or food poisoning. It is good in cases of jaundice when the liver is obstructed. Excellent for obesity. Increases the flow of urine and also increases the menstrual flow. Fennel oil may be rubbed over painful joints to relieve pain and may also be added to gargles for hoarseness and sore throat. Available in capsule or powder form. Take one or two capsules daily.

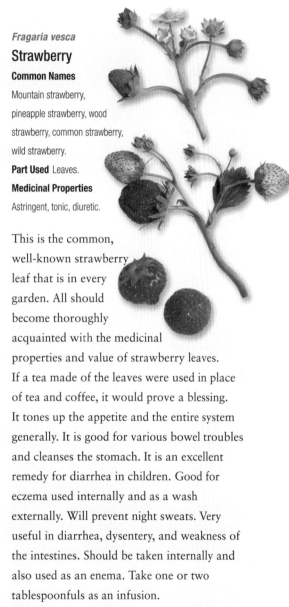

Fragaria vesca

Strawberry

Common Names

Mountain strawberry, pineapple strawberry, wood strawberry, common strawberry, wild strawberry.

Part Used Leaves.

Medicinal Properties

Astringent, tonic, diuretic.

This is the common, well-known strawberry leaf that is in every garden. All should become thoroughly acquainted with the medicinal properties and value of strawberry leaves. If a tea made of the leaves were used in place of tea and coffee, it would prove a blessing. It tones up the appetite and the entire system generally. It is good for various bowel troubles and cleanses the stomach. It is an excellent remedy for diarrhea in children. Good for eczema used internally and as a wash externally. Will prevent night sweats. Very useful in diarrhea, dysentery, and weakness of the intestines. Should be taken internally and also used as an enema. Take one or two tablespoonfuls as an infusion.

Fucus vesiculosus

Seawrack

Common Names

Bladder fucus, seaweed, bladderwrack, sea oak, kelpware, black tany, cutweed.

Part Used Entire plant.

Medicinal Properties

Alterative, diuretic.

The best remedy for obesity. Good in all glandular afflictions, goiter, and scrofula. Has an excellent effect on the kidneys. Steep a heaping teaspoonful to a cup of boiling water for 30 minutes. Drink three or four cups a day an hour before meals, and one final hot cup upon retiring.

Galium aparine

Cleavers

Common Names Bedstraw, clivers, coachweed, goose grass, goose's hair, grip grass, gravel grass, gosling weed, hedge-burrs, clabber grass, catchweed, milk sweet, poor robin, savoyan, scratchweed, cleaverwort, cheese rent herb.

Part Used Entire herb.

Medicinal Properties Refrigerant, diuretic, aperient, alterative, tonic.

One of the best remedies for kidney and bladder troubles, particularly burning or suppressed urine, especially when used with broom, uva-ursi, buchu, and marshmallow. Makes an excellent wash for the face to clear the complexion. Due to its refrigerant properties it is excellent in all cases of fever, scarlet fever, measles, and all acute diseases. Good in many skin diseases, such as cancer, scrofula, and severe cases of eczema. Also good for inflammatory stages of gonorrhea.

Excellent for stones in the bladder, scurvy, and dropsy. Cleavers is very astringent due to its high tannin content. It should be taken for only two weeks at a time, and then skip one or two weeks. Place 1 ounce in 1 pint of hot water and simmer for 20 minutes. Take one teaspoonful three times a day.

Gaultheria procumbens

Wintergreen

Common Names

Spring wintergreen, Canada tea, partridge berry, checkerberry, boxberry, wax cluster, spice berry, mountain tea, deerberry, spicy wintergreen, aromatic wintergreen, chink, ground berry, grouse berry, red pollom, redberry tea, hillberry, ivory plum.

Part Used Leaves.

Medicinal Properties Stimulant, antiseptic, astringent, diuretic, emmenagogue, aromatic.

This is an old-fashioned remedy. Taken in small frequent doses it will stimulate stomach, heart, and respiration. Useful in chronic inflammatory rheumatism, also rheumatic fever, sciatica, diabetes, all bladder troubles, scrofula, and skin diseases. Valuable in colic and gas in the bowels. Helpful in dropsy, gonorrhea, stomach trouble, and obstruction in the bowels.

The oil of the wintergreen is used internally and externally. It is very useful in liniments.

Used as a poultice, it is good for boils, swellings, ulcers, felons, and inflammation. A douche of the tea is excellent in whites and leukorrhea. The tea is also very beneficial as a gargle for sore throat and mouth. Good wash for sore eyes.

Gentiana lutea

Gentian Root

Common Names Bitterroot, bitterwort, gentian, yellow gentian, pale gentian, felwort.

Part Used Root, leaves.

Medicinal Properties Stomachic, tonic, anthelmintic, antibilious.

An excellent and reliable tonic. Purifies the blood. Good for liver complaints and dysentery. Most effective for jaundice. Excellent for the spleen. Gentian root will improve the appetite and strengthen the digestive organs. It is especially good for gastritis, indigestion, heartburn, and stomach aches. When used for these conditions, gentian should be taken 30 to 60 minutes before meals.

It increases the circulation, benefits the female organs, and invigorates the entire system. Useful in fevers, colds, gout, convulsions, scrofula, and dyspepsia. It will expel worms. Excellent in suppressed menstruation and scanty urine. Because of its bitterness, it is better to combine gentian root with some aromatic herb such as a small amount of licorice.

Allays poison from mad dog, insect, and snake bites. Take one-fourth to one-half teaspoonful of the powder in a cup of water three times a day 30 minutes before meals.

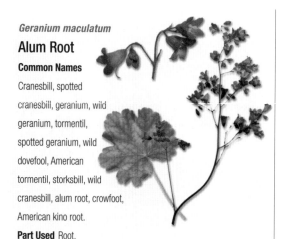

Geranium maculatum

Alum Root

Common Names
Cranesbill, spotted cranesbill, geranium, wild geranium, tormentil, spotted geranium, wild dovefool, American tormentil, storksbill, wild cranesbill, alum root, crowfoot, American kino root.

Part Used Root.

Medicinal Properties Astringent, styptic, antiseptic.

A powerful astringent. Rinse the mouth often with a strong tea for sores and bleeding gums. Excellent in hemorrhage, bleeding wounds, nosebleed, and profuse menstruation. The dry powder sprinkled on a wound will stop bleeding. Useful in old chronic ulcers. For hemorrhoids, inject as an enema two or three tablespoonfuls of the strong tea several times a day. Excellent for mucus and pus in the bladder and intestines, and for leukorrhea. Very useful in diabetes and Bright's disease. For mucous discharges, it is excellent when used with an equal part of golden seal. Use a teaspoonful of each to a pint of boiling water.

Let steep 30 minutes. Use as an injection for piles, as a douche, or take internally, a tablespoonful four to six times a day. For general use, steep a heaping teaspoonful in a cup of boiling water for 30 minutes.

Glycyrrhiza glabra

Licorice

Common Names Sweetwood, licorice root.

Part Used Root.

Medicinal Properties Laxative, tonic, expectorant, demulcent, pectoral, emollient.

Licorice is primarily used for lung and throat problems. It is useful in coughs, bronchitis, congestion, etc. It was used as a treatment for coughs as long ago as the third century BC. It is frequently added to other herbal combinations to make them more palatable and for its demulcent action. Acts as a mild laxative. A decoction of one teaspoonful of the root in one cup of water is a good strength to use for children. A mixture of licorice, wild cherry, and flaxseed makes a wonderful cough syrup. It is available as a powder or in capsules.

CAUTION
Do not take licorice if you have high blood pressure.

Hamamelis virginiana

Witch Hazel

Common Names Winter bloom, striped alder, spotted alder, hazelnut, snapping hazel, pistachio, tobacco wood.

Part Used Bark, leaves.

Medicinal Properties Astringent, tonic, antiphlogistic, sedative, styptic.

Very valuable for stopping either internal or external bleeding. Also good in the treatment of piles. It is unsurpassed for stopping excessive menstruation, hemorrhages from the lungs, stomach, uterus, and bowels. For piles or diarrhea, inject a teaspoonful into the rectum several times a day and after each stool. As a poultice or wash it is excellent for painful tumors, all external inflammations, bedsores, and sore and inflamed eyes. For use internally, steep a heaping teaspoonful in a cup of boiling water for 30 minutes. Take one or more cupfuls during the day as needed, a large mouthful at a time.

CAUTION

Do not drink witch hazel purchased from the drug store; it contains an alcohol that is not intended to be used internally.

Hedeoma pulegioides

Pennyroyal

Common Names Tickweed, squaw mint, stinking balm, thickweed, American pennyroyal, mock pennyroyal, mosquito plant, squaw balm.

Part Used Entire plant, oil.

Medicinal Properties

Sudorific, carminative, emmenagogue, stimulant, diaphoretic, aromatic, sedative.

It is excellent in burning fevers and will promote perspiration when taken hot. Excellent remedy for toothache, gout, leprosy, colds, consumption, phlegm in the chest and lungs, jaundice, dropsy, cramps, convulsions, headache, ulcers, sores in mouth, insect and snake bites, itch, intestinal pains, colic, and griping. If troubled with suppressed or scanty menstruation, take one or two cupfuls hot at bedtime along with a hot foot bath, several days before menstruation is expected.

It will relieve nausea, but SHOULD NOT BE TAKEN DURING PREGNANCY. Good as a poultice and wash for bruises or black eyes. Good for nervousness and hysteria. Useful for skin diseases and the oil is an excellent insect repellent. Take one or two cups a day or use one-half teaspoonful of the powder in a cup of hot water.

Helianthemum canadense

Rock Rose

Common Names Frostwort, frost weed, frost plant, sun rose, scrofula plant.

Part Used Oil from the herb.

Medicinal Properties Aromatic, tonic, alterative, astringent.

It is a valuable remedy for scrofula and has long been used for this purpose. Simmer a teaspoonful of the herb in a cup of water for 10 minutes. Cool, strain, and take from four to six large swallows. A poultice made from the leaves is good for scrofulous tumors and ulcers. Excellent gargle for sore throat and scarlatina. Good for diarrhea, syphilis, and gonorrhea. Helpful in treating some forms of cancer.

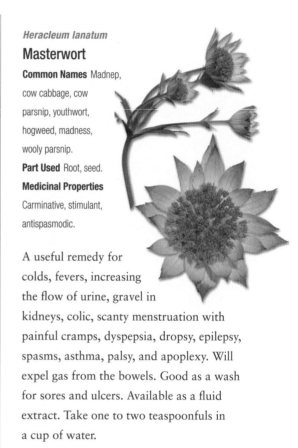

Heracleum lanatum

Masterwort

Common Names Madnep, cow cabbage, cow parsnip, youthwort, hogweed, madness, wooly parsnip.

Part Used Root, seed.

Medicinal Properties Carminative, stimulant, antispasmodic.

A useful remedy for colds, fevers, increasing the flow of urine, gravel in kidneys, colic, scanty menstruation with painful cramps, dyspepsia, dropsy, epilepsy, spasms, asthma, palsy, and apoplexy. Will expel gas from the bowels. Good as a wash for sores and ulcers. Available as a fluid extract. Take one to two teaspoonfuls in a cup of water.

Humulus lupulus

Hops

Common Names Common hops, European hops.

Part Used Flowers.

Medicinal Properties Febrifuge, tonic, nervine, diuretic, anodyne, hypnotic, anthelmintic, sedative.

Hops is an old-fashioned and very useful remedy. An excellent nervine. Will produce sleep when nothing else will. Two or three cups should be taken hot. Valuable in delirium tremens. Is a good remedy for toothache, earache, neuralgia, and like ailments. Will tone up the liver, increase the flow of urine and bile, and is good for excessive sexual desires and gonorrhea. Put a tablespoonful in a pint of water and simmer for 10 minutes. Drink a half pint morning and evening. A pillow stuffed with hops has long been used to produce sleep and is very effective. Good in diseases of the chest and throat. Hop poultices are very effective for inflammation, boils, tumors, painful swellings, and old ulcers.

Hydrangea arborescens

Hydrangea

Common Names Wild hydrangea, seven barks.

Part Used Leaves, root.

Medicinal Properties Root—diuretic, lithontryptic. Leaves—tonic, diuretic, sialagogue, cathartic.

This is an old remedy that is very valuable in bladder troubles. It will remove and also help prevent the formation of bladder stones and gravel; will ease the pains caused by the stones. Will relieve backache caused by kidney troubles. Good for chronic rheumatism, paralysis, scurvy, and dropsy. The hydrangea root has been used for a long time as a mild diuretic. This herb may act differently in different people.

In some it may act as a laxative. Therefore, it is better to start with a smaller dose and increase slowly as needed. The average dose is two capsules daily. To make tea, infuse 1 ounce of the root in 1 pint of boiling water and take in wineglass doses, either hot or cold.

Hydrastis canadensis

Golden Seal

Common Names Yellow paint root, orange root, yellow puccoon, ground raspberry, eye root, yellow Indian plant, tumeric root, Ohio curcuma, eye balm, yellow eye, jaundice root.

Part Used Root.

Medicinal Properties Laxative, tonic, alterative, detergent, opthalmicum, antiperiodic, aperient, diuretic, antiseptic, deobstruent.

This is one of the most wonderful remedies in the entire herb kingdom. It is especially valuable in all diseased states of the digestive system.

It is a wonderful remedy for all stomach disorders and acute inflammations and is a most excellent remedy for colds, la grippe, and all kinds of stomach and liver troubles. It exerts a special influence on all the mucous membranes and tissues with which it comes in contact. For open sores, inflammations, eczema, ringworm, erysipelas, or any skin disease, golden seal excels. Golden seal tea is made by steeping one teaspoonful in a pint of boiling water for 20 minutes. Use this tea as a wash. Then after the area is thoroughly clean, sprinkle on some of the powdered root and cover. It is beneficial also to use hydrogen peroxide for cleansing the area.

Taken in small but frequent doses, it will allay nausea during pregnancy. Steep a teaspoonful in a pint of boiling water for 20 minutes, stir well, let settle, and pour off the liquid. Take six tablespoonfuls a day. It equalizes the circulation and, when combined with skullcap and red pepper (cayenne), will greatly relieve and strengthen the heart. It has no superior when combined with myrrh, one part golden seal to one-fourth part myrrh, for an ulcerated stomach or duodenum or dyspepsia, and is especially good for enlarged tonsils and sores in the mouth. If the sore continues to enlarge, proper medical advice should be sought.

It is an excellent remedy for diphtheria, tonsillitis, and other serious throat troubles, and has a good effect when combined with a little myrrh and cayenne. Excellent for chronic catarrh of the intestines and all catarrhal conditions. Will improve the appetite and aid digestion.

Combined with skullcap and hops, it is a very fine tonic for spinal nerves and is very good in spinal meningitis. Very useful in all skin eruptions, scarlet fever, and smallpox.

To cure pyorrhea or sore gums, put a little of the tea in a cup, dip a toothbrush in it, and thoroughly brush the teeth and gums. The results will be most satisfactory. In any nose trouble, pour some tea in the hollow of the hand and snuff it up the nose. Very useful in typhoid fever, gonorrhea, leukorrhea, and syphilis. For bladder troubles, it should be introduced into the bladder through a catheter immediately after the bladder has been emptied and retained as long as possible, repeating two or three times a day. Have a physician or nurse inject it for you through a sterile rubber catheter.

Golden seal combined with alum root, taken internally, is an excellent remedy for bowel and bladder troubles, Use two parts of golden seal and one part of wild alum. This is a good laxative. Good for piles, hemorrhoids, and prostate trouble. When combined with equal parts of red clover blossoms, yellow dock, and dandelion, it has a wonderful effect on the gallbladder, liver, pancreas, spleen, and kidneys. Combined with peach leaves, queen of the meadow, cleavers, and corn silk, it is a reliable aid for Bright's disease and diabetes.

Golden seal is excellent for the eyes. Steep one small teaspoonful of golden seal and one of boric acid in a pint of boiling water, stir thoroughly, let cool, and pour off the liquid. Put a tablespoonful of this liquid in a half cup of water. Bathe the eyes with this, using an eye cup, or drop it in with an eye dropper.

Golden seal may be used alone. Take one-fourth teaspoonful of golden seal dissolved in a glass of hot water immediately upon arising, and one hour before the noon and evening meals. Or you may steep a teaspoonful in a pint of boiling water, stir thoroughly, let cool, pour the liquid

off and take a tablespoonful four to six times a day. Children should take less of all doses according to age.

There are many remedies advertised as containing golden seal; but the fact is that the herb is very expensive. Usually there is so little golden seal in commercial preparations that it does very little good.

Chronic catarrh (inflammation with a discharge) of the intestines, even to the extent of ulceration, is greatly benefited by golden seal. Golden seal is effective in treating hemorrhage from the rectum and will heal ulcerations of the mucous lining in this area. It is a remedy for chronic and intermittent malaria or enlarged spleen caused by malaria.

From the above it will be seen how applicable golden seal is in all catarrhal conditions, whether of the throat, nasal passages, bronchial tubes, intestines, stomach, bladder, or wherever there is a lining of mucous membrane. It kills and neutralizes many poisons. Take one or two capsules daily. Don't take too much, as golden seal may be quite strong.

CAUTION

Do not take either during pregnancy or continuously for a long period of time without some periods of rest.

Hypericum perforatum

St. John's Wort

Common Names

Johnswort, goat weed, amber, Klamath weed.

Part Used Tops, flowers.

Medicinal Properties

Aromatic, nervine, astringent, resolvent, sedative, diuretic, vulnerary.

Powerful as a blood purifier. Very good for tumors and boils, as well as for chronic uterine troubles, pains following childbirth, suppressed urine, diarrhea, dysentery, and jaundice. Will correct irregular menstruation. Good used externally as fomentations or as an ointment for caked breasts, all wounds, ulcers, and old sores. Will correct bedwetting in children when proper diet is given. The seeds steeped in boiling water will expel congealed blood from the stomach. Use a heaping teaspoonful of the seeds to a cup of boiling water and take a mouthful several times a day.

CAUTION

May be toxic. Use with care under competent medical supervision.

Hyssopus officinalis

Hyssop

Common Names Hisopo, curdukotu.

Part Used Entire plant.

Medicinal Properties Anthelmintic, aromatic, aperient, carminative, expectorant, febrifuge, pectoral, stimulant, sudorific.

Hyssop, in connection with water and deep breathing, is a most wonderful body cleanser.

Valuable in quinsy, asthma, colds, coughs, and all lung afflictions. Can be applied as a compress and used as a gargle. In fevers, give a glassful every hour of a tea made by simmering a tablespoonful of the herb in a pint of boiling water for ten minutes. It will start perspiration, relieve the kidneys and bladder, and is slightly laxative. Hyssop increases the circulation of the blood and will reduce blood pressure. It is excellent for scrofula, gravel in the bladder, various stomach troubles, jaundice, dropsy, and for the spleen.

A fine remedy for epilepsy in connection with other hygienic measures. It will expel worms. The leaves, applied to inflammations and bruises, will remove the pain and discoloration. Effective for insect stings and bites. Kills body lice. Hyssop is good for all kinds of fevers.

Inula helenium

Elecampane

Common Names Scabwort, elfwort, horseheal, horse-elder.

Part Used Root.

Medicinal Properties
Diaphoretic, diuretic, expectorant, aromatic, stimulant, stomachic, astringent, and tonic.

Useful in coughs, asthma, and bronchitis. When combined with echinacea, is an excellent remedy in tuberculosis. It is a stimulant and tonic to the mucous membranes. Warms and strengthens the lungs and promotes expectoration. A tea of elecampane is useful in whooping cough. It strengthens, cleanses, and tones up the mucous membranes of the lungs and stomach. It can also be used in urinary retention, kidney and bladder stones, and delayed menstruation. Take one capsule three times a day. Liquid extract, one-half to one teaspoonful.

Iris versicolor

Blue Flag

Common Names
Poison flag, water flag, water lily, flag lily, fleur-de-lis, liver lily, snake lily, flower-de-luce, iris.

Part Used Rhizome.

Medicinal Properties
Alterative, resolvent, sialagogue, laxative, diuretic, vermifuge.

Useful in cancer, rheumatism, dropsy, impurity of blood, constipation, syphilis, skin diseases, liver troubles, and as a laxative. It is very relaxing and stimulating.

Jeffersonia diphylla

Twin Leaf

Common Names Ground squirrel pea, rheumatism root, helmet pod, yellow root, twin leaf root.

Part Used Root.

Medicinal Properties Diuretic, alterative, antisyphilitic, antirheumatic, antispasmodic, tonic.

Very useful in chronic rheumatism, nervous, and spasmodic afflictions. Very successful in neuralgia, cramps, and syphilis. Splendid gargle for throat troubles. Fine in scarlet fever, scarlatina, and indolent ulcers. A poultice or hot fomentation made out of the strong tea, will relieve pain anywhere in the body. In severe pains, take the herb hot internally. Steep a teaspoonful in a cup of boiling water for 30 minutes; simmer for 10 minutes, then strain and drink one cupful. Follow with small frequent doses.

Juniperus communis

Juniper

Common Names
Juniper bush, Juniper bark.

Part Used Berries.

Medicinal Properties
Diuretic, carminative, tonic, antiseptic, stomachic.

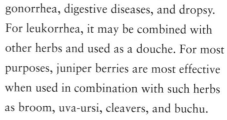

The tea is very effective for kidney, prostate and bladder trouble, gleet, leukorrhea, gonorrhea, digestive diseases, and dropsy. For leukorrhea, it may be combined with other herbs and used as a douche. For most purposes, juniper berries are most effective when used in combination with such herbs as broom, uva-ursi, cleavers, and buchu.

The dried berries are excellent as a preventive of disease, and should be chewed or used as a strong tea to gargle the throat when exposed to contagious diseases.

It is useful to inhale the steam for colds, respiratory infections, bronchitis, etc. The pure oil should not be rubbed on the skin as it can be very irritating. It is not recommended for pregnant women and should not be taken in large doses or over a prolonged period because of its possible irritating effect on the bladder and kidneys. Take one or two cups of the tea a day, a mouthful at a time, for one week.

Juglans cinerea

Butternut Bark

Common Names Oilnut, oilnut bark, white walnut, lemon walnut, Kisky Thomas nut.

Part Used Inner bark.

Medicinal Properties Tonic, astringent, cholagogue, anthelmintic, alterative, cathartic.

An excellent gentle laxative, very good for chronic constipation. Will expel worms from the intestines. Good for sluggish liver, fevers, colds, and la grippe. It is an old-fashioned remedy. As a powder, use five to ten grains or take one No. 00 capsule daily.

Lawsonia inermis

Henna

Common Names Jamaica mignonette, Egyptian privet, alcanna, henna plant.

Part Used Leaves, root.

Medicinal Properties Astringent.

The leaves can be used internally or externally for jaundice, leprosy, and other skin problems. It is occasionally used for headaches and a tea made from the leaves is useful as a gargle for sore throat. The bark is used as a dye.

Lavandula vera

Lavender

Common Names Garden lavender, spike lavender, common lavender.

Part Used Plant.

Medicinal Properties Stimulant, aromatic, fragrant, carminative.

A tea steeped from the flowers is tonic, prevents fainting, and allays nausea. Excellent when combined with other herbs to disguise their taste. The flowers are also used in making perfumes. The dried flowers and leaves are used to put in drawers and linen closets.

Sometimes used to keep moths from clothing and furs. Leaves are used as a culinary herb for seasoning. Not used very often as a medicine nowadays.

Leonurus cardiaca

Motherwort

Common Names Lion's tail, lion's ear, throwwort.

Part Used Entire plant.

Medicinal Properties Antispasmodic, nervine, emmenagogue, laxative, hepatic, tonic.

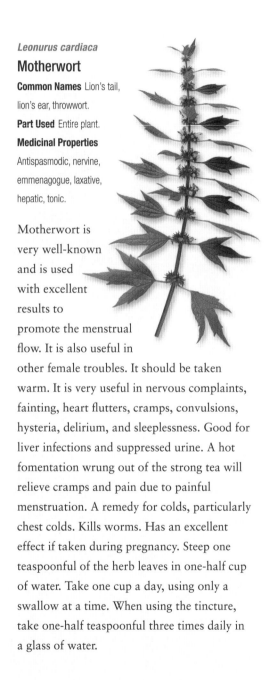

Motherwort is very well-known and is used with excellent results to promote the menstrual flow. It is also useful in other female troubles. It should be taken warm. It is very useful in nervous complaints, fainting, heart flutters, cramps, convulsions, hysteria, delirium, and sleeplessness. Good for liver infections and suppressed urine. A hot fomentation wrung out of the strong tea will relieve cramps and pain due to painful menstruation. A remedy for colds, particularly chest colds. Kills worms. Has an excellent effect if taken during pregnancy. Steep one teaspoonful of the herb leaves in one-half cup of water. Take one cup a day, using only a swallow at a time. When using the tincture, take one-half teaspoonful three times daily in a glass of water.

Leptandra virginica

Black Root

Common Names Culver's physic, tall speedwell, tall veronica, Culver's root, beaumont root, bowman's root, leptandra, hini, oxadoddy, physic root, whorlywort.

Part Used Root.

Medicinal Properties Cathartic, cholagogue, tonic, emetic, hepatic.

The fresh root is too toxic to use safely. The dried root is an excellent laxative and tonic and is useful in cases of sluggish liver to stimulate the normal flow of bile.

Even the dried root must be used with caution as it contains leptandrin, a very strong purgative and emetic. It is best to use only with medical supervision. Steep a teaspoonful of the dried root, cut into small pieces, in a cup of boiling water for half an hour. Drink cold, one mouthful before each meal. Start with a small dose and gradually increase the amount taken, as tolerated, to no more than one cup a day.

Linum usitatissimum

Flaxseed

Common Names Linseed, common flax, winterlien, lint bells.

Part Used Ripe seed.

Medicinal Properties Demulcent, pectoral, maturating, mucilaginous, emollient.

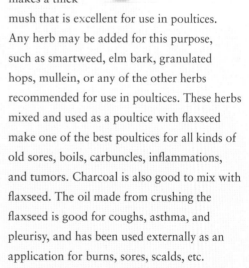

This is the common flaxseed with which almost everyone is familiar. The ground seed, when mixed with boiling water, makes a thick mush that is excellent for use in poultices. Any herb may be added for this purpose, such as smartweed, elm bark, granulated hops, mullein, or any of the other herbs recommended for use in poultices. These herbs mixed and used as a poultice with flaxseed make one of the best poultices for all kinds of old sores, boils, carbuncles, inflammations, and tumors. Charcoal is also good to mix with flaxseed. The oil made from crushing the flaxseed is good for coughs, asthma, and pleurisy, and has been used externally as an application for burns, sores, scalds, etc.

Place one teaspoonful of the seed in a cup of boiling water, let cool, and take one or two mouthfuls three times a day.

Lobelia inflata

Lobelia

Common Names Indian tobacco, bladderpod, wild tobacco, emetic herb, emetic weed, lobelia herb, puke weed, asthma weed, rag root, eye-bright, vomit wort.

Part Used Entire plant.

Medicinal Properties Emetic, expectorant, diuretic, nervine, diaphoretic.

Lobelia is one of the most extensively used herbs and is used chiefly as an emetic or in pulmonary complaints such as bronchitis, croup, whooping cough, asthma, etc., antispasmodic, stimulant.

Lobelia is the most powerful relaxant known among the herbs that have no harmful effects when used externally. Lobelia acts differently upon different people, but it will not hurt anyone. It makes the pulse fuller and slower in cases of inflammation and fever. Lobelia reduces palpitation of the heart. It is fine in the treatment of all fevers and in pneumonia, meningitis, pleurisy, hepatitis, peritonitis, periostitis, and nephritis. Lobelia alone cannot cure, but it is very beneficial if given in connection with other measures, such as an enema of catnip infusion morning and evening. The enema should be given even if the patient is delirious. It will relieve the brain.

Pleurisy root is a specific remedy for pleurisy, and it is also excellent if combined with lobelia for its relaxing properties.

The use of lobelia in fevers is superior to any other remedy. It is excellent for very nervous patients. Poultices or hot fomentations of lobelia are good in external inflammations, such as rheumatism. It is excellent to add lobelia to poultices for abscesses, boils, and carbuncles. Use one-third lobelia to two-thirds slippery elm bark or the same proportion to any other herb you are using.

While lobelia is an excellent emetic, it is a strange fact that when given in small doses for an irritated stomach it will stop vomiting. In cases of asthma, give a lobelia pack, followed the next morning by an emetic. The pack will loosen the waste material and it will be cast out with the emetic. In bad cases where the liver is affected and the skin yellow, combine equal parts of pleurisy root, catnip, and bitterroot.

Lobelia is excellent for whooping cough. There is nothing that will as quickly clear the air passages of the lungs as lobelia. A TINCTURE, made as follows, will stop difficult breathing and clear the air passages of the lungs if taken a tablespoonful at a time:

lobelia herb	2 ounces
crushed lobelia seed	2 ounces
apple vinegar	1 pint

Soak for two weeks in a well-stoppered bottle, shaking every day. Then strain, and it is ready for use. This is also good used as an external application, rubbing between the shoulders and chest in asthma. A lobelia poultice is excellent for sprains, felons, bruises, ringworm, erysipelas, stings of insects, and poison ivy.

The following paragraphs are quoted from *The Medicines of Nature*, pages 65–69, and are the opinions of Drs. Thompson, Scudder, Lyle, Greer, Stephens, and other physicians.

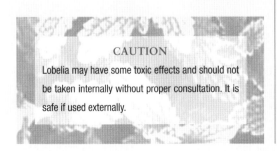

CAUTION

Lobelia may have some toxic effects and should not be taken internally without proper consultation. It is safe if used externally.

Lobelia inflata

The herb and seeds of this plant are largely used by all herbal practitioners. It is employed in quite a number of cases and has won a richly deserved place in the annals of herbal writers. To Dr. Samuel Thompson is due the credit of first bringing this article into real use. It had, no doubt, been used to produce emesis in some localities previously, but its great uses were made known by him.

Now for the uses of this plant. The herb and seed have similar properties, the seed, however, being much the stronger. In infusing the seeds, it is best to crush them. Both herb and seed contain a volatile oil, and if the seed is kept in paper, some of the oil will be absorbed by the paper.

Lobelia is a most efficient relaxant, influencing mucous, serous, nervous, and muscular structures. IT IS A GOOD RULE, TO ALWAYS GIVE A STIMULANT BEFORE ADMINISTERING LOBELIA, OR TO COMBINE A STIMULANT WITH IT.

It is used in coughs, bronchitis, asthma, whooping cough, pneumonia, hysteria, convulsions, suspended animation, tetanus, febrile troubles, etc.

It may be used in substance, i.e., the powdered herb or seed, in fluid extract, acid tincture, infusion, decoction, pills or capsules, in syrup, by enema, and in poultices.

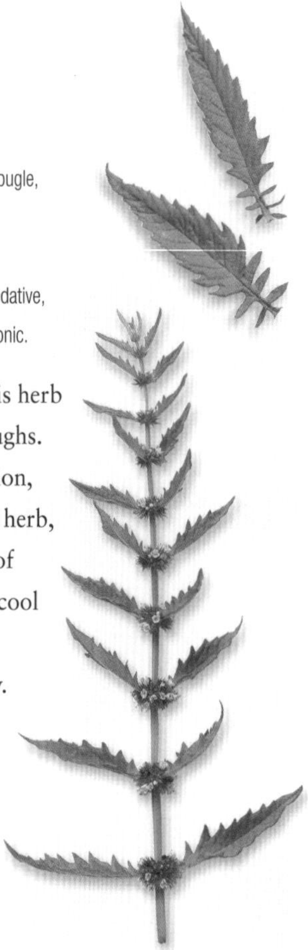

Lycopus virginicus

Bugleweed

Common Names Sweet bugle, water bugle, gipsywort.

Part Used Entire plant.

Medicinal Properties Sedative, astringent, mild narcotic, tonic.

The infusion of this herb is excellent for coughs. To make the infusion, use 1 ounce of the herb, cut fine, to a pint of boiling water. Let cool and take a cupful several times a day.

Majorana hortensis

Marjoram

Common Names Sweet marjoram, knotted marjoram.

Part Used Entire plant.

Medicinal Properties Aromatic, tonic, condiment, emmenagogue.

This is a good tonic. Very effective in combination with camomile and gentian. Excellent for sour stomach, loss of appetite, cough, consumption, eruptive diseases, suppressed menstruation, to increase the flow of urine, for poisonous insect bites and snake bites, dropsy, scurvy, itch, jaundice, toothache, headache, and indigestion. Taken hot, it produces perspiration. This herb is not commonly used in medicine, but is largely used in cooking as a seasoning agent. The dose is one to two capsules daily.

Marrubium vulgare

Horehound

Common Names White horehound, hoarhound, marrubium.

Part Used Plant.

Medicinal Properties Pectoral, aromatic, diaphoretic, tonic, expectorant, diuretic, hepatic, stimulant.

Horehound will produce profuse perspiration when taken hot. Taken in large doses, it is a laxative. When taken cold, it is good for dyspepsia, jaundice, asthma, hysteria, and will expel worms. Very useful in chronic sore throat, coughs, consumption, and all pulmonary infections. If the menses stop abnormally, it will bring them back.

Horehound is one of the old-fashioned remedies and should be in every home ready for immediate use. Horehound syrup is excellent for coughs, colds, asthma, and difficult breathing. For children with coughs or croup, steep a heaping tablespoonful in a pint of boiling water for 20 minutes; strain, add honey, and let them drink it freely. Horehound is one of the bitter herbs that the Jews eat at Passover time, the others being nettle, horseradish, coriander, and lettuce.

Melissa officinalis

Balm

Common Names Garden balm, sweet balm, lemon balm, honey plant, cure-all, balm mint, bee balm.

Part Used Herbs, flowers.

Medicinal Properties Diaphoretic, carminative, febrifuge, tonic.

A warm tea of balm will produce perspiration. To make the tea, pour 1 pint of boiling water on 1 ounce of the herb, let stand for 15 minutes, cool, strain, and then drink freely. Liquid extract can be used; one-fourth to one teaspoonful. It is very helpful in painful or suppressed menstruation. Aids digestion and is valuable in nausea and vomiting. Useful in low-grade fever, liver, spleen, kidney, and bladder troubles, griping in the bowels, and dysentery. A warm poultice of balm will bring a boil to a head and then it will break. For insect stings and rabid dog bites, take the tea internally and make a poultice to apply to the bite or sting. It is good also as a toothache and headache remedy.

Mentha piperita

Peppermint

Common Names Brandy mint, balm mint, curled mint, lamb mint.

Part Used Leaves, oil.

Medicinal Properties
Aromatic, stimulant, stomachic, carminative, rubefacient.

Excellent remedy for chills, colic, fevers, dizziness, flatulence, nausea, vomiting, diarrhea, dysentery, cholera, heart trouble, palpitation of the heart, influenza, la grippe, and hysteria. Applied externally, it is good for rheumatism, neuralgia, and headache. Peppermint enemas are excellent for cholera and colon troubles.

Peppermint is a general stimulant. A strong cup of peppermint tea will act more powerfully on the system than any liquor stimulant. It is good in cases of sudden fainting or dizziness with extreme coldness and pale countenance. Useful for griping pains caused by eating unripe fruit or irritating foods.

Peppermint tea cleanses and strengthens the entire body. If the tea is not at hand, take some of the leaves and chew them up until you can swallow them easily. This will start your food digesting and assist the entire body in doing its work more normally.

Mentha viridis

Spearmint

Common Names Mint, peamint, mackerel mint.

Part Used
Entire plant.

Medicinal Properties
Antispasmodic, aromatic, diuretic, diaphoretic, carminative.

A highly esteemed remedy for colic, gas in the stomach and bowels, nausea and vomiting, dyspepsia, spasms, and dropsy. It will relieve suppressed, painful, or scalding urine, and is also good for gravel in the bladder. Locally applied, it is excellent for piles and hemorrhoids. For this purpose, inject a small amount into the rectum several times a day with a soft-tipped syringe. Good in inflammation of the kidneys and bladder. Excellent for treating vomiting during pregnancy. Very good to quiet and soothe the stomach after an emetic. Very soothing and quieting to the nerves. NEVER BOIL SPEARMINT. Is added to many compounds for its pleasing taste. No home should be without this excellent home remedy. (See also preceding paragraph on Peppermint.) An infusion of 1 ounce in a pint of boiling water can be taken in doses of a wineglassful as needed.

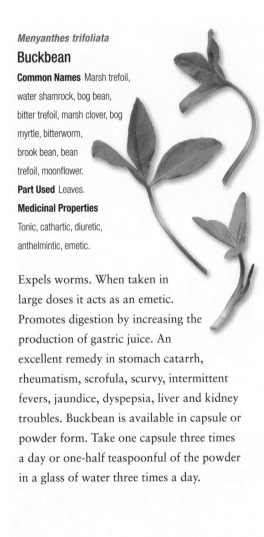

Menyanthes trifoliata

Buckbean

Common Names Marsh trefoil, water shamrock, bog bean, bitter trefoil, marsh clover, bog myrtle, bitterworm, brook bean, bean trefoil, moonflower.

Part Used Leaves.

Medicinal Properties Tonic, cathartic, diuretic, anthelmintic, emetic.

Expels worms. When taken in large doses it acts as an emetic. Promotes digestion by increasing the production of gastric juice. An excellent remedy in stomach catarrh, rheumatism, scrofula, scurvy, intermittent fevers, jaundice, dyspepsia, liver and kidney troubles. Buckbean is available in capsule or powder form. Take one capsule three times a day or one-half teaspoonful of the powder in a glass of water three times a day.

Mitchella repens

Squaw Vine

Common Names Partridgeberry, checkerberry, deerberry, winter clover, twin-berry, one-berry, hive vine, one-berry leaves, squawberry.

Part Used Entire plant.

Medicinal Properties Diuretic, astringent, tonic, alterative, parturient.

This herb is an excellent medicine to take during the last few weeks of pregnancy and will make childbirth much easier. It is better than red raspberry leaves, but it is good to combine the two. Good in scanty or painful menstruation. An excellent wash for sore eyes in infants. For this purpose combine with equal parts of raspberry leaves and witch hazel leaves. If the witch hazel leaves cannot be secured, use wild strawberry leaves. This is also an excellent injection for mild leukorrhea, dysentery, and gonorrhea. This herb is good for gravel, urinary troubles, uterine troubles, female complaints, and increases the menstrual flow. A strong tea made from the berries is good to bathe sore nipples. Add a little olive oil or cream. Stir thoroughly and apply. As a decoction, use 2 ounces in 1 pint of water and take in wineglass doses. As a tincture, 5 to 10 drops three times a day.

Monarda punctata

Mint

Common Names Horsemint,
American horsemint, monarda.

Part Used Leaves, tops.

Medicinal Properties
Stimulant, carminative, sudorific,
diuretic, emmenagogue.

Very quieting
and soothing.
Eases pain. Excellent
for suppressed
urine, nausea
and vomiting,
gas in the stomach and
intestinal tract,
decreased menstrual
flow, rheumatism, diarrhea, and other
digestive problems. Take 10 to 30 drops of
the tincture daily in a glass of water.

Monotropa uniflora

Fit Root

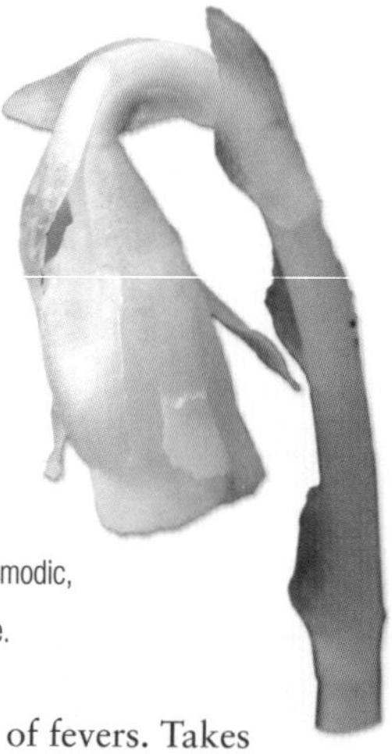

Common Names Ice plant,
Indian pipe, fit root plant, pipe
plant, Dutchman's-pipe, bird's
nest plant, ova ova, bird's nest,
corpse plant, nest root,
convulsion weed.

Part Used Root.

Medicinal Properties Antispasmodic,
nervine, tonic, sedative, febrifuge.

Is splendid in all kinds of fevers. Takes
the place of quinine and opium. An excellent
remedy for restlessness, fainting, nervous
irritability, muscle spasm, and convulsions.
Should be used in place of opium and quinine.
It will cure intermittent and remittent fevers.
Oh, why will not people use this wonderful
remedy in place of poisonous drugs? It is
efficient and harmless. A teaspoonful of fit
root and fennel seed, steeped in a pint of
boiling water for 20 minutes, is an excellent
douche for inflammation of the vagina and
uterus, also good used as a wash for sore
eyes. A valuable remedy for epilepsy and
lockjaw in children.

Myrica cerifera

Bayberry

Common Names

Bayberry bush, American bayberry, American vegetable tallow tree, bayberry wax tree, myrtle, wax myrtle, candleberry, candleberry myrtle, tallow shrub, American vegetable wax, vegetable tallow.

Part Used Bark, leaves, flowers.

Medicinal Properties Astringent, tonic, stimulant. Leaves—aromatic, stimulant.

One of the most valuable and useful herbs. The tea is a most excellent gargle for sore throat. It will thoroughly cleanse the throat of all putrid matter. Steep a teaspoonful in a pint of boiling water for 30 minutes, gargle thoroughly until the throat is clear, then drink a pint of lukewarm tea to thoroughly cleanse the stomach. If it does not come up easily, tickle the back of the throat. This restores the mucous secretions to normal activity.

Bayberry is excellent as an emetic after narcotic poisoning of any kind. Bayberry is also valuable when taken in the usual manner for all kinds of hemorrhages, whether from the stomach, lungs, or excessive menstruation, and when combined with capsicum it is an unfailing remedy for this. Very good in leukorrhea. Has an excellent general effect on the female organs, also has an excellent influence on the uterus during pregnancy, and makes a good douche. Excellent results will be obtained from its use in goiter. In diarrhea and dysentery, use the tea as an enema.

For gangrenous sores, boils, or carbuncles, use as a wash and poultice, or apply the powdered bayberry to the infection. The tea is an excellent wash for spongy and bleeding gums.

The tea taken internally is useful in jaundice, scrofula, and canker sores in the throat and mouth. The tea taken warm promotes perspiration, improves the whole circulation and tones up the tissues. Taken in combination with yarrow, catnip, sage, or peppermint, it is unexcelled for colds.

An excellent formula for colds, fevers, flu, colic, cramps, and pains in the stomach:

bayberry	4 ounces
ginger	2 ounces
white pine	1 ounce
cloves	1 dram
capsicum	1 dram

This is prepared by mixing the herbs (in powdered form) and passing them through a fine sieve several times. Use one teaspoonful, more or less as the case may require, in a cup of hot water. Allow the herbs to stand so they will settle, then drink the clear liquid. Bayberry is high in tannin content. Taking some milk with the herb will tend to counteract the effect of the tannin.

Myristica fragrans

Nutmeg

Common Names Nutmeg flower, black caraway, flower seed, black cumin, nigella seed, bishop's wort, small fennel flower.

Part Used Seed.

Medicinal Properties

Carminative, expectorant, deobstruent, sialagogue, emmenagogue, aromatic.

Nutmeg is commonly used for seasoning foods. It helps prevent gas and fermentation in the intestinal tract. It improves the appetite and digestion and is good in nausea and vomiting. It is mildly hallucinogenic. Nutmeg is no longer commonly used for medicinal purposes as there are other less toxic herbs having greater effect on the system. Serious symptoms of poisoning can result from eating only a few of the nutmegs.

Myroxylon pereirae

Balsam

Common Names

Balsam of Peru.

Part Used Balsam, twigs, bark.

Medicinal Properties

Tonic, expectorant, exanthematous, herpatic.

The balsam evergreen tree, which we use for Christmas trees and which develops big blisters on the outside of the bark, is filled with a very wonderful medicine called balsam fir. This liquid exudes from the bark of the tree after it has been injured. It is useful in all chronic mucous afflictions, catarrh, leukorrhea, as well as diarrhea and dysentery. It is useful externally in ulcers, wounds, ringworm, eczema, and other skin infections. The twigs and the bark have wonderful medicinal properties that are good for rheumatism, kidney trouble, gleet, inflammation of the bladder, and urinary complaints.

Nepeta cataria

Catnip

Common Names
Catmint, catrup, cat's-wort, field balm.

Part Used Herb.

Medicinal Properties
Anodyne, antispasmodic, carminative, aromatic, diaphoretic, nervine.

Catnip is wonderful for very small children and infants. Use the tea as an enema for children with convulsions. Useful in pain of any kind, spasm, gas pains, hyper-acidity in the stomach, and for the prevention of griping in the bowels. A tablespoonful steeped in a pint of water and used as an enema is soothing, and effective in convulsions, fevers, and for expelling worms in children. A high enema of catnip will relieve headaches; good to restore menstruation. Catnip, sweet balm, marshmallow, and sweet weed make an excellent baby remedy. A little honey or malt honey may be added to make it palatable. Steep. Take internally freely. A warm enema of catnip will help free the flow of urine when it is blocked.

CAUTION
Never boil catnip.

Nymphaea odorata

White Pond Lily

Common Names White water lily, sweet-scented pond lily, sweet-scented water lily, toad lily, pond lily, water lily, cow cabbage, sweet water lily, water cabbage.

Part Used Root.

Medicinal Properties Deobstruent, astringent, vulnerary, discutient, demulcent, antiseptic.

This is one of the old-fashioned home remedies. Very astringent. Use as a douche in leukorrhea. Take internally for leukorrhea, diarrhea, bowel complaints, scrofula. Excellent remedy in mucous troubles and inflamed tissues in various parts of the body and also for bronchial troubles. Very effective in dropsy, kidney troubles, catarrh of the bladder, or irritation of the prostate. Excellent for infant bowel troubles. Very healing to inflamed gums. In making poultices for painful swellings, boils, ulcers, etc., mix the ingredients with a strong tea of this herb. Valuable as a gargle for sore throat. The leaves are very healing to wounds and cuts. Apply the powder, combined with flaxseed, as a poultice.

Ocimum basilicum

Basil

Common Names

Common basil, sweet basil, St. Josephwort, garden basil.

Part Used Leaves.

Medicinal Properties

Stimulant, condiment, nervine, aromatic.

The tea taken hot is good in suppressed menses. It helps to stop vomiting and eases stomach cramps. It is effective when applied to snake bites and insect stings. It is a well-known culinary herb and is used in cooking as a flavoring agent.

Use two teaspoonfuls steeped in a cup of hot water. Take one cup a day.

Origanum vulgare

Origanum

Common Names

Wild marjoram, winter marjoram, mountain mint, winter sweet, oregano.

Part Used Entire plant.

Medicinal Properties

Aromatic, pungent, stomachic, tonic, stimulant, emmenagogue, carminative, diaphoretic.

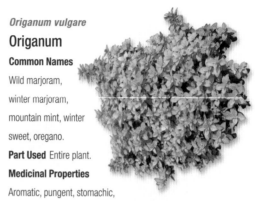

Very strengthening to the stomach and increases the appetite. Excellent for relieving sour stomach. Good in suppressed urine, suppressed menstruation, dropsy, yellow jaundice, scurvy, and itch. The extracted juice is excellent for deafness or pain and noise in the ears. The oil dropped in the hollow of an aching tooth will stop the pain. Will expel gas from the stomach and bowels.

Very helpful in dyspepsia. Good for rheumatism, colic, nausea, and neuralgia. A poultice is very beneficial for painful swellings, sprains, felons, boils, and carbuncles. Good to use in salves and liniments. It is excellent for a sore throat when applied as a heating compress. Steep a heaping tablespoonful in a pint of boiling water for 30 minutes. Dip a cloth in this hot tea, apply to the neck, binding snugly with a dry cloth. It is well to cover the compress with oiled silk or a piece of plastic, which will keep it moist.

Panax quinquefolia

Ginseng

Common Names Five-fingers root, American ginseng, ninsin, red berry, garantogen, sang.

Part Used Root.

Medicinal Properties Demulcent, stomachic, mild stimulant, tonic.

The word "panax" in the botanical name means "all-healing." Ginseng is very commonly used in hot, moist climates as a preventive against all manner of illnesses, and is also used in severe diseases of all types. Promotes appetite and is useful in digestive disturbances. Flavored with any flavoring you like, ginseng makes an agreeable and very effective drink for colds, chest troubles, and coughs.

If taken when hot, it will produce perspiration. It is also good for stomach troubles and constipation. Has been used frequently in lung troubles and inflammation of the urinary tract. Ginseng has been used for thousands of years in China to treat all kinds of illnesses and is held in high regard by the Chinese as an aphrodisiac. A good systemic tonic, but don't use it if you have high blood pressure. Take one capsule a day, and adjust to fit your needs. Of the powder, take one No. 00 capsule or 15 grains in water after each meal.

Petroselinum sativum

Parsley

Common Names Garden parsley, rock parsley, common parsley, march.

Part Used Leaves, root, seed.

Medicinal Properties Diuretic, aperient, expectorant, carminative. Juice—antiperiodic. Seed—febrifuge, emmenagogue.

The roots or leaves are one of the most excellent remedies for difficult urination, dropsy, jaundice, fevers, stones or gravel in the urinary tracts, obstructions of the liver and spleen, strangury, syphilis, and gonorrhea. Also excellent for cancer and should be classed among the preventive herbs. Simmer a tablespoonful to a pint of boiling water for 10 minutes, let stand, strain, and drink one to three cups a day, a large swallow at a time, more or less, as needed. For painful or scanty menstruation combine the leaves with equal parts of buchu, black haw, and cramp bark.

A hot fomentation wrung out of the tea and applied to insect bites will cure them.

CAUTION
Do not use parsley if you have a kidney infection.

Pilocarpus microphyllus

Jaborandi

Common Names Pernambuco jaborandi, arruda.

Part Used Leaves.

Medicinal Properties Stimulant, expectorant, sialagogue, antivenomous, diaphoretic.

This is excellent for breaking up colds, for rheumatism, asthma, influenza and Bright's disease. It causes profuse perspiration. Effective in various fevers, in diabetes, dropsy, pleurisy, catarrh, and jaundice. An excellent remedy for mumps, taken internally as a tea, and applied externally as a fomentation or poultice to reduce swelling. Fold the cloth three or four thicknesses and dip in the hot tea and apply. Very effective in asthma and diphtheria. It will stop hiccoughs. Excellent to stimulate the growth of the hair. Dip the fingers in tea made of the leaves several times a day and massage the scalp thoroughly. Infuse 1 ounce of leaves in 1 pint of boiling water and take a wineglassful or less as needed.

Pilocarpus selloanus

Indian Hemp

Part Used Leaves and root.

Medicinal Properties Same as Jaborandi (see above).

Piper cubeba

Cubeb Berries

Common Names Java pepper, cubebs, tailed cubebs, tailed pepper.

Part Used Dried unripe berries.

Medicinal Properties Aromatic, purgative, stimulant, diuretic, antisyphilitic, carminative, stomachic.

Is excellent in chronic bladder troubles, burning urine, leukorrhea, gonorrhea, bronchial troubles, cough, colic. Gives tone to the stomach and bowels. Heretofore has been used largely for seasoning soups. Increases the flow of urine. Of the fluid extract, take one-fourth to one teaspoonful in a glass of water.

Pimpinella anisum

Anise

Common Names
Anise seed,
common anise.

Part Used Seed, root.

**Medicinal
Properties** Aromatic,
diaphoretic,
relaxant, stimulant,
tonic, carminative,
stomachic.

Anise is one of the old-fashioned herbs and has many valuable properties. It will prevent fermentation and production of gas in the stomach and bowels, check griping in the bowels when taken as a hot tea, and relieves flatulence. Anise is a very good stomach remedy to overcome nausea and colic. It is useful when mixed with or taken with other herbs to give them a palatable flavor and is frequently used in cough medicines.

Pimpinella saxifraga

Burnet

Common Names Burnet
saxifrage, small saxifrage, pimpernel,
small pimpernel, European burnet
saxifrage, small burnet saxifrage.

Part Used Root.

Medicinal Properties
Aromatic, stimulant, stomachic,
pungent, carminative.

It is very useful for cleansing the chest, lungs, and stomach. Will aid in expelling stones from the bladder. Good for cuts, wounds, running sores, toothache, earache, and piles. Steep a teaspoonful of the root in a cup of boiling water, let cool, strain, and drink one or two cups a day cold, a large swallow at a time. Best remedy known for sour stomach.

Plantago major

Plantain

Common Names Waybread, round-leaved plantain, Englishman's foot, common plantain, ribwort, ripple grass, snake weed.

Part Used Entire plant.

Medicinal Properties Alterative, diuretic, antisyphilitic, antiseptic, astringent, deobstruent, styptic, vulnerary.

Plantain is an old-fashioned herb. The Indians used it to great advantage. It grows practically all over the United States.

Every family should gather some and have it ready for use. It has wonderful properties and many uses. There are two kinds of plantain—narrow and wide leaf. Both are good. The whole plant should be used.

Plantain has a soothing, cooling, and healing effect on sores and ulcers. The fresh leaves, when pounded into a paste and applied to wounds, will check the bleeding. They may also be rubbed directly onto insect bites and stings. It is extremely useful in erysipelas, eczema, burns, and scalds. Make a strong tea and apply to the affected parts, using frequently in bad cases. For piles and hemorrhoids, make a strong tea with an ounce of granulated plantain to a pint of boiling water. Let steep for 20 to 30 minutes.

For hemorrhoids, inject one tablespoonful of this tea three or four times a day at least, and especially after each stool, using more frequently in bad cases. Apply externally with a soft gauze or cotton as needed. A saturated piece of gauze may be kept on the piles by using a belt or band around the body to which has been attached a narrow strip of cloth for holding the saturated gauze against the piles.

An ointment for piles may be made by boiling slowly for about two hours 2 ounces of granulated plantain in 1 pint of soybean oil, peanut oil, or any other soluble oil.

For use in leukorrhea, make a strong tea and use as a douche.

For diarrhea, kidney, and bladder trouble, aching in the lumbar region, and bedwetting, plantain is wonderful. Make a tea by using one teaspoonful of granulated herbs in one cup of boiling water. Let steep for 20 or 30 minutes. If powdered herbs are used, place one small teaspoonful in a cup of hot water.

Let stand about 15 or 20 minutes. Drink a cupful of this tea four or five times a day until relief is obtained.

For use in tuberculosis and syphilis, use both internally and externally.

The green leaves give wonderful relief if mashed up and applied as a poultice to any part of the body stung by poisonous insects, or to snake bites, boils, carbuncles, and tumors.

Plantain tea will ease pain in the bowels. It will help clear the head of mucus and slows all manner of flowings, even excessive menstruation. The plantain seed is good for dropsy, by making a tea of one teaspoonful to a cup of boiling water. The roots, beaten into powder, are good for toothache. A tea made with distilled water is good for inflamed eyes. The tea kills worms in the stomach and bowels. Equal parts of plantain and yellow dock make a very excellent wash for itch, ringworms, and all running sores. Plantain is excellent for healing fresh or old wounds or sores, either internal or external.

Plantago psyllium

Psyllium

Common Names
Branching plantain, flea seed, fleawort, spogel.

Part Used Seed.

Medicinal Properties Demulcent, purgative, detergent.

Psyllium assists greatly in cases of colitis, anal fissures or ulcers, and hemorrhoids by relieving the stress occasioned during difficult evacuation of the bowel. It relieves autointoxication, the cause of many diseases, by cleansing the intestines and removing the putrefactive toxins. Psyllium, being a purely vegetable product, causes no harmful effects, either physiological or chemical. It is superior to emulsions, oils, and agar compounds, which are widely known and used. For adults, take two teaspoonfuls after meals or an hour before meals in a glass of water, warm water being preferred. For children the dose is one-half to one teaspoonful after meals. Vary the dose according to the individual needs.

When soaked in water the seeds swell into a jelly-like mass that lubricates the intestines and stimulates the normal muscular activity without causing cramps and griping in the bowels. Psyllium could really be called a colon broom. Some psyllium preparations come with natural flavors, such as lemon, which makes it easier for children to take.

Phytolacca decandra

Poke Root

Common Names Red weed, red ink plant, poke weed, garget, pigeon berry, scoke, coakum, Virginia polk, pocan bush, American nightshade, red ink berries.

Part Used Root, leaves, berries.

Medicinal Properties Alterative, resolvent, deobstruent, detergent, antisyphilitic, antiscorbutic, cathartic.

The tender leaves are excellent as greens for the dinner table, especially in the early spring. They are eaten by many people for the purpose of toning up the whole system. The green root of poke is a most useful agent. Very good in enlargement of the glands, particularly the thyroid gland. Very good for hard liver, biliousness, inflammation of the kidneys, enlarged lymphatic glands. It is effective in goiter, either taken internally or applied as a poultice or liniment. Excellent in skin diseases, scrofula, and eczema. If a tea is made of the root and applied to the skin, it will cure itching.

Poke root makes a good poultice for caked breasts. It has also been used as an aid in advanced cancer of the breast as a poultice. First, grind fine the fresh root. Roll this out to make a plaster to cover the breast completely, cutting out a hole for the nipple. Use a piece of cheese cloth or other thin material to put this on the breast, and once daily moisten the poultice with poke root tea, made fresh each time. Do this for three days, putting on a fresh poultice daily, and continuing the treatment for fifteen days. The skin will be covered with little sores with pus. In about four to six weeks the hardness should then leave the breast. Then cleanse the skin thoroughly and cover with boric acid powder, and allow the entire surface to become dry. In about ten days the sores will be completely healed.

Care should be taken in using roots that are insufficiently cooked or fresh.

CAUTION

The seeds, which are present in the berries, are poisonous and should not be eaten. Do not eat this plant raw or inadequately cooked. Poke root should be boiled before eating and the water drained off and discarded; boil it again in fresh water and drain off the water again. It may then be eaten.

Podophyllum peltatum

Mandrake

Common Names Hog apple, May apple, American mandrake, Indian apple, duck's foot, ground lemon, wild lemon, racoonberry.

Part Used Root.

Medicinal Properties Antibilious, cathartic, emetic, diaphoretic, cholagogue, alterative, resolvent, vermifuge, deobstruent.

Excellent regulator for liver and bowels. In chronic liver diseases it has no equal. Valuable in jaundice, bilious, or intermittent fever. Good physic; is often combined with senna leaves. It is very beneficial in uterine diseases. It acts powerfully upon all the tissues of the body. Use wherever a powerful cathartic is required.

Small doses given frequently should be used in order to prevent severe purgative action. Steep a teaspoonful in a pint of boiling water and take a teaspoonful of this tea at a time. Children less according to age. Take one capsule a day for no longer than one week at a time.

CAUTION

Mandrake is a potent herb; *it should be taken with care.* Other herbs can give the same results and are much safer to use.

Polygonatum multiflorum

Solomon's Seal

Common Names Dropberry, sealwort, seal root.

Part Used Root.

Medicinal Properties Tonic, expectorant, astringent, mucilaginous.

A fine remedy for all kinds of female troubles. Excellent as a wash for poison ivy, erysipelas, and other sores on the body. Will allay pain and heal piles. Inject four or five tablespoonfuls of the tea several times a day into the rectum. Take internally the same as other tea for neuralgia. Use 1 ounce of the cut herb in a cup of hot water. Solomon's seal makes an excellent poultice for external inflammations, wounds, and piles.

Polygonum bistorta

Bistort Root

Common Names Patience dock, snake weed, sweet dock, dragonwort, red legs, Easter giant.

Part Used Root.

Medicinal Properties Astringent, diuretic, styptic, alterative.

Bistort is one of the strongest herb astringents. It is excellent for gargles, injections, and is used for cholera, diarrhea, dysentery, and leukorrhea. Excellent wash for sore mouth or gums and running sores. Combined with equal parts of red raspberries, it will cleanse internal ulcers. Makes a good wash for the nose. Useful in smallpox, measles, pimples, jaundice, ruptures, insect stings, snake bites, and expels worms. Combined with plantain, it is useful in gonorrhea. The powdered bistort will stop bleeding of a cut or wound when applied directly to the injury. Used in a douche to decrease or regulate the menstrual flow.

Polygonum punctatum

Water Pepper

Common Names Smartweed, American water pepper, water smartweed, pepperwort, culrage.

Part Used Entire plant.

Medicinal Properties Astringent, diaphoretic, tonic, stimulant, emmenagogue, antiseptic.

Useful remedy for scanty menstruation, all womb troubles, gravel in the bladder, colds, coughs, bowel complaints, and kidney troubles. Can be used internally and externally. A poultice made of charcoal and moistened with water pepper tea is an excellent remedy for pain in the bowels and ulcers; is one of the best known remedies for this purpose. Also take the tea internally. Give high enemas, fruit juice, and liquid diet for a few days. A most wonderful remedy in appendicitis.

For cholera, the tea should be used as an enema. A fomentation should also be wrung out of the hot tea and applied over the abdomen. Use the tea as a wash in erysipelas and for sore nipples in nursing mothers.

Populus candicans
Balm of Gilead

Common Names

Balsam poplar, American balm of Gilead, balm of Gilead buds, Mecca balsam.

Part Used Buds, bark, leaves.

Medicinal Properties Bark—stimulant, tonic, diuretic, antiscorbutic. Buds—balsamic, vulnerary.

The beautiful Balm of Gilead tree which we admire so much for its wonderful fragrance, contains excellent properties in its bark and leaves for coughs, colds, lung troubles, kidney, and urinary troubles.

When the buds are boiled in olive oil, cocoa fat, or some other good oil, they make an excellent salve that is especially good for the healing or soothing of inflamed parts, the healing of fresh cuts, wounds, or bruises, and for the healing of bedsores. The buds and bark are also excellent for scurvy, as a stimulating tonic and to increase the flow of urine.

The buds are very valuable for dry asthma, coughs and colds, and as a gargle for sore throat. Add an equal part of any one of the following herbs to add to this tea's efficiency: chickweed, coltsfoot, horehound, hyssop, licorice, lobelia, ragwort, anise, or red sage.

Populus tremuloides
Poplar

Common Names Quaking aspen, American aspen, quaking asp, quiver leaf, trembling tree, trembling poplar, white poplar, aspen poplar, abele tree.

Part Used Bark, buds, leaves.

Medicinal Properties Stomachic, febrifuge, tonic, antiperiodic, balsamic.

Poplar is very useful for disease of the urinary organs, especially if weak. An excellent aid to digestion and to tone up run-down conditions, either in disease or old age. Very good in all cases of chronic diarrhea. Excellent for acute rheumatism. Good for fever caused by influenza. It is useful in neuralgia, jaundice, liver trouble, diabetes, hay fever, cholera infantum, and will expel worms.

It is splendid when used externally as a wash for cancer, bad ulcers, gangrenous wounds, eczema, strong perspiration, burns, and sores caused by gonorrhea and syphilis. It is more effective than quinine in fever. Place a teaspoonful of the buds, bark, or leaves in a pint of boiling water. Use cold, and take one or two cupfuls a day, one swallow at a time.

The buds from the poplar tree may be boiled in olive oil and made into an ointment for cuts, wounds, burns, and scratches.

Quercus alba

Oak

Common Names

White oak, Tanner's bark.

Part Used Inner bark, leaves, acorn cups.

Medicinal Properties Tonic, astringent, antiseptic, anthelmintic.

The leaves and bark are used: the inner white bark is best and is a very strong astringent. A strong tea made from white oak bark is excellent for vaginal discharge and womb troubles. It will also expel pin-worms. Simmer a tablespoonful in a pint of water for ten minutes. Drink up to three cups a day. It is one of the best remedies for piles or hemorrhoids, hemorrhages, or any trouble in the rectum. It may be used internally or taken as an enema. For enemas and douches, steep a heaping tablespoonful in a quart of boiling water for thirty minutes and strain through a cloth. Use as hot as possible. Stops hemorrhages in the lungs, stomach, and bowels, spitting of blood, and bleeding in the mouth. Increases the flow of urine and helps remove kidney stones. It is helpful for an ulcerated bladder or bloody urine. Checks excess menstrual flow.

For goiter, fold a small towel to make a compress and moisten with the tea as made for enemas. Tie the compress around the neck, leaving it on all night and covering well with a woolen or flannel cloth. For varicose veins, take the tea internally and bathe the veins externally with a strong tea three or four times a day. It is also good to moisten a cloth with the tea, wrap it around the legs, and cover well with flannel. This will also reduce swelling and hard tumors.

A tea made from the bark, with the powder of the acorn cups added, is excellent for bleeding from the mouth, spitting of blood, and to stop vomiting. It resists the force of poisonous medicines and is excellent for ulcerated bladder and bloody urine. The powder of the acorn made into a tea helps to counteract the poison of venomous creatures. The distilled liquid of the buds can be used either outwardly or inwardly for inflammations, fevers, and infections. The water from the leaves is especially excellent to normalize the kidneys, liver and spleen, goiter, tumors, and swellings. Dose is 1 ounce of the bark steeped in a pint of water. Use one teaspoonful of the tea three or four times a day for dysentery or diarrhea. Use as a douche for vaginal discharge or as a gargle for sore throat and mucous discharge.

Use the powdered bark on ulcers. It is astringent and antiseptic. It is good in enemas for colon trouble, gonorrhea, gleet (urethritis), leukorrhea, and stomach troubles.

Prunella vulgaris

Self-heal

Common Names

Wound wort, all heal,
heal all,
Hercules wound wort,
brownwort, sickle wort, blue
curls, panay, hook heal, hood
weed, carpenter's herb.

Part Used Entire plant.

Medicinal Properties Pungent,
tonic, antispasmodic, vermifuge, diuretic,
astringent, styptic, vulnerary.

Excellent for epilepsy, convulsions, falling sickness, and obstructed liver. Especially useful for wounds, both internal and external.

For internal wounds, take the tea. Use as a poultice and as a wash in all external wounds and sores. Will stop bleeding. Also very cleansing. Will cleanse and heal ulcers of the mouth. An old Italian proverb says: "He that hath self-heal and sanicle needs no other physician." Make an infusion of 1 ounce of the herb to a pint of boiling water. Take one wineglassful several times a day.

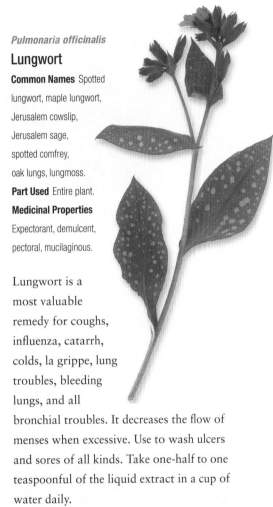

Pulmonaria officinalis

Lungwort

Common Names Spotted
lungwort, maple lungwort,
Jerusalem cowslip,
Jerusalem sage,
spotted comfrey,
oak lungs, lungmoss.

Part Used Entire plant.

Medicinal Properties

Expectorant, demulcent,
pectoral, mucilaginous.

Lungwort is a most valuable remedy for coughs, influenza, catarrh, colds, la grippe, lung troubles, bleeding lungs, and all bronchial troubles. It decreases the flow of menses when excessive. Use to wash ulcers and sores of all kinds. Take one-half to one teaspoonful of the liquid extract in a cup of water daily.

Rhamnus frangula

Buckthorn Bark

Common Names

European buckthorn, black alder dogwood, black alder tree, alder buckthorn, black dogwood, Persian berries, European black alder, arrow wood.

Part Used Bark, fruit.

Medicinal Properties Purgative, diuretic, emetic, vermifuge. Fruit—purgative.

Buckthorn bark is a very well-known cure for constipation. It is important to note that freshly cut bark should NOT be used: the bark should be dried for one to two years before using. It is not habit-forming. It is an effective remedy for appendicitis. Good in rheumatism, gout, dropsy, and skin diseases. Will produce profuse perspiration when taken hot. Expels worms. Take both internally and apply externally as a wash. Ointment made of buckthorn is very effective in reducing itching. Will remove warts. Good used as a fomentation or poultice.

Rhamnus purshiana

Cascara Sagrada

Common Names

Purshiana bark, Persian bark, sacred bark, chittem bark, bearberry, California buckthorn.

Part Used Bark.

Medicinal Properties Purgative, bitter tonic.

One of the most reliable remedies for chronic constipation. An excellent remedy for gallstones and increases secretion of bile. Good for liver complaints. Mix four teaspoonfuls in a quart of boiling water, steep for one hour, and drink one or two cupfuls a day one hour before meals or on an empty stomach.

The bark can be procured from drugstores in three and five grain chocolate-coated tablets, called extract of cascara sagrada. When there is a bad taste in the mouth, or the bowels do not move, take one or more of these tablets. Take immediately after meals, or upon retiring. Excellent remedy for constipated children. Also available as a tincture. Use 15 to 30 drops.

CAUTION
Bark should be at least one year old.

Rheum palmatum

Rhubarb

Common Names Turkey rhubarb, Chinese rhubarb.

Part Used Root.

Medicinal Properties
Vulnerary, tonic, stomachic, purgative, astringent, aperient.

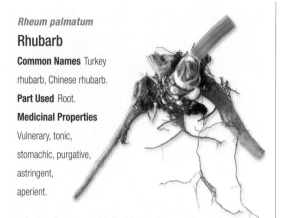

Rhubarb is an old-fashioned remedy and is very useful in small doses for diarrhea and dysentery in adults and children. In larger doses, it is an excellent laxative for infants, as it is very mild and tonic. Excellent to increase the muscular action of the bowels and for use in stomach troubles. Will relieve headache. It stimulates the gallbladder, thereby causing the ejection of bilious material. Excellent for scrofulous children with distended abdomens. Good for the liver. Cleanses and tones the bowels. Rhubarb is very high in oxalates and therefore should not be used by those who develop kidney stones. Available as the powdered root or as a tincture, 10 to 20 drops in water.

CAUTION
Never eat the leaves, which are poisonous.

Rhus glabra

Sumach Berries

Common Names Scarlet sumach, smooth sumach, dwarf sumach, upland sumach, Pennsylvania sumach, sleek sumach, mountain sumach.

Part Used Bark, leaves, berries.

Medicinal Properties Bark and leaves—tonic, astringent, alterative, antiseptic. Berries—diuretic, refrigerant, emmenagogue, diaphoretic, cephalic.

A valuable treatment to try in gonorrhea and syphilis when others have failed is the following: equal parts sumach berries and bark, white pine bark, and slippery elm. This tea is very cleansing to the system, and is very useful in leukorrhea, scrofula, and for inward sores and wounds. A tea of sumach berries alone is excellent for bowel complaints, diabetes, and all kinds of fevers; and for sores in the mouth there is no superior. Use also as a gargle and mouthwash. As a tincture take 5 to 15 drops in water two times a day.

Rosemarinus officinalis
Rosemary

Common Names Garden rosemary, rosemary plant.

Part Used Leaves, flowers.

Medicinal Properties Stimulant, antispasmodic, emmenagogue, tonic, astringent, diaphoretic, carminative, nervine, aromatic, cephalic.

An old-fashioned remedy for colds, colic, and nervous conditions. Very good in headaches caused by nervousness. Should be taken warm for these complaints. Good as a wash for mouth, gums, halitosis (foul breath), and sore throat. Is useful for female complaints. The leaves are used for flavoring. The oil is used as a perfume for ointments and liniments. This is an excellent ingredient for shampoos and is reported to prevent premature baldness. Rosemary is helpful in some cases of mental disturbance. It aids digestion, cough, consumption, and strengthens the eyes.

Rubus strigosus
Red Raspberry

Common Names Wild red raspberry, reapberry.

Part Used Leaves, berries.

Medicinal Properties Leaves—antiemetic, astringent, purgative, stomachic, parturient, tonic, stimulant, alterative. Fruit—laxative, esculent, antacid, parturient.

Will heal canker sores that develop on mucous membranes. Take one cup of tea every hour until the canker sores disappear.

During this time drink only juice. The tea has been reported to speed up delivery as well as easing labor pains. Excellent for dysentery and diarrhea, especially in infants. It decreases the menstrual flow. Good to combine in such cases with prickly ash, blue cohosh, wild yam, and cinnamon. Will allay nausea. When the bowels are greatly relaxed, use in place of coffee or tea. Good for intestinal problems in children.

To make red raspberry tea, take 1 ounce of the dried herb or one handful of fresh leaves and pour over them a pint of boiling hot water. Cover and let steep for 15 to 20 minutes. Then strain and drink one or two cups a day. A little honey may be added. The leaves are available in powder form also.

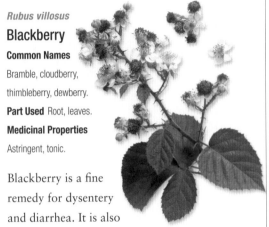

Rubus villosus

Blackberry

Common Names

Bramble, cloudberry, thimbleberry, dewberry.

Part Used Root, leaves.

Medicinal Properties

Astringent, tonic.

Blackberry is a fine remedy for dysentery and diarrhea. It is also good for bleeding; either internally or from the rectum or mouth. This herb has a high tannin content and should be taken for a limited time only, not more than one week at a time. A little honey or cinnamon makes it a more palatable medication. It is available as a tincture, one-half to one teaspoonful twice daily in water.

Rumex acetosa

Sorrel

Common Names

Common field sorrel, red top sorrel, garden sorrel, meadow sorrel, sourgrass.

Part Used Leaves, root.

Medicinal Properties

Diuretic, antiscorbutic, refrigerant, vermifuge.

The leaves are used like greens, as spinach, and are very high in life-giving properties.

It kills putrefaction in the blood, expels worms, and is warming to the heart. The root boiled is good for profuse menstruation or stomach hemorrhage. Also expels gravel from the kidneys, and is good in jaundice. A tea made from the flowers is good for internal ulcers, scurvy, scrofula, and all skin diseases. Steep 1 ounce of the cut herb in a cup of hot water. A sorrel poultice is excellent for cancer, boils, and tumors. As a cold drink, it is good to reduce fevers.

The leaves eaten as a salad in the spring are an excellent preventive for scurvy.

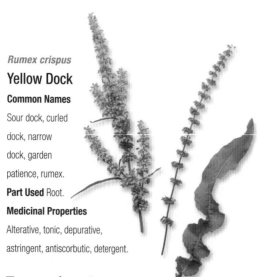

Rumex crispus

Yellow Dock

Common Names

Sour dock, curled dock, narrow dock, garden patience, rumex.

Part Used Root.

Medicinal Properties

Alterative, tonic, depurative, astringent, antiscorbutic, detergent.

Tones up the entire system and is an excellent and effective remedy for the following: impure blood, eruptive skin diseases, scrofula, glandular tumors, swellings, leprosy, cancer, ulcerated eyelids, syphilis, and running ears. Makes a valuable ointment for itch and sores. For glandular tumors and swellings, apply fomentations wrung from the hot tea. Most wonderful blood purifier. Yellow dock is high in tannin content and should be taken only every other week. As a capsule, one a day. As a decoction, one teaspoonful in a cup of water, one to two cups a day.

Ruta graveolens

Rue

Common Names Herb of grace, garden rue, countryman's treacle.

Part Used Entire plant.

Medicinal Properties Aromatic, pungent, tonic, emmenagogue, stimulant, antispasmodic.

This herb should be in every garden. Rue is very much like hyssop as a fine remedy for the many ills of humanity. It will relieve congestion of the uterus, lending a very stimulating and tonic effect. Excellent in suppressed menstruation.

Steep a tablespoonful in a pint of boiling water for half an hour. DO NOT BOIL. Strain, drink warm, a teacupful every two to four hours. Also good for painful menstruation. Excellent remedy for stomach trouble, cramps in the bowels, nervousness, hysteria, spasms, convulsions, will expel worms, relieve pain in the head, confusion, and dizziness. Excellent for colic and convulsions in children. A poultice of rue is good for sciatica, pain in the joints, and gout. It resists poison.

CAUTION
Do not boil rue. Do not use if pregnant. Do not use in large doses.

Salix alba

White Willow

Common Names Willow, salacin willow, willow bark, withe, withy.

Part Used

Leaves, bark.

Medicinal Properties

Tonic, antiperiodic, astringent, antiseptic, anodyne, diaphoretic, diuretic, febrifuge.

The ability of willow bark to reduce fever and alleviate pain has been known for centuries. It is closely related to the common aspirin. It is useful in all stomach troubles, sour stomach, and heartburn. Excellent in all kind of fevers, chills, ague, acute rheumatism. The tea made from the leaves or buds is good in gangrene, cancer, and eczema. Use internally and externally. Good for bleeding wounds, nosebleeds, or spitting of blood, as an antiemetic, eyewash, and to increase the flow of urine. Excellent to use in place of quinine and far more effective.

To prepare a decoction, soak one to three teaspoonfuls of bark in a cup of cold water for three or four hours and then bring the water to a boil. Take a mouthful at a time of the unsweetened decoction, to a total of about one cup a day.

Salix negra

Black Willow

Common Names Pussy willow, catkin's willow.

Part Used Bark, buds.

Medicinal Properties Bark— anodyne, antiseptic, astringent, antiperiodic, tonic, febrifuge. Buds—antiaphrodisiac.

A decoction of willow bark is a great aid in reducing fever and relieving pain. Willow bark is also good for the treatment of joint pains and to reduce inflammation and swelling. The decoction can also be used for sores in the mouth and as a gargle for sore throat. The decoction is made by soaking one to three teaspoonfuls of the bark in a cup of water for two or three hours and then bringing the water to a boil. A mouthful at a time should be taken to a total amount of about a cup a day. If you prefer the capsules, take one a day.

Black willow exerts a good influence on the sex organs, as in cases of incontinence, excessive sexual desire, and acute gonorrhea.

When combined with saw palmetto berries or skullcap, it is good for nocturnal emissions.

Salvia officinalis

Sage

Common Names Garden sage, red sage, purple top sage.

Part Used Leaves.

Medicinal Properties Sudorific, astringent, expectorant, tonic, aromatic, antispasmodic, nervine, vermifuge, emmenagogue, diuretic, stimulant, diaphoretic, stomachic, antiseptic.

Sage is a wonderful remedy for many diseases. A strong sage tea is an excellent gargle for tonsillitis or ulcers in the throat or mouth. This tea, drunk cold during the day, will prevent night sweats. For quinsy, use the tea externally and also as a gargle for the throat. One of the best remedies for stomach troubles, dyspepsia, biliousness, gas in the stomach, and bowels. Will expel worms in adults and children. Also used in liver and kidney troubles. Will stop bleeding of wounds and is very cleansing to old ulcers and sores. Wounds of any kind will heal more rapidly when washed with sage tea. Good when used in a poultice for inflammation of all kinds; very useful for typhoid and scarlet fever, measles, and smallpox. It is very soothing in nervous troubles and will relieve headaches. Good in high fevers of all kinds.

A most effective hair tonic. Will make hair grow if the roots have not been destroyed. Will remove dandruff. Is a good substitute for quinine. For all kinds of lung trouble, colds, influenza, asthma, coughs, bronchitis, or pneumonia, first take a high enema; next take a big dose of body cleanser or laxative. Then go to bed and take three, four, or five cups of hot sage tea at short intervals—say a half hour apart. This will cause free perspiration, make the whole body active, produce a strong circulation, and will throw off the infection. Fine remedy for female troubles. Will increase menstruation when too scanty and check it when profuse. When it is desired that the milk should cease in the breast, sage tea drunk cold will cause the flow of milk in the breasts to cease.

For any throat trouble, red root or wood betony, half-and-half, can be added to the sage. The tea should not be boiled, but just steeped. The ordinary dose is a heaping teaspoonful to a cup of hot water. Let it steep for 20 or 30 minutes. Then strain and drink three or four cups a day, one hour before meals and upon retiring, more or less as the case requires.

CAUTION

Never steep herbs in aluminum containers.

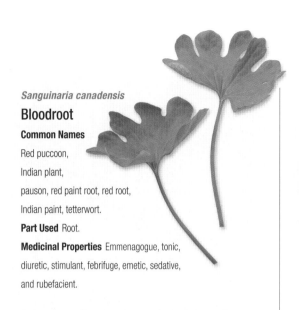

Sanguinaria canadensis

Bloodroot

Common Names
Red puccoon,
Indian plant,
pauson, red paint root, red root,
Indian paint, tetterwort.

Part Used Root.

Medicinal Properties Emmenagogue, tonic,
diuretic, stimulant, febrifuge, emetic, sedative,
and rubefacient.

It is an excellent agent in adenoids, nasal polyps, sore throat, and syphilitic troubles. When the condition is not easily overcome, combine with equal parts of golden seal. Bloodroot is also excellent for piles by using the strong tea as an enema. Effective remedy in coughs, colds, laryngitis, bronchitis, typhoid fever, pneumonia, catarrh, scarlatina, jaundice, dyspepsia, ringworm, whooping cough, running sores, eczema, and skin diseases. Small doses stimulate the digestive organs and heart. Large doses act as a sedative and narcotic. Bloodroot was used as a body paint by the American Indians.

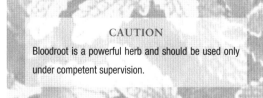

CAUTION
Bloodroot is a powerful herb and should be used only under competent supervision.

Sanicula marilandica

Sanicle

Common Names Black sanicle,
black snake root, wood sanicle,
sanicle root, American sanicle, pool
root, butterwort.

Part Used Root, leaves.

Medicinal Properties Vulnerary,
astringent, alterative, expectorant, discutient, depurative.

Sanicle possesses powerful cleansing and healing properties. Both the leaves and roots are used. It heals both internal and external wounds and tumors. Use a heaping teaspoonful of the granulated herb to a cup of water. Let it steep for 20 or 30 minutes. Drink five or six cups a day. When using the powder, use a good half-teaspoonful to a cup of hot or cold water.

It will help to check excessive menstruation. It is also good to reduce hemorrhage from the lungs, bowels, and kidneys. It will stop pain in the bowels. It is excellent in gonorrhea and syphilis, as it is strong enough to cleanse the body of mucous and poisonous waste matter. It is very healing for sores in the mouth, for sore throat, quinsy, and to cleanse the throat of mucus when the strong tea is used as a gargle. It is very healing to ulcers in the stomach and is an effective remedy for the dreadful disease, consumption (tuberculosis).

Sassafras officinale
Sassafras
Common Names Ague tree,
saxifrax, cinnamon wood, saloip.
Part Used Bark of the root.
Medicinal Properties Aromatic,
stimulant, alterative, diaphoretic,
diuretic.

Sassafras is often called a spring medicine
to purify the blood and cleanse the entire
system. Good to flavor other herbs that have
a disagreeable taste, and commonly used in
combination with other blood-purifying herbs.
Useful as a tonic for stomach and bowels.
Will relieve gas and colic. Taken warm, it is
an excellent remedy for spasms. Valuable in
all skin diseases and eruptions. Good wash
for inflamed eyes. Good for kidneys, bladder,
chest, and throat troubles. Oil of sassafras is
excellent for toothache. Good in varicose
ulcers as a wash externally and also when taken
internally. Take for no more than a week at a
time. As a tincture, use 10 to 20 drops in water.

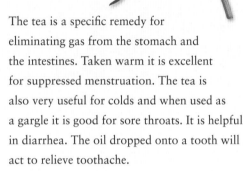

Satureja hortensis
Summer Savory
Common Names
Savory, bean herb.
Part Used Entire plant.
Medicinal Properties Aromatic,
stimulant, carminative, condiment,
emmenagogue, aphrodisiac.

The tea is a specific remedy for
eliminating gas from the stomach and
the intestines. Taken warm it is excellent
for suppressed menstruation. The tea is
also very useful for colds and when used as
a gargle it is good for sore throats. It is helpful
in diarrhea. The oil dropped onto a tooth will
act to relieve toothache.

As a culinary herb, the leaves are used for
flavoring, usually combined with sage.

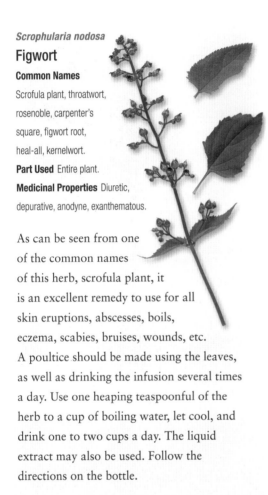

Scrophularia nodosa
Figwort

Common Names

Scrofula plant, throatwort, rosenoble, carpenter's square, figwort root, heal-all, kernelwort.

Part Used Entire plant.

Medicinal Properties Diuretic, depurative, anodyne, exanthematous.

As can be seen from one of the common names of this herb, scrofula plant, it is an excellent remedy to use for all skin eruptions, abscesses, boils, eczema, scabies, bruises, wounds, etc. A poultice should be made using the leaves, as well as drinking the infusion several times a day. Use one heaping teaspoonful of the herb to a cup of boiling water, let cool, and drink one to two cups a day. The liquid extract may also be used. Follow the directions on the bottle.

Scutellaria lateriflora
Skullcap

Common Names

Scullcap, blue skullcap, blue pimpernel, hoodwart, hooded willow herb, side-flowering skullcap, mad dogweed, mad weed, helmet flower, American skullcap.

Part Used Entire plant.

Medicinal Properties Antispasmodic, nervine, tonic, diuretic.

It is one of the best nerve tonics we have and is often combined with other herbs. Very quieting and soothing to the nerves of people who are easily excited. For those with delirium tremens, it will produce sleep. Good in neuralgia, aches, and pains. Useful in St. Vitus's dance, shaking palsy, convulsions, fits, rheumatism, hydrophobia, epilepsy, and bites of poisonous insects and snakes. Splendid to suppress excessive sexual desire.

The following combination is a positive remedy for wakefulness: equal parts skullcap, nerve root, hops, catnip, and black cohosh. Take a tablespoonful of each, mix together, and use a heaping teaspoonful to a cup of boiling water. This combination is very useful in aiding a morphine addict to sleep. As a substitute for quinine, skullcap is more effective and is not as harmful.

Senecio aureus

Ragwort

Common Names

Uncum root, waw weed, uncum, liferoot, liferoot plant, false valerian, golden sececio, cough weed, squaw weed, female regulator, cocash weed, ragweed, staggerwort, St. James wort.

Part Used Entire plant.

Medicinal Properties Expectorant, diaphoretic, febrifuge, emmenagogue, pectoral, tonic.

Has a very powerful influence upon the female organs. Combined with white pond lily, it is one of the most certain and safe cures known for severe cases of leukorrhea, and also for suppressed menstruation.

Good in all urinary diseases and gravel. Useful for rheumatism, sciatica, joint pains, coughs, and colds. As a fluid extract, take one-half to one teaspoonful in a cup of water.

Serenoa serrulate

Saw Palmetto Berries

Common Names Pan palm, dwarf palmetto.

Part Used Berries.

Medicinal Properties

Antiseptic, sedative, cardiac, tonic, diuretic.

A very useful article in asthma and all kinds of throat troubles, colds, bronchitis, la grippe, whooping cough, and when the throat is irritated and painful. Especially useful when there is excessive mucous discharge from the sinuses and nose. Valuable in all diseases of the reproductive organs, ovaries, prostate, testes, etc. Very useful in Bright's disease and diabetes. Excellent as a general tonic to regain strength and weight following a debilitating illness. Thought by some to be an aphrodisiac. Excellent to use in diseases of the prostate gland. Available as capsules or as a tincture, 20 to 40 drops in water daily.

Smilax officinalis

Sarsaparilla

Common Names Jamaica sarsaparilla, guay-quill sarsaparilla, red sarsaparilla.

Part Used Root.

Medicinal Properties Alterative, diuretic, demulcent, antisyphilitic, stimulant, antiscorbutic.

Very useful in rheumatism, gout, skin eruptions, tetters, ringworm, scrofula, and psoriasis. An excellent antidote after taking a deadly poison. Drink copiously after thoroughly cleaning out the stomach with an emetic. Excellent for internal inflammations, colds, catarrh, and fever. Will increase the flow of urine. Good eyewash. Will promote profuse perspiration when taken hot. Powerful to expel gas from the stomach and bowels. One of the best herbs to use for infants infected with venereal disease. Experience has taught us that it is not a sure remedy for this disease in either children or adults. Wash the local pustules or sores with a tea made of the root, and administer inwardly by mixing the powdered root with their food. An excellent blood purifier. Take only for two weeks out of every three. If the tincture is used, take 25 to 50 drops in water twice a day.

Simaba cedron

Cedron

Common Names Cedron, rattlesnake's beans.

Part Used Seeds.

Medicinal Properties Antispasmodic, nervine, stomachic.

Cedron strengthens and invigorates the entire system. It is excellent for the stomach, prevents gas and fermentation. A good remedy in intermittent fevers, spasms, convulsions, and nervous troubles. Make a strong tea of it and apply to a snake bite or a poisonous insect bite by moistening a cloth in the tea and keeping it over the bite.

Keep the area well saturated with the tea. In addition, take the tea internally, one tablespoonful four times a day. Make the infusion with 1 ounce of the herb in 1 pint of boiling water.

Sinapis alba

Mustard

Common Names White mustard seed, yellow mustard, kedlock, yellow mustard seed, white mustard.

Part Used Seeds.

Medicinal Properties Pungent, laxative, stimulant, condiment, emetic, irritant, digestive.

Mustard is an old-fashioned remedy used to produce vomiting. Steep a teaspoonful of mustard in a large cup of boiling water, stir well, let cool to lukewarm, drink all at one time. Mustard is excellent when put in a foot bath to draw the blood to the lower part of the body in congestion of the lungs or head. It is excellent to use in a poultice for pneumonia, bronchitis, and other diseases of the respiratory tract.

Mustard plaster is also excellent in irritation of the kidneys. A good mustard plaster is made as follows: one part mustard and four parts whole wheat flour. Make into a paste by mixing with warm water. Have it thick enough to nicely spread on a piece of cloth. Be careful not to blister the skin. When the burning becomes too uncomfortable, the mustard plaster should be removed. Thoroughly cleanse the skin, making sure that no mustard remains.

Solanum dulcamara

Bittersweet

Common Names Woody nightshade, wolfe grape, nightshade, violet bloom, scarlet berry, bittersweet herb, bittersweet twigs, nightshade vine, garden nightshade, fever twig, felonwort, staff vine, felonwood.

Part Used Root, twigs.

Medicinal Properties Emetic, anodyne, deobstruent, herpatic, resolvent, depurative, aperient, laxative.

Has a splendid effect on the liver, pancreas, spleen, and other glandular organs of the body. Excellent in all skin troubles, and will purify the blood. It is very soothing and allays general irritability. Good in piles, jaundice, syphilis, gonorrhea, and rheumatism. It makes the skin and kidneys active, increases the menstrual flow, is helpful in leprosy, and is an important part of many salves. The tea is very healing to sores when they are bathed with it, and it is especially good for burns and scalds.

CAUTION

Bittersweet may have some toxic effects and should be used with caution when taken internally. It is usually used externally.

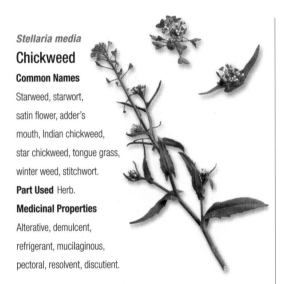

Stellaria media

Chickweed

Common Names

Starweed, starwort, satin flower, adder's mouth, Indian chickweed, star chickweed, tongue grass, winter weed, stitchwort.

Part Used Herb.

Medicinal Properties

Alterative, demulcent, refrigerant, mucilaginous, pectoral, resolvent, discutient.

Chickweed may be used fresh, dried, powdered, in poultices, fomentations, or made into a salve. Excellent in all cases of bronchitis, pleurisy, coughs, colds, hoarseness, rheumatism, inflammation, or weakness of the bowels and stomach, lungs, bronchial tubes—in fact, any form of internal inflammation.

It is one of the best remedies for external application to inflamed surfaces, skin diseases, boils, scalds, burns, inflamed or sore eyes, erysipelas, tumors, piles, cancer, swollen testes, ulcerated throat and mouth. Chickweed salve should be applied after bathing any external part with tea and left on as long as possible. Apply at night and leave on. Give several applications during the day if possible. It will cure burning and itching genitals. Anyone who is covered with any kind of sores should take a chickweed herb bath, and then apply the salve.

Symphytum officinale

Comfrey

Common Names

Blackwort, bruisewort, gum plant, healing herb, knitback, slippery root, wallwort, nipbone.

Part Used Root.

Medicinal Properties

Demulcent, astringent, pectoral, vulnerary, mucilaginous, static, nutritive.

Powerful remedy in coughs, catarrh, ulceration or inflammation of the lungs, consumption, hemorrhage and excessive expectoration in asthma and tuberculosis. Very valuable in ulceration or soreness of the kidneys, stomach, or bowels. The best remedy for bloody urine.

Apply a fomentation wrung out of the strong hot tea for bad bruises, swellings, sprains, fractures: it will greatly reduce the swelling and relieve the pain. Also use as a fomentation on boils.

A poultice of the fresh leaves is excellent for ruptures, sore breasts, fresh wounds, ulcers, burns, bruises, gangrenous sores, insect bites, and pimples. The tea taken internally is useful in scrofula, anemia, dysentery, diarrhea, leukorrhea, and female debility. Also has an excellent effect on internal sores and pains. Take one or two capsules daily for one or two weeks, then take a week's rest.

Symplocarpus foetidus

Skunk Cabbage

Common Names Meadow
cabbage, skunk weed, collard,
stinking poke, fetid hellebore,
polecat weed, swamp cabbage.

Part Used Root, seed.

Medicinal Properties

Sudorific, expectorant, pectoral,
antispasmodic, stimulant, diaphoretic.

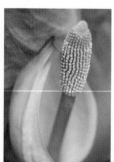

One of the old-fashioned, well-known
remedies. Very reliable in tuberculosis, chronic
catarrh, all bronchial and lung infections,
whooping cough, spasmodic asthma, hay fever
and pleurisy. Excellent remedy in chronic
rheumatism, nervous troubles, dysentery,
spasms, convulsions, dropsy, hysteria, epilepsy,
and for use during pregnancy. When made into
an ointment, it greatly relieves the pain of all
external tumors and sores.

Tanacetum vulgare

Tansy

Common Names Hindheel,
common tansy, bitter buttons,
parsley fern, ginger plant, golden
buttons, bachelor's buttons.

Part Used Entire plant.

**Medicinal
Properties**

Aromatic, tonic,
emmenagogue,
diaphoretic, vulnerary,
anthelmintic. Seed—vermifuge.

Tansy is excellent taken hot
for colds, fevers, la grippe, and ague. Good
for dyspepsia. One of the best remedies to
promote menstruation. Tansy seed will expel
worms. Useful in hysteria, jaundice, dropsy,
worms, and kidney troubles. Strengthens weak
veins. Hot fomentations wrung out of tansy
tea are excellent for swellings, tumors,
inflammations, bruises, freckles, sunburn,
leukorrhea, sciatica, toothache, and inflamed
eyes. Good in heart trouble. Will check
palpitation of the heart in a very short time.
Tansy should be taken in moderate doses only.

CAUTION
An overdose may prove fatal.

Taraxacum officinale

Dandelion

Common Names
Lion's tooth, swine
snout, puff ball,
wild endive, priest's
crown, white endive.

Part Used Root, leaves.

Medicinal Properties
Hepatic, aperient, diuretic,
depurative, tonic, stomachic.

Dandelion contains
twenty-eight parts
sodium. The natural
nutritive salts purify the blood and help to
neutralize the acids in the blood. Anemia is
caused by a deficiency of proper nutrients in
the blood and really has little to do with the
quantity of blood. Dandelion is one of the old
well-known remedies. The root is used to
increase the flow of urine in liver problems.
It is slightly laxative. It is a splendid remedy
for jaundice and skin diseases, scurvy, scrofula,
and eczema. Useful in all kinds of kidney
troubles, diabetes, dropsy, inflammation of the
bowels, and fever.

Has a beneficial effect on the female organs.
Increases the activity of the liver, pancreas, and
spleen, especially in enlargement of the liver
and spleen. Promotes bile formation. The
roasted, ground roots are especially good in
cases of dyspepsia and rheumatism.

Teucrium scorodonia

Wood Sage

Common Names Garlic sage.

Part Used Entire plant.

Medicinal Properties Tonic,
vermifuge, alterative, diuretic,
slightly diaphoretic.

Stimulates the
appetite. When
combined with
chickweed it is
a good external
wash to cleanse old sores,
indolent ulcers, swellings,
and boils. As a poultice
for cancer and tumors, it should be combined
with comfrey and ragwort. This will often
assist in effecting a cure. It is very useful in
palsy, quinsy, sore throat, colds, fevers, kidney,
and bladder troubles. Increases the flow of
urine and also the menstrual flow. This may be
purchased as a fluid extract. Use one-half to
one teaspoonful daily.

Thymus vulgaris

Thyme

Common Names

Common garden thyme, mother of thyme.

Part Used Entire plant.

Medicinal Properties

Tonic, carminative, emmenagogue, resolvent, antispasmodic, antiseptic.

One of the old-time household remedies. Usually used in combination with other herbs. Excellent taken hot for suppressed menstruation. Good in fevers. Will produce profuse perspiration when taken hot. A reliable nervine and excellent for relief of nightmares. Valuable in whooping cough, asthma, and lung troubles. For small children, give small and frequent doses. Good remedy for weak stomach, dyspepsia, gas, griping, cramps in the stomach, and diarrhea. Better taken cold for these purposes. Will relieve headache and acts as a mood elevator. Use 1 ounce of the dry herb to one pint of boiling water. Take two tablespoonfuls two times a day.

Use sparingly. Do not make a habit of using thyme.

Trigonella foenum-graecum

Fenugreek

Common Names

Foenugreek seed.

Part Used Seed.

Medicinal Properties

Mucilaginous, emollient, febrifuge, restorative.

Excellent when made into a poultice and used on wounds and inflammations. Grind the seed, mix it with powdered charcoal, and make it into a thick paste. The charcoal will make the poultice more effective. Treating ulcers and swellings in this manner will prevent blood poisoning. The tea is an excellent gargle for sore throat and will help clear the mucous from the bronchial passages. The seed is jelly-like when moistened and has a very cooling and healing effect on the bowels, as well as providing lubrication. The tea is excellent in fevers. The seeds boiled in soybean or nut milk are very nourishing.

Trifolium pratense

Red Clover

Common Names Wild clover, cleaver grass, marl grass, cow grass, trefoil, purple clover.

Part Used Flowers.

Medicinal Properties Depurative, detergent, alterative, mild stimulant.

Red clover is very pleasant to take and a wonderful blood purifier. Combined with equal parts of blue violet, burdock, yellow dock, dandelion root, rock rose, and golden seal, it is a great help in treating cancerous growths, leprosy, and pellagra. Used without other herbs, it is good for cancer of the stomach, whooping cough, and various spasms. The warm tea is very soothing to the nerves.

Red clover blossoms were also one of Mrs. E. G. White's home remedies. Mrs. White wrote several books on health and good diet. Red clover is effective in bronchial troubles and whooping cough.

It is healing to fresh wounds as well as old ulcers and makes an excellent healing salve. Red clover is splendid for syphilis. A good prescription is the following:

1 ounce red clover

1 ounce burdock seed

2 ounces wild Oregon grape

½ ounce bloodroot

Use the granulated herbs, mixing them well in one pint of hot water and one pint of hot apple cider. Cover and let stand for two hours. The dose is one wineglassful four times a day.

Red clover is exceedingly good for cancer on any part of the body. If in the throat, make a strong tea and gargle four or five times a day, swallowing some of the tea. If in the stomach, drink four or more cups of red clover tea a day on an empty stomach. If there are sores on the outside of any part of the body, bathe them freely with the tea. If in the rectum, inject with a syringe, five or six times a day. If in the uterus, inject with a bulb syringe, holding the vagina closed after the syringe is inserted so the tea will be forced well around the head of the womb. This should be held in for several minutes before expelling.

Every family should have a good supply of red clover blossoms. Gather them in the summer when in full bloom and dry them in the shade on paper. Put them in paper bags when dry and hang in a dry place. Use this tea in place of ordinary tea and coffee and you will have splendid results. Use it freely. It can be taken in place of water. If used as a capsule, take one, two, or three times a day.

Trifolium repens

White Clover

Common Names White shamrock, shamrock.

Part Used Blossoms.

Medicinal Properties Depurative, detergent.

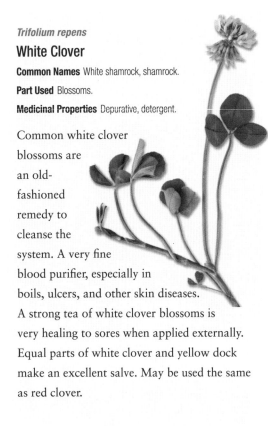

Common white clover blossoms are an old-fashioned remedy to cleanse the system. A very fine blood purifier, especially in boils, ulcers, and other skin diseases. A strong tea of white clover blossoms is very healing to sores when applied externally. Equal parts of white clover and yellow dock make an excellent salve. May be used the same as red clover.

Trillium pendulum

Beth Root

Common Names

Birthroot, milk ipecac, three-leaved nightshade, trillium, Indian shamrock, cough root, nodding, wakerobin, lamb's quarters, ground lily, snake bite, rattlesnake's root, Jew's harp plant.

Part Used Root.

Medicinal Properties Astringent, tonic, antiseptic, emmenagogue, diaphoretic, alterative, pectoral.

Useful in coughs, bronchial troubles, pulmonary consumption, hemorrhages from the lungs, excessive menstruation, leukorrhea, lax conditions of the vagina, and fallen womb. Remedy for diarrhea and dysentery. One of the common names for this herb, birthroot, is an indication of its use by the American Indians as an aid during childbirth. Beth root is available in whole, cut, or powdered form. It may also be obtained as a tincture and used in a solution of ¼ teaspoonful daily in a cup of water.

Tussilago farfara

Coltsfoot

Common Names

Bull's foot, horsefoot, horsehoof, butterbur, British tobacco, foal's-foot, flower velure, coughwort, ginger root.

Part Used Root, leaves.

Medicinal Properties Emollient, demulcent, expectorant, pectoral, diaphoretic, tonic.

An excellent remedy for catarrh, consumption, and all lung troubles. Very soothing to the mucous membranes. Good results are obtained when a tea is made by steeping a heaping tablespoonful in a quart of water and using as a fomentation or just moisten a cloth in the tea and apply it to the chest and throat. Excellent to relieve the chest of phlegm in all coughs, asthma, bronchitis, whooping cough, and spasmodic cough. It is good for inflammation and swelling, piles, stomach troubles, and fever. For scrofula or scrofulous tumors, take internally, one or two capsules a day, or make a poultice and apply externally. Has also been used internally for diarrhea and applied externally for burns, sores, ulcers, and insect bites. Make a decoction by placing 1 ounce of the leaves in a quart of water and letting it boil down to a pint. Sweeten with honey and take one cupful three or four times a day.

Ulmus fulva

Slippery Elm

Common Names Red elm, moose elm, Indian elm, sweet elm, American elm, rock elm, winged elm.

Part Used Inner bark.

Medicinal Properties

Mucilaginous, demulcent, emollient, nutritive, diuretic, pectoral.

Slippery elm is highly nourishing and very soothing to the stomach as a tea. It is very effective in diarrhea, bowel, stomach, bladder, and kidney troubles. It is soothing and healing wherever it is used. Slippery elm will stay in an ulcerated and cancerous stomach when nothing else will.

For excellent poultices, mix two parts of powdered slippery elm with one part of any one or all of the following powdered herbs: cornmeal, bloodroot, blue flag, comfrey, ragweed, chickweed. Mix well together, add warm water to make a thick paste, and use for abscesses, dirty wounds, inflammations, congestions, or eruptions. The face of the poultice should be smeared with olive oil if it is to be applied to a hairy surface. This poultice is also good for an enlarged prostate, swollen glands of the neck, groin, etc.

As a diet, take a teaspoonful of the powdered slippery elm bark and pour upon it a cupful of boiling soybean milk. Sweeten to taste.

Urtica dioica

Nettle

Common Names Common stinging nettle, stinging nettle, common nettle.

Part Used Entire plant.

Medicinal Properties
Pectoral, diuretic, astringent, tonic, styptic, rubefacient.

This herb is an excellent remedy for kidney trouble. It will expel gravel from the bladder and increase the flow of urine. Splendid for neuralgia. The tea increases the menstrual flow. It will kill and expel worms. For diarrhea, dysentery, piles, hemorrhages, hemorrhoids, gravel, or inflammation of the kidneys, make a decoction using a teaspoonful to a cup of water and simmer for ten minutes. For chronic rheumatism, take the bruised leaves and rub on the skin. Tea made from the root will cure dropsy in the first stages and will stop hemorrhage from the urinary organs, lungs, intestines, nose, and stomach. The boiled leaves applied externally will stop bleeding almost immediately. Nettle tea is good for fever, colds, and la grippe.

Very fine for eczema. Tea made from the leaves will expel phlegm from the lungs and stomach and clean out the urinary passages.

Valeriana officinalis

Valerian

Common Names English valerian, German valerian, great wild valerian, Vermont valerian, vandal root, all-heal, setwall, American English valerian (grown in U.S.)

Part Used Root.

Medicinal Properties
Aromatic, stimulant, tonic, anodyne, antispasmodic, nervine, emmenagogue.

Excellent nerve tonic— very quieting and soothing. Useful in hysteria. Will promote menstruation when taken hot. Useful in colic, low fevers, to break up colds, and also for gravel in the bladder. Healing for stomach ulcers and very good for prevention of fermentation and gas. The tea is very healing when applied to sores and pimples externally, and must also be taken internally at the same time. Relieves palpitation of the heart. DO NOT BOIL THE ROOT. Poisoning may result if large amounts of the tea are taken for more than two to three weeks. As a tincture use one to two teaspoonfuls in a glass of water. When used in capsule form, take one or two a day.

Verbascum thapsus

Mullein

Common Names Velvet plant, white mullein, verbascum flowers, woolen blanket herb, bullock's lungwort, flannel flower, shepherd's club, hare's beard, pig taper, cow's lungwort.

Part Used Leaves, flower, roots.

Medicinal Properties Anodyne, diuretic, demulcent, antispasmodic, vulnerary, astringent, emollient, pectoral.

The root has been successfully used for many years in asthma. For this purpose, burn the root and inhale the fumes. A tea of the leaves is very valuable in asthma, croup, bronchitis, all lung afflictions, bleeding from the lungs, difficult breathing, and hay fever.

A tea made from the flowers will induce sleep, relieve pain, and in large doses act as a laxative. The freshly crushed flowers will remove warts. Fomentations wrung from hot tea made from the leaves are helpful for inflamed piles, ulcers, tumors, mumps, acute inflammation of the tonsils, and sore throat.

This is a splendid remedy when taken internally for dropsy, catarrh, or swollen joints. Fomentations are good for any kind of swelling or bad sores. Excellent pain killer without being habit-forming. Helps to calm the nerves.

Verbena officinalis

Vervain

Common Names American vervain, wild hyssop, blue vervain, false vervain, simpler's joy, traveler's joy, Indian hyssop, purvain.

Part Used Entire plant.

Medicinal Properties Tonic, sudorific, expectorant, vulnerary, emetic, nervine, emmenagogue, vermifuge.

Vervain is very powerful to produce profuse perspiration. Excellent in fevers. Will often cure colds overnight. Take a warm cup of vervain tea often. An excellent remedy in whooping cough, pneumonia, consumption, asthma, ague, and will expel phlegm from the throat and chest. In fevers, take a cup of the hot tea every hour. Good in all female troubles. Will increase menstrual flow. Also good in scrofula and skin diseases. Will often expel worms when everything else fails. Very useful in nervousness, delirium, epilepsy, insanity, sleeplessness, and nervous headache. Will tone up the system during convalescence from heart diseases. Will remove obstruction in the bowels, colon, and bladder. Good in stomach troubles, shortness of breath, and wheezing. Used in combination with equal parts of smartweed and peppermint leaves. Is excellent for appendicitis. In fevers, use in combination with boneset, willow bark, or water pepper.

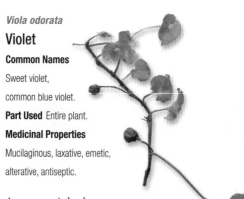

Viola odorata

Violet

Common Names
Sweet violet,
common blue violet.
Part Used Entire plant.
Medicinal Properties
Mucilaginous, laxative, emetic,
alterative, antiseptic.

As a tea, violet leaves are used as a blood purifier. Violet leaves are very effective in healing and give prompt relief in internal ulcers. They have been used as a treatment for cancer. Use externally for this purpose as a poultice and take the tea internally. For cancerous growths and other skin diseases, violet is especially beneficial when combined with red clover and vervain. Violet is a successful remedy in gout, coughs, colds, sores, sore throat, ulcers, scrofula, syphilis, bronchitis, and difficult breathing due to gas and morbid matter in the stomach and bowels. Violet is wonderful for nervousness or general debility when combined with nerve root, skullcap, or black cohosh. Relieves severe headache and congestion in the head. Very effective for whooping cough.

Viscum album

Mistletoe

Common Names Birdlime,
all-heal, European
mistletoe, devil's fuge.
Part Used Leaves, young
twigs.
Medicinal Properties Nervine,
antispasmodic, cardiac, tonic, narcotic.

This is a different plant from American mistletoe, *Phoradendron flavescens*. It is a fine nervine, effective in epilepsy, convulsions, hysteria, delirium, and St. Vitus's dance. Persons with heart trouble should be careful when using mistletoe, particularly in large doses. It raises the blood pressure and speeds up the pulse. Use only one teaspoonful to a pint of boiling water.

CAUTION

The berries are poisonous and should not be eaten. Large doses have an adverse effect on the heart. Take this herb with care and preferably under proper supervision.

Zea mays

Corn Silk

Common Names Corn, Indian corn, maize jagnog, Turkish corn.

Part Used Fresh or dried flower pistils.

Medicinal Properties Anodyne, diuretic, demulcent, alterative, lithotriptic.

Corn silk is one of the best remedies for kidney, bladder, and prostate troubles. Especially useful for pain or burning during urination and for difficulty in starting urination. May also be useful in helping to prevent bedwetting. Infuse two ounces of the herb in one pint of boiling water and drink several wineglassfuls a day.

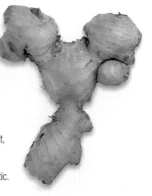

Zingiber officinale

Ginger

Common Names Black ginger, race ginger, African ginger.

Part Used Root.

Medicinal Properties Stimulant, pungent, carminative, aromatic, sialagogue, condiment, diaphoretic.

When taken hot, ginger is excellent in cases of suppressed menstruation. Chewing a little of the root stimulates the salivary glands and is very useful in paralysis of the tongue and is also good for sore throats. Prevents griping and is good for diarrhea, colds, la grippe, chronic bronchitis, coughs, dyspepsia, gas and fermentation, cholera, gout, and nausea when combined with stronger laxative herbs. Produces sweat when taken hot.

Specific Herbs
for Various
Medical Problems

Stress & Anxiety

Relieving nervous problems with herbs

Insomnia

Causes Common causes are overeating, indigestion, eating late at night just before retiring, stress, tension, worry, fear of something that might happen, etc. Cold feet, poor circulation, nervousness, and poor ventilation in the bedroom are also causes. A constant loss of sleep, whatever the cause, is always injurious to health.

Treatment A full warm bath or a hot footbath taken with a cup of hot tea, as given in the next paragraph, will often bring sleep immediately. If the person is very tired, nervous, and worn out, a fomentation to the spine, liver, and stomach will help produce sleep. The extremities should be kept warm, and a hot water bottle or electric heating pad should be used if necessary. Some people are put to sleep by having their hair brushed, or sometimes by having their feet gently rubbed.

The following herbs are very effective in producing sleep: lady's slipper, valerian, catnip, skullcap, and especially hops. Use a teaspoon of any one of the above, steep in a cup of boiling water for 20 minutes and drink hot. These herbs will not only produce sleep, but they have many other good qualities: they tone up the stomach and nerves, without ever leaving any bad aftereffects. Instead, they act as a tonic to the entire system. Aspirin or bromides taken for this purpose may seem to help for a time, but as their effect is to deaden the nerves, every dose taken makes the condition decidedly worse, and finally they lose their effectiveness altogether.

If you do not have herbs on hand, either hot sour lemonade or hot grapefruit juice may be tried. A cup of warm soybean milk is also sometimes helpful.

Herb list for sleep (to induce) Hops, motherwort, mullein, vervain, skullcap, peppermint. Equal parts of skullcap, nerve root, hops, catnip, and black cohosh.

Herb list for nightmares Bugleweed, thyme, lily of the valley, catnip, peppermint.

Hops work particularly well in relieving insomnia.

Eat a light meal early in the evening if you have problems sleeping; one of the commonest causes of insomnia is indigestion.

NIGHTMARES

Anyone who eats a heavy evening meal or midnight supper is likely to have nightmares. They are caused by overloading the stomach just before bedtime, and are made worse by sleeping on the back. No food should be taken for four or five hours before bedtime, as it normally takes about this long for the stomach to empty. Anyone who has frequent nightmares should sleep on his right side or stomach.

Children troubled with bad dreams, sometimes termed night terrors, frequently have trouble digesting their food properly. If they are bothered by constipation, they should be given catnip enemas and catnip tea to drink. They must also have a well-balanced diet.

Nervousness

Causes A large variety of circumstances and conditions may cause nervousness. The stomach and intestinal tract are very closely connected with the nervous system. Many times a woman becomes extremely nervous because of overwork, worry, care of children, improper food, lack of sleep, and in many instances it is true that a woman's work is never done. Many times the husband finds fault and makes unpleasant remarks, which make her more nervous and which would be unnecessary if he understood the situation and lent a helping hand. Excessive novel reading, sedentary or dissipating habits, and lack of exercise and fresh air are also causes.

Waste matter in the system gets into the blood and affects the nervous system, especially the nerves of the brain, causing irritability and

Nervousness can be the underlying cause of insomnia, headaches, and other obstinate health problems.

headaches. We must never forget that the food we eat affects all the nervous system, because what we eat and drink is what feeds and nourishes the nerves.

Treatment Hot and cold fomentations, to the spine, stomach, liver, and spleen, are very beneficial for nervous people. A prolonged warm bath of an hour's duration or longer if agreeable, finishing with a cool bath or spray and vigorous rubbing, is excellent. Gentle massage after a bath, or for that matter at any time, will help greatly.

A nervous person must also get the system cleaned out. Use high enemas and herb laxatives. The bowels must move freely to maintain good health. Plenty of rest in a well-ventilated room is essential. Skullcap is one of the best herbs for nerves. Red sage is excellent for nervous headaches. Take a cup of the tea, strong, as often as necessary.

The following herbs are excellent for strengthening the nerves, or for any nervous disorder: horehound, lady's slipper, motherwort, mugwort, marshmallow, poplar bark, catnip, spearmint, camomile, ginger, peach leaves, vervain, blue and black cohosh. Prepare and take according to the directions for use of herbs.

Herb list for nervousness Camomile, celery, cinchona bark, dill, fit root, skullcap with golden seal and hops, lobelia, motherwort,

Ginger is helpful in nervous disorders and is also a digestive tonic.

origanum, peach leaves, pennyroyal, queen of the meadow, red clover, rosemary, rue, sage, skullcap, skunk cabbage, spearmint, squaw vine, St. John's wort, thyme, twin leaf, valerian, vervain, wild cherry, wood betony, blue violet, sanicle, buchu, mistletoe, red sage, catnip, peppermint, marshmallow root, mugwort, nettle, poplar bark, Solomon's seal, lady's slipper, lobelia tincture for quick results.

Herb list for dizziness Peppermint, catnip, rue, wood betony.

Herb list for fainting Lavender (prevents fainting), cayenne, peppermint, antispasmodic tincture, motherwort.

Headaches

There are three common kinds of headaches:

1 Sick Headache

This type of headache occurs if undigested food stays in the stomach, during times of increased stress, if there is a disordered liver, or when there is mental or physical overwork. In women, disorders of menstruation may cause a sick headache.

Treatment Relief is sometimes obtained by taking a hot footbath with a tablespoon of mustard in it, or use just plain water as hot as can be borne. Keep the feet and legs in the hot water nearly up to the knees. Place a cold washcloth on the forehead and one on the back of the neck. Drink a cup of hot peppermint, spearmint, valerian, black cohosh, or skullcap tea. If you do not have these herbs, drink a

Lemon juice taken in hot water is effective against a sick headache.

cupful of hot water, adding the juice of a lemon, but no sweetening.

2 Bilious Headache

Caused from indigestion, disordered liver, overeating, wrong food combinations, and insufficient exercise. People who overeat of rich heavy foods and take little or no exercise at all are the frequent sufferers of this type of headache. Unless the diet is changed and a regular exercise program established, this may develop into a chronic type of headache.

Symptoms Dull pain in the forehead, sore and throbbing temples.

Treatment Avoid all harmful articles of diet. High enemas initially, to cleanse the colon, may be helpful in bilious headaches. Often the stomach is overloaded when the headache comes on. If this is the case, use an emetic, as described on pages 32–3. Take the treatment as given for sick headache.

3 Nervous (Tension) Headache

Nervous people and those whose work is sedentary usually suffer from this form of headache. Mental strain and worry will cause a nervous headache. Bright lights or noises of any kind usually make the headache worse.

Quiet rest is the best remedy for a nervous headache; a gentle massage may be helpful, too.

Treatment Lie down and rest where it is quiet, and where there is plenty of fresh air. Take a cupful or two of hot peppermint, catnip, red sage, or spearmint tea. Upon retiring, take a cupful of hot hops tea, or if it is possible to retire when the headache comes on, take it then; it will soothe the nerves and produce sleep. Red sage is one of the best herbs for headache.

The herbal liniment that is recommended on page 28, when thoroughly applied to the forehead, temples, and back of the neck, will many times give prompt relief.

If the headache continues, use an enema of catnip, blue cohosh, or black cohosh tea. The enema should be very warm and retained as long as possible, using a pint or more of liquid.

Herb list for headache Blue violet, catnip, coltsfoot, peppermint, rhubarb, rosemary, rue, sweet balm, thyme, vervain, virgin's bower, wood betony, elder, marjoram, calamint, pennyroyal, fringe tree, red root, holy thistle, mountain balm, yerba santa, camomile, tansy.

Head & Hair Conditions

A reflection of your general health

Hair & Scalp

Any disease that impairs the vitality of the body has an effect upon the hair. When the circulation is diminished by a general nervous condition, the scalp cannot be properly nourished. Diseases of the scalp and loss of hair are expressions of bodily ailments. A poisoned or impure bloodstream carries little or no nourishment to the hair. The color, luster, dryness or oiliness, and brittle condition of the hair are all due to the condition of the system.

The best medicine for your hair is a good, nutritious diet.

Your lifestyle will be reflected in the condition of your hair and scalp.

The real treatment for diseases of the hair and scalp lies not in the many tonics that are used, but in the attention to the foods that are eaten, many of which cause diseases of the body, thereby affecting the hair and scalp. The blood that nourishes the hair must be purified by using wholesome, nourishing foods, that will build a healthy body.

Loss of hair may be caused by catarrh, nervous diseases, fevers, worry, mental disorders, skin diseases, injurious tonics, eczema, and anesthetics. Curling and crimping with metal curlers and hot irons dries the hair and breaks it.

Since an analysis of the hair shows it to be composed of iron, oxygen, hydrogen, nitrogen, carbon, and sulphur, the blood must be supplied with these minerals so that nourishment will be carried to the scalp. Raw foods contain the highest percentage of minerals obtainable. Many of the best foods are prepared in such a way that most of the minerals are drained off in the water. Proper nourishment and good health will do more to make beautiful hair than any external treatment it is possible to give.

A thorough brushing of the hair every day keeps it free from lint and makes it silky. To manipulate the scalp lightly with the tips of the fingers, always using a rotary movement, is good. It should be done very thoroughly.

The leaves and bark of the willow tree, made into a tea, will cure dandruff. A tea made of marshmallow leaves and thoroughly applied to the scalp will do much to prevent falling hair.

Any of the following herbs are useful to nourish and brighten the hair and make it grow: nettle, pepper grass, sage, henna leaves, or burdock.

Steep a tablespoon in a pint of boiling water for one-half hour and add a level tablespoon of boric acid. Massage the scalp with this solution. It may also be used before a shampoo or between shampoos.

Herb list for scald head Sanicle. Make a tea of 2 ounces of raspberry leaves in 1 quart of water. Steep for 30 minutes and add one-half ounce of lobelia powder. Take both morning and

Hair should be brushed regularly and thoroughly to maintain its condition.

evening. Use witch hazel extract to allay itching. Also take a good blood purifier.

Herb list for dandruff Burdock, nettle, sage.

Herb list for hair health Nettle, rosemary (prevents hair from falling out), sage, peach, burdock.

Stomach & Digestion
Balancing your digestive system

Stomach Trouble

Stomach troubles arise from eating and drinking harmful foods, wrong combinations of foods, eating fruits and vegetables together, milk and cane sugar together, pies, cakes, white flour products, greasy and fried foods, taking too much fluid with meals, and poor mastication. No matter what or how much you eat, if it is not properly masticated it will not digest properly. Drinking with meals will dilute the digestive juices so that they cannot do their work properly. Ice cold drinks are especially harmful, because they chill the stomach as well as dilute the digestive juices.

The best thing to do for any kind of stomach trouble is to go on a fruit diet for at least a week or more. Give the stomach a chance to rest so that the normal gastric juices may become strong enough to digest the food.

When on the fasting or fruit diet, do not drink anything but pure water and the prescribed herbs. Upon arising, drink one-fourth teaspoonful of golden seal or take one No. 00 capsule in a glass of very warm water, before taking anything else into the stomach. This is one of the best remedies. Continue doing this after you have completed taking the fruit diet. If this is taken regularly, good results will follow.

Herb list for stomach (indigestion and gas)
Angelica, strawberry, thyme, valerian, vervain, witch hazel, wild cherry, willow, wintergreen, wood betony, camomile, marjoram, echinacea, bethroot, chickweed, aloes, chicory, bayberry bark, balmony, blue violet, buckbean, calamus, caraway seed, catnip, cayenne, cinchona bark, comfrey, colombo, cubeb, fennel, ginseng, golden seal, golden thread, sage, sassafras, slippery elm, giant Solomon's seal, spearmint, St. John's wort, gum arabic, hyssop, milkweed, mint, mugwort, nettle, origanum (especially for sour stomach), peach leaves, pimpernel, plantain, rue, anise, bay leaves, cedron.

Golden thread acts as a powerful cure for dyspepsia.

Stomach Inflammation (Gastritis)

See also **gas in the stomach** or **bowels**

Causes One of the most common causes of gastritis is the drinking of alcohol. Another frequent cause is aspirin or other anti-inflammatory medicines. People with ulcers also frequently have gastritis. The ingestion of strong acid or alkali products causes severe gastritis. Excessive use of spices, mustard, condiments, and all stimulating foods, also favor the development of gastritis.

Symptoms Frequent symptoms are pain in the upper abdomen, nausea, loss of appetite, weight loss, gas, burning sensation in the chest or upper abdomen.

Treatment Discontinue all irritating medicines, particularly aspirin. Drink no alcoholic beverages. Eat a bland, nourishing diet.

Take oatmeal, bran, or barley water. Oatmeal water with soybean milk is an excellent nourishing drink when mixed half-and-half. To get the stomach into shape to retain food, steep a teaspoonful of golden seal in a pint of boiling water. Take six or more large swallows a day.

Hot and cold applications to the stomach, liver, and spine are helpful.

The following herbs are excellent in stomach trouble. Look up their descriptions and use the ones best suited to your condition. They may be taken singly, or combined. Sage, wood betony, poplar bark, bitterroot, cayenne, slippery elm (excellent), columbo, pleurisy root, hyssop, plantain, wild yams, sweet flag, yarrow, strawberry leaves, wild alum root, rue, violet leaves.

Red raspberry tea is very soothing to the stomach. Excellent results will be obtained by drinking chickweed tea or red clover tea in place of water, six or eight glasses a day. Slippery elm tea should be used in all stomach troubles. It heals, strengthens, and nourishes.

An excellent stomach remedy is to mix equal parts of golden seal, echinacea, burnet, wood betony, myrrh, and spearmint (use powdered herbs). After thoroughly mixing these together, take one-half teaspoonful in a glass of hot water an hour before meals and one upon retiring.

Indigestion—See heartburn.

Dysentery (Diarrhea) or Summer Complaint

Causes Inflammation of the rectum and large intestine, insufficient foods, improper diet, drinking too much liquid with meals, overeating, wrong combinations of food, stimulating foods, liquor, tea, coffee, drinking impure water, unhygienic surroundings, eating fruits or vegetables that have begun to decompose, eating foods that have been standing in pantries that are not well ventilated, and eating improperly refrigerated, contaminated foods. Irritable bowels, habitual constipation, and taking certain medicines, such as laxatives, may also be the cause.

Mild symptoms Frequent, small, and painful passages from the bowels, or the passage of mucus streaked with blood. A constant desire to evacuate the bowels. Great straining. Fever, loss of appetite, sleeplessness, and restless at night. Sometimes the abdomen is distended.

Severe Symptoms Increasing fever, great thirst, red tongue, the abdomen may appear sunken in some cases, straining ceases, and the bowels become more relaxed and may protrude. Passage of urine is infrequent and is accompanied by a burning sensation. The pulse becomes slow, breathing is rapid, and generally the patient looks pale and emaciated. Do not let this condition continue. Give the following treatment in either mild or severe cases and good results will be obtained.

Treatment The patient should be put to bed. Take equal amounts of slippery elm, lady's slipper, gentian, wild yam, bayberry bark, and skullcap. Mix thoroughly. Use a heaping teaspoonful to a cup of boiling water; steep for one-half hour; drink a half cupful every half hour until relieved; then take three to four cups a day. The addition of calamus root will prevent griping, fermentation, and gas. These herbs can usually be obtained in either powder or capsule form, which makes their administration quite easy.

Another excellent combination of herbs is equal parts of red raspberry and witch hazel

Eating food that is no longer fresh can be the cause of diarrhea.

A combination of whole-wheat flakes and soybean milk is soothing to the stomach and can help to alleviate symptoms.

leaves. If the kidneys are affected, add peach leaves. Mix thoroughly together. Use a heaping teaspoonful to a quart of boiling water and drink four or five cups a day as hot as possible.

The diet must be light. Use potassium broth, soybean milk, or oatmeal milk, and drink at least a pint a day of slippery elm water and barley water. Whole wheat flakes can be completely dissolved in soybean milk; a diet of this is most nourishing and highly alkaline. It contains all the elements the system requires. Chew your food thoroughly, until it is a cream, before swallowing.

Give hot fomentations to the abdomen and spine, continuing for half an hour. If the case is severe, repeat three or four times a day.

The herbal liniment, as described on page 28, when thoroughly applied to the abdomen and spine after the fomentations, is excellent.

Give a high enema, using either white oak bark, bayberry bark, or wild alum root tea. All of these act as an astringent. Give the enema as hot as the patient can tolerate without burning. This will usually be between 102 and 108°F. It may be hard to retain the tea at this temperature, but it will give great relief.

Dyspepsia (Sour Stomach)

Causes Nonnourishing and devitaminized food, eating too many soft foods, irregular meals, highly seasoned foods, iced drinks, overeating. People who lead a sedentary life need plenty of outdoor exercise and deep breathing, and a proper amount of rest.

Symptoms Heartburn, headache, pain in the chest, heaviness in the stomach, irregularity of bowels, cold feet, weak pulse, general prostration in chronic cases, irritability, nausea, bloating, and gas. In long-standing cases, there may be a hacking cough, intermittent fever at times, or palpitation of the heart.

Treatment The herbs listed below will prove soothing and add tone to the system. Any one, two, or three of them may be used together and will be of great advantage in treating dyspepsia.

Herb list for dyspepsia (sour stomach) Tansy, gentian root, thyme, wild cherry, boneset, summer savory, origanum, buckbean, yarrow, magnolia, horehound, golden seal, sweet flag, quassia, white oak, masterwort, spearmint, peach leaves, golden thread, wahoo, myrrh.

Golden seal, taken one-quarter of a teaspoonful to a glass of water an hour before meals, will help the digestion greatly. A cup of skullcap or gentian tea taken every three hours

Crisp whole wheat or bran crackers are a good antidote to dyspepsia.

will prove beneficial, since many cases are primarily caused by nervous troubles.

When overeating is the cause, a mild emetic will often bring immediate relief. This can be done by drinking as much warm water with a little salt in it as the stomach can hold. Put the finger down the throat after drinking. You will not have to strain if plenty of water is taken.

Diet The old idea of starving dyspepsia is a wrong one. Ordinarily dyspeptics should eat more than the usual amount of food, but it should be light, nourishing, and easy to digest. Quick elimination is essential. Eat regularly with no late meals.

Acid Dyspepsia

Causes Meats, fish, tea, coffee, tobacco, alcohol, spices, vinegar, excessive salt, desserts and candy, pastries, fried foods, irregular eating, excess starch, improperly cooked foods, poorly baked bread, foods too hot or cold, and foods cooked in aluminum utensils.

Symptoms Loss of appetite, headaches, sleeplessness, acid urine, acid or strong perspiration, acid taste in the mouth, sour stomach, lassitude, occasional vomiting, a burning, hot feeling in the chest or abdomen, gas on the stomach.

Treatment Soybean products are excellent as a remedy. A diet of soybean milk, buttermilk, or orange juice for a few days or a week is excellent. Chew until your food becomes thoroughly saturated with saliva, which is alkaline. Do not drink with meals.

Do not eat between meals or for several hours before going to bed!

After you have been on this diet for a few days to a week, eat one good vegetable meal every day, preferably at noon. Be careful of combinations. Avoid eating fruits and vegetables at the same meal; when the two are combined digestion is delayed. Do not use any of the foods listed under Causes in the first paragraph of this section.

ALL OF THESE SYMPTOMS ARE THE RESULT OF YEARS OF WRONG LIVING. YOU MUST NOT EXPECT THEM TO DISAPPEAR IMMEDIATELY.

The following foods should be eaten in abundance: oranges, apples, beets, cherries, carrots, strawberries, celery, radishes, cucumbers, figs, okra, string beans.

Burnet, sanicle, wood betony, calamus, and peppermint are very beneficial herbs. Golden seal powder, taken one-fourth teaspoon in a glass of water an hour before meals, is healing.

Herb list for acid dyspepsia Beech, buckbean, calamus, cayenne, colombo, gentian root, golden seal, gold thread, horehound, magnolia, origanum, peach leaves, quassia, sage, spearmint, tansy, thyme, wahoo, wild cherry, yarrow, balmony, bloodroot, camomile, Peruvian bark, ginger, charcoal, boneset, motherwort, bitterroot, St. John's wort.

Herb list for heartburn Balmony, bay leaves, beech, bitterroot, buckbean, cayenne, gentian root, ginseng, golden seal, gold thread, poplar, Peruvian bark, coltsfoot, lobelia, wild cherry bark, bayberry bark, skullcap, nutmeg, balm, bloodroot, marjoram, rosemary, wood betony, wormwood, red root, willow, angelica, burnet, origanum.

Colitis

Causes There are many causes of colitis, most of which are known but some are unknown. Many cases are caused by infectious organisms, others by faulty diet, constipation, improper mixtures of food that irritate the stomach and bowels, too much cane sugar and too many cane sugar products, grease, white flour, eating too hastily, too much liquid and very soft foods, taking of excessive cathartics, and stress.

Symptoms Running off of the bowels or constipation. Mucus passes in the feces and discharges are stringy. There is a feeling of weakness through the abdomen, at times headache, often great pain and dizziness, emaciation, weakness, and pains in various parts of the body. In severe cases of colitis, there may be severe abdominal cramps, bleeding from the rectum, and fever.

Treatment Take a high enema made of one tablespoonful of bayberry bark to every quart of water. Yellow dock root and burdock root are also good and are very healing. Cover and let simmer for a few minutes; then steep for 15 or 20 minutes.

After the herbs settle, pour off the tea and take it as hot as you can stand (from 100°F to 108°F—or in some cases even hotter).

Wild alum root, golden seal, or myrrh are also excellent herbs to use as an enema. Use a heaping teaspoonful of golden seal and a heaping teaspoonful of myrrh to four quarts of boiling water. Steep and let the mixture settle.

A liquid diet for a short time is advisable. When eating solid food, thoroughly chew it, drinking no liquids with meals. All roughage should be avoided until the condition is better. Puree any vegetables. Soybean milk, zwieback, and wheat flakes are good.

Herbs to be taken internally Use a teaspoonful of golden seal and one-fourth teaspoonful of myrrh to a pint of boiling water. Let it steep and take a tablespoonful of this mixture six or eight times a day. If the case is severe, take a tablespoonful every hour; or take from one-fourth to one teaspoonful, as per directions for taking herbs, one hour before each meal and upon retiring. In places where sumach grows, a tea may be made from the bark, leaves, or berries. For an enema, take a handful of any of these in four quarts of water and steep for an hour.

Herb list for colon trouble Colombo, fireweed, fleabane, peppermint, vervain, aloes, slippery elm bark, bayberry bark, white oak bark, golden seal, myrrh.

Herb list for bowel trouble Water pepper, white pond lily, wintergreen, dandelion, wood sanicle, bethroot, chickweed, myrrh, witch hazel, echinacea, bayberry bark, birch, bitterroot, blue violet, caraway seeds (expels gas), catnip (for acid), chickweed, comfrey, coriander, cubeb berries, fenugreek, golden seal, gum arabic, hyssop, magnolia, masterwort, milkweed, mugwort, mullein, origanum, pilewort, rhubarb, rue, sage, sanicle, sassafras, slippery elm, spearmint, strawberry, sumach berries, tansy, vervain, marshmallow.

Herb list for appendicitis Buckthorn bark, vervain, water pepper, lady's slipper. Proper medical attention is also necessary.

Excess roughage can exacerbate bowel problems so use soybean products instead, which are easier to digest.

Constipation

Causes Nearly the entire human race is afflicted with constipation. Wrong diet is the main cause. Eating refined foods; too many varieties of food at one meal; eating food that is too concentrated; using coffee, tea, and liquor of all kinds; sedentary life and lack of exercise are other contributing factors to this ailment.

Constipation, diverticulosis, and cancer of the colon are all prevalent diseases in North America and European countries where the diet contains large amounts of refined foods and is low in bulk. In Africa, where the diet contains large amounts of bulk, these diseases of the colon are rarely found.

Excessive use of drugs as well as patent medicines is a frequent cause of constipation, tumors, etc.

Symptoms Coated tongue, foul breath, backache, headache, mental dullness, depression, insomnia, loss of appetite, and various pains.

Treatment Regulate the diet. Eat your food as dry as possible. When food is eaten dry and thoroughly saturated with saliva, it is a wonderful help to lubricate the bowels. It will make the system alkaline and will greatly increase the rapidity of digestion.

Do your drinking one hour before or two or three hours after eating. No liquid of any kind should be taken with the meals. Eat freely of fresh and stewed fruits, selecting the fruits that agree best with you. It is best not to eat fruits and vegetables at the same meal.

Get plenty of outdoor exercise. Practice deep breathing while walking, and in the morning before getting up, lie on your back, knees flexed, and pant, breathing in short rapid gasps. Roll on your right side, stomach, and

Too much coffee or other stimulants can be a cause of constipation.

left side, and continue panting. This exercise massages the bowels.

The following is an excellent formula for a laxative: mix thoroughly one tablespoon each of mandrake, buckthorn bark, rhubarb root, fennel seed, and calamus root, and one teaspoonful of aloes. This is a real body cleanser. Mandrake is one of the finest herbs to cleanse the liver. If powdered, take one-fourth teaspoonful in a half glass of cold water followed by a glass of hot water. This can be taken after meals or upon retiring. Take more or less than the one-fourth teaspoonful according to your individual needs.

Another laxative herb formula that is very good is this: mix thoroughly one ounce mandrake root, one ounce cascara sagrada bark, one ounce buckthorn bark, one ounce fennel seed, one ounce calamus root, and one-fourth ounce aloe. Putting this mixture through a fine sieve is a good way to mix it thoroughly. The above herbs are available in powdered form. Take one-fourth teaspoonful or one No. 00 capsule with one glass or more of hot water upon retiring. Increase or decrease the amount taken so as to keep the bowels moving normally.

Plenty of liquids are imperative in the treatment of constipation. Try to drink six to eight glasses of water or fruit juice a day, and be sure the diet contains an abundance of fiber and bulk-forming foods.

Herb list for constipation Balmony, buckthorn bark, cascara sagrada, chickweed, ginger, fennel seed, origanum, psyllium, white ash, elder, blue flag, wild Oregon grape, rhubarb root, butternut bark, licorice, calamus root, aloes.

NAUSEA AND VOMITING

If the nausea is due to undigested food or fermentation in the stomach, take an emetic and clean out the stomach. (See emetics on pages 32–3.) A cup of hot peppermint or spearmint tea, taken after the stomach is cleansed, will strengthen and settle it. A hot fomentation applied over the stomach or a hot water bottle with a moist towel under it will often prove beneficial.

The following herbs are excellent for nausea and vomiting: spearmint, peppermint, catnip, sweet balm.

To stop severe vomiting, use origanum, peppermint, spearmint, or peach leaves. Sweet balm settles the stomach. Use one teaspoon of the herbs to a cup of boiling water and steep. Lobelia is also good. Use a teaspoon to a pint of boiling water and steep. Take a teaspoon of this tea every 15 minutes until relief is obtained.

Antispasmodic tincture given in small doses is very good; use ten drops in a glass of warm water.

Gas in the Stomach or Bowels

Causes Gas in the stomach and bowels is the result of improper digestion. Most of the gas in the intestinal tract is composed of nitrogen, carbon dioxide, and methane. The amount of hydrogen and carbon dioxide in the intestines largely depends upon the diet, since these gases are mostly produced by bacteria in the colon acting on unabsorbed carbohydrates and proteins in the diet. Approximately 600 cc of gas is passed each day, and about two-thirds of this is produced in the intestines. Air that is swallowed during routine everyday activities contributes only a small amount to the total gas content of the intestinal tract. Certain conditions, such as strictures or spasm in the small intestine or colon, may cause some obstruction to the bowel, thereby producing "gas pains."

Large amounts of gas in the intestinal tract may be produced by eating certain foods, by improper absorption of some foods, particularly carbohydrates, or by an overgrowth of gas-producing bacteria. Eating wrong combinations of food will cause gas to form in the stomach and bowels.

Drinking with meals causes a sour stomach and fermentation, as does hasty eating and poor mastication.

Treatment Peppermint and spearmint tea are excellent for reducing gas in the stomach. Equal parts of calamus root, valerian, and granulated or powdered peppermint or spearmint should be taken: mix these together using a teaspoon to a cup of boiling water; steep, strain, and drink one-half cupful an hour before meals, and another half cupful after meals.

The above herbs can be used in powdered form, as well as in capsules, if desired.

Mint tea is appetizing at any time of day, and a proven remedy for gas.

Regular energetic activity helps the digestive system and works against excess gas or heartburn.

To strengthen the stomach and cleanse it so that this condition will be overcome, take one-fourth teaspoon of powdered golden seal in one-half glass of warm water an hour before each meal. You may also take it as follows if you prefer: one heaping teaspoon of golden seal and one-fourth teaspoon of myrrh to a pint of boiling water, steep, and take a swallow just a few minutes before eating.

Rinse the mouth and throat thoroughly with this every morning, swallowing a little.

If you find that certain foods such as beans, sauerkraut, apples, etc., form excessive gas, eat these foods sparingly or omit them entirely from your diet.

It has also been found that as a person grows older, different foods may react differently in the body, whereby foods that could previously be eaten without any trouble may, as the person reaches middle and older age, begin to produce considerable gas. If this occurs, the diet must be adjusted accordingly.

Herb list for gas (see also **heartburn**) Anise, calamus, caraway seed, catnip, dill, fennel, mint, origanum, peppermint, sage, sarsaparilla, sassafras, spearmint, thyme, wild yam, wintergreen, yarrow, ginger, nutmeg, valerian, angelica, wood betony.

Herb list for griping (in bowels) Anise, caraway seed, catnip, coriander, ginger, pennyroyal, thyme, nutmeg, balm, bay leaves.

Herb list for intestines Fenugreek, golden seal, mint, nettle, pennyroyal, psyllium, slippery elm, giant Solomon's seal, strawberry, wild alum root, cascara sagrada.

Piles (Hemorrhoids)

Hemorrhoids are dilated veins around the anus and rectum. They may be either internal (not visible from the outside) or external. Approximately half the population of the United States over fifty years of age has them.

Causes Wrong eating habits may be a cause of hemorrhoids. Eating a diet that contains a large amount of refined foods that are low in bulk (fiber), tends to cause small, hard stools, resulting in straining and constipation; this causes the pressure inside the colon to increase.

Taking commercial laxatives that are on the market may also be a cause, as many of them irritate the membranous lining of the colon.

Symptoms Swollen veins are present around the anus or inside the rectum. These swollen blood vessels frequently become irritated and bleed.

Sometimes the bleeding is quite severe and may even result in anemia and weakness. If a blood clot forms in a hemorrhoid, it becomes swollen, blue, tense, and extremely painful. At times the veins inside the rectum are so swollen that when the stool passes they are forced to the outside. In this case, some oil should be used and they should be replaced inside. Often there is extreme itching.

Treatment First take a high hot enema at a temperature of from 102° to 108°F. Use white oak bark, bayberry bark, or white alum root tea. This will cleanse the entire colon.

Make a strong tea of witch hazel bark and one teaspoon of catnip, one-half teaspoon of bloodroot and one teaspoon of yellow dock root. If you do not have the other herbs, you may use just the witch hazel bark and catnip. Use a tablespoon of witch hazel bark and a teaspoon of catnip to a cup of boiling water.

A sedentary lifestyle may be a contributing factor in hemorrhoids.

Steep for 20 minutes. If the hemorrhoids are external, dip a small piece of cotton in this tea and bathe the affected parts. If the hemorrhoids are internal, use a soft rubber enema tip and inject two tablespoons at a time into the rectum. This will give relief in a short time.

When taking the enemas you will find it less painful, and the piles will go back inside easier, if you take the knee-chest position; this causes the intestines to drop forward.

Another herb tea injection that is very effective is powdered white oak bark or alum root tea. Use a teaspoon of either to a cup of boiling water, steep for 20 minutes, strain, bathe the affected parts, and inject a little into the rectum. This will give relief.

I have cured bad cases with kerosene alone. Apply to the affected parts either inside or out. If inside, inject a little. Lemon juice is also excellent when used in the same way.

Take the following tea internally: use equal parts of mullein, yarrow, wild alum root, and pilewort. Mix thoroughly and use one teaspoon to a pint of boiling water. Boil and then let steep for one-half hour. Take half a cup three or four times a day. The following is excellent for healing when used as a suppository:

2 ounces powdered hemlock bark

1 ounce golden seal

1 ounce powdered wheat flour

1 ounce boric acid

1 ounce bayberry bark

Mix with glycerine until stiff enough to form suppositories. Insert and leave in overnight.

Diet: It should be simple and light. All heavy and stimulating foods should be avoided, as should tobacco, tea, coffee, vinegar, alcoholic drinks, and meat. Potassium broth is very excellent. So is soybean milk, soybean zwieback, thoroughly ripe bananas, and vegetable broths of any kind. Staying on a fruit diet for a few days is very helpful.

In using all these treatments, good judgment must be exercised. There are perhaps other things that could be eaten, but a simple alkaline diet will hasten a cure.

A hot sitz bath, as hot as can be borne, should be taken. Sit in this bath for 15 minutes or longer. Have another tub ready containing cold water, and sit in this for a minute or two. Return to the hot water and repeat. If you use a bathtub, have the water well over the hips. Place the other tub alongside the bathtub, and tilt it by using wood or some other solid article under one side. Continue this treatment for one hour.

Herb list for piles (hemorrhoids) Bittersweet, chickweed, fireweed, golden seal, mullein, myrrh, nettle, plantain, shepherd's purse, Solomon's seal, spearmint, uva-ursi, white oak bark, witch hazel, wild alum root, yarrow, bloodroot, pilewort, pimpernel, aloes, burdock, psyllium.

Gout

Gout is not a very common disease, although there are certain groups of people, such as the Philippinos living in the United States, in whom there is a very high incidence. It usually affects adult males; only five to ten percent occurring in women. Patients with gout comprise approximately five percent of all patients having arthritis.

Causes While the cause of most cases is not known for sure, about 10 to 20 percent of patients with gout have an inherited form of the disease. All patients with gout have increased urates in the blood. These are deposited in crystalline form in the joints and may produce severe arthritis. Many patients with gout also have kidney stones.

Symptoms The peak age for the onset of symptoms in men is between forty and fifty, while in women gout is rarely seen before the onset of menopause.

Gout is responsive to a wide range of herbs, blue violet among them, which may be taken singly or together in a mixture.

More than half the patients with gouty arthritis experience their first attack of pain in the great toe. Other common sites are the ankle, knee, wrist, fingers, and elbow. The pain usually occurs suddenly and frequently begins at night. The affected joint becomes red, hot, and exceedingly painful. Overindulgence in an abundance of rich foods and alcohol frequently brings on an attack, which may last anywhere from a few hours to weeks. Between attacks the patient usually has no symptoms, but subsequent attacks occur at unpredictable intervals. In a small percentage of patients (about five percent), after the first attack no further attacks occur. As the episodes of gout become more frequent and severe, the joints become more deformed and painful.

Treatment The diet is of great importance. During an acute attack of gout, the diet should be high in carbohydrates and low in fat and protein. Meat should be eliminated and peas, beans, and lentils should be limited. The calories must be strictly limited so that the patient does not gain weight, and if the patient is obese he must be placed on a diet to lose weight. Alcohol must be eliminated. A large fluid intake is very helpful.

Take equal parts of granulated skullcap, yarrow, and valerian, and mix thoroughly together. Use a heaping teaspoon to a cup of boiling water.

Steep, and drink a cupful an hour before meals and one upon retiring. Take laxative herbs to keep the bowels open; this is important. Liniment, see pages 28–9, if applied freely and thoroughly rubbed in, will greatly allay the pain. The herbs given in the section on Rheumatism and Arthritis, on page 212, may also be taken for gout with good effect. Study each herb separately, and take the one or combination that suits your case best.

Any one of the following herbs will be found beneficial and may be taken singly or in any combination you desire. Use a teaspoon to the cup of boiling water, steep for 20 minutes, and take four a cups a day, an hour before each meal and at bedtime: blue violet, burdock, gentian root, mugwort, rue, birch, broom, sarsaparilla, buckthorn, ginger, pennyroyal, plantain, wood betony, and balm of Gilead.

For an acute attack of gout, colchicine has been used successfully for hundreds of years. Colchicine is obtained from the meadow saffron (*Colchicum autumnale*). This plant is poisonous and should be used only under medical supervision.

Herb list for gout Blue violet, birch, burdock, gentian root, mugwort, rue, sarsaparilla, broom, buckthorn bark, ginger, pennyroyal, plantain, wood betony, balm of Gilead.

Diabetes

Causes Diabetes is essentially a disease of degeneration of some part of the digestive tract, nearly always the pancreas. When the pancreas fails to function normally and does not produce enough insulin, you have diabetes. Call on your family physician for an examination and diagnosis. In diabetes mellitus, when starchy foods are broken down to sugar in the body, the pancreas is unable to rid the system of the excess sugar.

Most people know that diabetes has something to do with the function of a large gland called the pancreas, which lies just behind the stomach. However, from study and research into the cause of diabetes, it has been found that failure of the pancreas to function normally is not the only cause for this condition. Another, but less common, cause of diabetes in some persons is obesity caused by eating an unbalanced diet, consisting largely of sugars, fats, and starches, prepared so as to delight the eye and palate, but which are to a great extent denatured (refined). The greater part of the food, as eaten by the majority of people from day to day, is denatured in one way or another.

Resulting from a large consumption of meat, sugar, white flour products, etc., diabetes has become a common disease in the United States. Diabetes will continue to increase as long as people partake of artificial sweets, white flour products, tea, coffee, tobacco, liquor, Coca Cola, soft drinks, and all denatured food and harmful drinks.

Many of the food preparations that are used daily are prepared with baking powder and soda. Soda decreases the activity of the pancreatic juices. These juices are used in the body to digest protein, fat, and carbohydrates. The pancreas is one of the most important organs of digestion.

A diet high in refined sugar can heighten the risk of diabetes.

Symptoms Constant hunger, frequent urination, great thirst, progressive weakness, loss of flesh, inordinate appetite, mental depression, dyspepsia, and a dry red tongue. The patient is irritable, restless, and morose. Not all these symptoms are present in every case.

Treatment There is no known remedy for diabetes. Generally, there is some colon trouble; therefore, using either powdered burdock root, yellow dock root, or bayberry bark, a high enema should be taken to help cleanse and heal the colon. Pour four quarts of boiling water over one tablespoonful of the powdered herb, stir thoroughly and use when cool enough. Daily hot baths followed by cold towel rubs are very beneficial. For best results, take the enema before the bath. Lying in a tub of hot water for one-half hour to two hours will greatly help to eliminate the sugar and waste matter from the system. Excellent results are obtained in diabetes by having the water as hot as the patient can comfortably stand, and have him drink a hot tea while in the tub, made either from red raspberry leaves, blueberry leaves, dandelion root, or pleurisy root. Raise the patient up when he feels too warm or if there is slight palpitation of the heart, and sponge off with cool water. If you have a shower bath, have the patient stand and shower off with cool water, getting right back into the hot water. Repeat a number of times, then finish with a cool shower and vigorous towel rub.

A salt glow is very beneficial. I recommend this highly, as it will increase the circulation and remove the old dead skin from the body so that the pores are open and the skin is more active. Much of the poison in the system will escape through the skin. A general massage after the bath is very restful and beneficial, as it also helps the circulation. When massaging, always stroke towards the heart.

Fomentations should be applied to the spine, stomach, liver, spleen, and pancreas daily. Do not fail to take a cold bath upon arising, thoroughly rubbing the body with a cold wet towel, and then vigorously with a dry towel.

The bowels should be kept loose with one to three good eliminations every day. Do not take harsh cathartics. Use an herbal laxative compound as given on page 29, or other laxative herbs.

Diet The general health must be improved if the patient expects to keep the diabetes under control. Correct the diet, which is one cause of diabetes. The food question is an important item to be considered in the treatment of this disease. There are many herbs which have medicinal properties that can be used and will greatly aid the vegetables and fruits that are eaten in supplying the needed alkaline elements for the body. All those foods that can be enjoyed in their natural state are best adapted for normal nutrition.

Meat of all kinds must be excluded from the diet. Milk and eggs should be reduced to a

Soybeans, naturally alkaline, are a good addition to the diet.

minimum. Stimulating foods are strictly forbidden, as well as such foods as oysters, chickens, clams, crabs, etc. Avoid all starches and sugars, except natural sweets such as juices of ripe fruit.

Bran, oatmeal, and slippery elm water are very beneficial in diabetes. A very wholesome dish, that is high in life-giving properties and is also an alkaline food, is the soybean. Prepare by using soybeans that have been sprouted a half inch or more, boil until tender, and then place in a baking dish and bake a little. Flavor with vegetable extract, onions, garlic, or tomatoes to suit the taste.

The following list of foods is very good in diabetes: Greens of all kinds, Chinese cabbage, red cabbage, cauliflower, watercress, cucumbers, okra, brussel sprouts, asparagus,

onions (baked or boiled), sprouted lentils, peas (tender and young), ripe olives, lettuce, beets and tops (tender, young), string beans, carrots, carrot juice, celery, spinach, eggplant, radishes, endive, parsnips, sprouted lima beans, green corn (very tender), soybean milk, soybean cottage cheese, whole wheat, zwieback, buttermilk, cream, baked Irish potatoes, coconut milk, peanuts, almonds, walnuts, pecans, and Brazil nuts. Do not eat roasted peanuts or peanut butter made from roasted peanuts. Raw peanuts and butter made from them is good. Avocados are excellent in diabetes. When thoroughly ripe, they are almost a specific.

Use all kinds of fresh fruits that are ripened in the sun. Fruits should never be sweetened with sugar. The natural sugar contained in grapes and other fruits is beneficial.

Never eat fruits and vegetables at the same meal. Eat as many raw fruits and vegetables as possible. Those requiring cooking should not be cooked more than just enough to make them palatable. It is best to steam or bake vegetables, but when boiled, boil them in as little water as possible. Beet tops and young tender beets are very desirable. The full-grown beets contain an excessive amount of sugar and should not be eaten by diabetics.

Deep breathing and as much vigorous outdoor exercise as the condition of the patient will permit must be taken.

The following list of herbs is helpful and beneficial in diabetes. Use either one or a combination of several that best suit your needs. Beech, blue cohosh, golden seal, white pine, poplar, queen of the meadow, saw palmetto berries, sumach berries, uva-ursi, wild alum root, wintergreen, yarrow, buchu (in first stages of diabetes), dandelion root (especially good), white pine combined with uva-ursi, equal parts of marshmallow and poplar bark, raspberry leaves (very good), and pleurisy root. If the kidneys or nerves are affected, use one of the following herbs: cornsilk, cubeb berries, fennel, skullcap, wild cherry bark, and nerve root.

Herb list for diabetes Beech, blue cohosh, golden seal, white pine, poplar, queen of the meadow, saw palmetto berries, sumach berries, uva-ursi, wild alum root, wintergreen, yarrow, buchu (first stages of diabetes), dandelion root (especially good), bittersweet, red root, blueberries and blueberry leaves (especially good), raspberry leaves (very good), pleurisy root, white pine combined with equal parts of uva-ursi, marshmallow, and poplar bark.

Herb list for appetite (to improve) Agrimony, beech, calamus, camomile, colombo, gentian root, ginseng, golden seal, origanum, strawberry, wood sage, wormwood, balmony, marjoram.

ADDENDUM

Many new and important discoveries have been made in regards to the cause and treatment of diabetes since the preceding section was first written by Jethro Kloss in the 1930s. While diabetes mellitus has many different causes, they all share an intolerance to glucose (sugar) as a major feature. It has been estimated that up to five percent of the American population will at some time be affected with diabetes. While eating a special diet remains the mainstay of the proper treatment of diabetes, some patients with more severe diabetes will require additional help in the form of insulin injections, or medicine given orally, to control the amount of glucose in the blood and urine. It is very important for obese persons to lose weight. Because of the severe complications that commonly occur in diabetics, it is extremely important that this disease be kept under proper control. These complications occur earlier and with greater frequency and severity if diabetes is not controlled properly. Some of these complications are: an increased incidence of coronary artery disease and strokes, gangrene and infection in the feet due to poor circulation, cataracts, kidney disease and high blood pressure, various neurological diseases, poor digestion, and various skin diseases. Because of the prevalence and seriousness of this disease and the need for constant monitoring and control of the sugar in the blood and urine, qualified medical advice is recommended.

Heart & Circulation

Strengthening the systems

Heart Trouble

There are many causes of heart trouble. Frequently there are wrong eating habits that cause obesity, thereby placing an extra strain on the heart. Too much salt in the diet also causes a strain on the heart by elevating the blood pressure. Palpitation of the heart is often due to gas and fermentation in the stomach. Much so-called heart trouble is not due to actual damage to the heart muscle or valves, but rather the heart has been weakened by impure blood caused by a wrong diet, lack of exercise, and

Tansy tea is a popular traditional remedy for palpitations.

poor circulation. Thus, the blood that should be circulating near the surface of the body is diverted to the inside and overburdens the digestive organs and heart.

Sometimes heart trouble is caused by eating too much food made of white flour and cane sugar products. When a large amount of food is eaten that has been robbed of its life-giving properties, the heart grows weaker and weaker.

Diet in heart trouble: Salt in the diet must be severely restricted and a good diet must be followed to get rid of any excess weight.

Herbs: A number of herbs are a great help in any kind of heart trouble. Tansy is very good for palpitation of the heart. Make it into a tea by using one heaping teaspoonful to a cup of boiling water and take three or four cups a day; or it may be taken in half cup doses an hour before meals and upon retiring.

When the heartbeat is irregular or there is weakness of the heart, the following tea may be used with excellent results. Take one teaspoon each of black cohosh, skullcap, valerian, lobelia, and a pinch of cayenne. Mix thoroughly and use a heaping teaspoonful to a cup of boiling water. Steep for one-half hour. Drink four cups a day, one an hour before each meal and one upon retiring; or you may take a swallow every two hours or a half cupful as needed. This is very beneficial.

Look up the following herbs and use the one that best suits your condition. Any one may be combined with others.

Lily of the valley is excellent in palpitation and for quieting the heart. Angelica, blue cohosh, borage, cayenne, golden seal, wood betony, hawthorn, valerian, vervain.

For any kind of heart failure, physical and mental rest is a necessity. In case of severe heart trouble, call your physician.

Herb list for heart Angelica, blue cohosh (for palpitation), borage (strengthens heart), cayenne (stimulant), coriander, golden seal, peppermint, sorrel, valerian, vervain, wintergreen, wood betony, bloodroot, motherwort, sorrel, mistletoe, holy thistle, tansy. Combination: golden seal, skullcap, cayenne, lily of the valley.

Witch hazel can be taken to improve sluggish circulation.

Herb list for circulation (to increase) Cayenne, gentian, golden seal, hyssop, witch hazel, holy thistle. Combination: golden seal, skullcap, cayenne, bayberry bark.

CIRCULATION—TO INCREASE

Take deep breathing exercises each morning and evening and during the day. In the morning, a cold towel rub, followed by a thorough rubbing with a dry, coarse towel, is beneficial. Get plenty of outdoor exercise, breathing deeply while exercising. For constipation, which is one cause of poor circulation, go on an eliminating diet and use herbal laxatives as given in this book. The following herbs are good to increase the circulation: gentian root, skullcap, colombo, rue, valerian, vervain, peppermint, catnip, spearmint.

Take African red pepper in No. 1 size gelatin capsules, one capsule one hour before each meal, drinking a full glass of water or more with each capsule. This can be taken any time during the day or with other herbs. It is fine to increase the circulation; however, cayenne, as well as most other herbs, should not be taken continuously over a long period of time.

Dropsy (Edema)

Causes Dropsy (edema) is an accumulation of fluid in the cellular tissues or the cavities of the body, such as the chest or abdomen, and it may be due to disease of the heart, lungs, liver, or kidneys. Anything that will cause the blood to become poisoned or the red corpuscles to die may result in dropsy. In most cases, it is caused by a crippled heart. Sometimes the liver and gallbladder are so diseased that they will not function normally and a dropsical condition will arise, causing the abdominal cavity to fill with fluid. It may be that the kidneys are the cause, as is the case in Bright's disease when the kidneys do not function properly, and dropsy results. Tumors in the abdomen may irritate the lining membrane (peritoneum), causing it to produce a large amount of fluid.

Eat fruit and vegetables separately when following a diet for dropsy.

Treatment Generally a complete change should be made in the diet, leaving off all alcoholic drinks, cocoa, chocolate, tea, coffee, cola, and other such drinks. No flesh foods, pies, cakes, or rich pastries should be indulged in. All foods should be eaten as dry as possible. No fluids should be taken with the meals, but water can be taken one hour after meals. Do not use any salt. Fruits or tomatoes should occupy a large part of the diet. One vegetable meal a day (preferably at noon), should compose the diet of all patients. It is best to avoid eating fruits and vegetables at the same meal. Sprouted lentils and sprouted soybeans are very good. Eat freely of vegetables, such as eggplant, young beets, parsley, celery, okra, kale, asparagus, collards, mustard, lettuce, spinach, parsnips, onions, cucumbers, watercress, pumpkin, potatoes, yellow corn, Swiss chard, cauliflower, endive, fresh beans, and peas.

Fresh grapes should be eaten freely in season. Thoroughly ripe bananas may be eaten often. Nuts can help to take the place of meat. Coconut is also good. If a patient cannot take the whole, the coconut milk is excellent. Whole wheat zwieback should be eaten. Never eat bread made with soda or baking powder.

Drink plenty of water and fruit juices to flush the kidneys and bladder. A hot bath daily (preferably at night) to produce perspiration will help rid the body of impurities. Cold morning baths and washing the limbs and abdomen two or three times a day with cold water are also very beneficial.

Drinking plenty of herb tea made of red raspberry or pleurisy root will produce perspiration. If the herbs are in powdered form, take a half-teaspoonful in one cup of boiling water. Let it steep for 30 minutes and drink; or the powder may be taken in capsules four to six times a day.

An excellent herb combination for this purpose is one-half teaspoonful each of wild yam and black cohosh, with a pinch of cayenne pepper, to a cup of water. Keep the bowels active so that they move one to three times a day by using herbal laxatives, see page 29. A tea made of the following may be taken freely with benefit, as much as four to six cups a day: wild carrot (blossoms or seeds, ground), dandelion root, yarrow, burdock root, queen of the meadow, dwarf elder, and broom. You may use equal parts of these herbs, adding one teaspoonful of the mixture to a cup of boiling water, and steeping for 20 or 30 minutes.

Burdock and broom make a good combination. They are also prepared in the same way. Dwarf elder is especially good since it cleanses the kidneys.

The following remedy has been known to cure dropsy many times: take grapevine root and burn to ashes. Use one dessertspoonful of these ashes in a glass of water three or four times a day, always drinking plenty of water with it. The inner bark of the vine is good too, prepared in the same way.

Frequent bathing in the ocean is very helpful for dropsy. If one cannot do this, take one pound of Epsom salts and one pound of table salt and add these to your bath.

Wild carrot, which grows so abundantly in many of the states of the United States, has been known to cure dropsy, together with the proper diet, after leaving off the harmful drinks, food, and habits.

Since dropsy is actually not a disease in itself, but merely a reflection of some trouble in another organ, such as the heart or kidneys, the cause for the dropsy should be determined and proper treatment directed to this cause.

Herb list for dropsy Wood betony, hemlock, buchu, blue flag, celandine, juniper berries, holy thistle, lobelia, iris (excellent), bitterroot, black cohosh, blue cohosh, broom, buckthorn, carrot, celery, cleavers, dandelion, elder, hydrangea, milkweed, mullein, nettle, origanum, parsley, queen of the meadow, skunk cabbage, spearmint, tansy, twin leaf, wahoo, white ash, white pond lily, wintergreen, camomile, hyssop, marjoram, masterwort, pennyroyal, plantain, lily of the valley, dwarf elder (excellent).

High Blood Pressure (Hypertension)

Causes There are many causes of high blood pressure. The blood pressure in normal individuals rises about one point each year until the seventh decade and then it usually levels off. Early in life, women usually have slightly lower blood pressures than men, but after the fourth decade this is reversed. A range of normal pressures exists, but the average pressure for a young adult is 120/80 mm/Hg.

Overeating, which usually results in obesity, contributes to high blood pressure, as does eating the wrong diet, particularly a diet that is

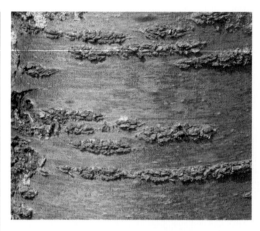

Wild cherry bark can be efficacious against the effects of hypertension.

high in salt. Some forms of high blood pressure are inherited; in some groups this may be the cause in as many as 80 percent of the cases.

Symptoms Patients with high blood pressure frequently complain of headaches, particularly in the morning, difficulty breathing, dizziness, flushed complexion, and blurred vision. They may first be seen with symptoms of heart failure or a stroke. In fact, one of the most frequent causes of a stroke or heart attack (myocardial infarction) is hypertension.

Treatment Please see also the section on Impure Blood (How to Cleanse), on page 168. High herbal enemas should be given, for there is always putrid waste matter in the colon.

Gentle, regular exercise is most helpful in reducing high blood pressure.

Put one teaspoon of golden seal in a pint of boiling water, and take a swallow of this at least six times a day. Take plenty of red clover tea, as this will purify the blood; it is good to drink this in place of water. The following herbs are useful for high blood pressure: wild cherry bark, vervain, rue, broom, black cohosh, boneset, peppermint, blue cohosh, red pepper, valerian, hyssop, sanicle, and skullcap.

Diet and rest White flour products, cane sugar products, meat, tea, coffee, pepper, vinegar, mustard, pickles, alcohol, and all other stimulating foods and drinks should be omitted from the diet. Tobacco should also be eliminated. A fruit diet for a few days is one of the best things you can take. Then use a simple nourishing diet, get plenty of outdoor exercise, and practice deep breathing. Most people with high blood pressure do not get enough rest. Rest is imperative. A warm bath at night and plenty of sleep in a well-ventilated room will do a great deal to lower the blood pressure. If troubled with sleeplessness, take an herb tea that induces sleep. If you follow the above treatment and instructions, your blood pressure will surely come down.

The following treatment will greatly aid recovery: hot and cold applications to the spine, liver, spleen, and stomach; cold towel rubs in the morning upon arising; warm baths at night and salt glows; hot and cold showers.

A general massage will help work the waste matter out of the system, equalize the circulation, and relieve the heart and nerves.

The blood pressure reflects the contractile powers of the heart and the resistance of the blood vessels. The blood pressure increases slowly during life so that the normal pressure at age thirty is approximately 125 and at age sixty it is about 140 mm/Hg. Persons who are weak physically have a slightly lower pressure. The blood pressure rises to some degree during exercise, depending upon the amount you are accustomed to taking. The more regularly you exercise the less the blood pressure will rise.

If the blood pressure is too high or too low, there may be something wrong with the circulation of the blood; therefore a course of treatment must be followed. Two important things you can do to lower your blood pressure are: (1) restrict the amount of salt in your diet and (2) make sure you are not overweight.

If after using the above measures your blood pressure does not fall within the normal range, medical help should be sought because of the great frequency of strokes and heart attacks in people who have high blood pressure.

Herb list for high blood pressure (hypertension)
Broom, black cohosh, blue cohosh, hyssop, wild cherry bark, valerian, vervain, sanicle, boneset, skullcap, golden seal, myrrh, herbal laxative.

Low Blood Pressure (Hypotension)

The diagnosis of low blood pressure must be made with care. In adults, the blood pressure is usually considered low if it is below 110/70 mm/Hg. But many healthy adults consistently have a systolic pressure (the highest number) of 90 to 100 mm/Hg.

Causes Lack of proper nourishment, rest, and exercise; lack of vitality and loss of blood. Certain neurological and muscular diseases.

Treatment Increase the circulation by means of deep breathing, hot baths, and cold morning baths, thoroughly rubbing with a coarse towel when drying. Any one of the following herbs, mixed with a very little red pepper, will greatly increase the vitality: hyssop, golden seal, vervain, prickly ash, blue cohosh, gentian, wood betony, burnet, and skullcap. Take any of the tonic herbs listed on page 30.

Diet Eat plenty of nourishing food; potassium broth and mashed potatoes, baked potatoes (skin and all), soybean milk, soy cottage cheese, plenty of leafy vegetables, and vegetables of all kinds. Do not eat any devitaminized or stimulating foods. If you are troubled with indigestion, drink peppermint or spearmint tea. You will not likely have indigestion if you eat proper food, and eat it dry. Drinking water and other liquids with meals causes fermentation and slows digestion. If you thoroughly cleanse your system, and follow the above instructions, your blood pressure will soon become normal. Regular exercise out-of-doors is very necessary.

Echinacea is an excellent tonic for the blood and is available in capsule form; take one capsule three times a day.

Historically, wood betony was regarded as a "cure-all" among herbs.

Paralysis (Stroke)

Causes Strokes (cerebrovascular accidents) are the third most frequent cause of death in the United States. They are the result of a decreased blood supply to a portion of the brain, usually caused by plaques forming in the arteries and blocking off the normal circulation of blood to the brain, or by the rupture of a blood vessel in the brain.

Symptoms The entire body or only a portion of the body may be paralyzed. Often in cases of paralysis half of the body will be paralyzed so that the patient is entirely helpless, unable to talk, and there is no sign of life, even when pricked with a needle. I have successfully treated and cured such cases.

Treatment The following treatment can be used with benefit no matter what part or parts of the body are affected. I have restored feeling in a single day to the affected part by using hot and cold fomentations, massage, liniments, and herbs when the attack first came on. A stimulating liniment used on the part affected is always beneficial. Liniment, as recommended on page 28, should be thoroughly rubbed in, and the part well saturated.

Give a cleansing and nourishing diet. Massage and exercise, as tolerated, are also beneficial. When giving hot fomentations, be sure you do not burn the skin, since the patient may have no pain sensation in the area affected by the stroke.

A gentle exercise program can get the patient moving again.

Blood conditions
Working toward healthy blood & circulation

Hemorrhages

Causes Whenever a blood vessel is cut, or ruptures from any other cause, hemorrhage (bleeding) will start at once. If an artery is cut, the blood spurts and is usually bright red in color. If a vein is cut, the blood will be dark and the flow slower and more constant. When the wound is small, the blood usually clots rapidly, provided that the proper blood components, especially the platelets, are present in sufficient amounts.

Golden seal tea, applied directly, may stop a nosebleed.

Hemorrhage from the stomach

Quiet and rest are required. Put an application of ice over the stomach for a short time and have the patient swallow small bits of ice. Shepherd's purse, made into a tea, is very reliable. Witch hazel leaves, wild alum root, bistort root, red raspberry, and sumach are also good. Make any one into a tea by steeping a teaspoon in a cup of boiling water for 30 minutes, strain, and drink. Ulcers, tumors, and inflammation (gastritis), are the most common causes of bleeding from the stomach.

Hemorrhage from the lungs

Give a hot footbath and have the patient refrain from coughing as much as possible. A tea made of hemlock spruce with a pinch of cayenne has been known to stop bleeding. Also use the same herbs as for stomach hemorrhage. Cancer of the lung is a frequent cause.

Hemorrhage from the uterus

Have the patient lie down and elevate the foot of the bed. Give a hot douche made of bayberry

---

CAUTION

Continued bleeding, even if only in small amounts, from any place in the body, may indicate a serious problem such as cancer, and the exact cause for the bleeding should be found as soon as possible.

bark or bistort root. Use either in powdered or granulated form. Steep one tablespoon in a quart of boiling water for a few minutes. Use a spiral douche if available; if not, use a regular douche tip.

A tea made from red raspberry leaves, white oak bark, witch hazel bark, or wild alum root is also good. If used in the granulated form, use two tablespoons to a quart of boiling water; steep for twenty minutes; let settle, strain, and drink as hot as possible.

Hemorrhage from the bowels

Keep the patient lying down. Give an enema of warm wild alum root tea. White oak bark or red raspberry tea may be used. Inject two or three ounces of the tea through the enema tip and have the patient retain this as long as possible. Repeat. Shepherd's purse, raspberry leaves, bistort root, witch hazel, bayberry, or

An ice compress can help to stop a stomach hemorrhage.

sumach, may be taken as a tea. Use either one of the herbs by itself, or make a mixture of any two or three and take according to the directions given on page 16.

Hemorrhage from the nose

Make a tea of golden seal, using one teaspoon to a pint of boiling water. Steep for a few minutes, let settle, and when cold pour a little into the palm of the hand and sniff it up the nostrils. Sometimes cold or pressure applied to the back of the neck helps to prevent the free flow of blood to the head. Use the golden seal tea a number of times during the day. If this is done thoroughly, the hemorrhage will rarely recur. Tea made from a combination of wild alum root, blackberry leaves, witch hazel leaves, and white oak bark is also very useful to check nosebleeds, as these herbs are astringent.

Pinching the nostrils together tightly for three to five minutes, while breathing through the mouth, will stop most ordinary nosebleeds.

Herb list for anemia Comfrey, dandelion, fenugreek, barberry bark, agrimony, centaury, raspberry leaves, quassia chips.

Herb list for bleeding Self-heal, mullein (stops bleeding from the lungs), shepherd's purse (for lungs, stomach, kidneys, and bowels), wild alum root, golden seal, blackberry leaves, comfrey, bayberry, uva-ursi, yellow dock.

Impure Blood (How to Cleanse)

Causes A wrong diet, constipation, overeating, eating a combination of food at the same meal that causes fermentation, or devitalized foods. The very elements that would keep the blood pure are removed from many foods by the way they are prepared; for example, the heart and the outside of the wheat, the eyes and peelings of potatoes, the outside of rice, and the heart of corn, which is taken out of the meal. These are wonderful alkaline medicines and do a great deal toward keeping the blood pure.

Some other causes of impure blood are improper breathing, sleeping in rooms that are not properly ventilated, and lack of exercise. Often the muscles are poisoned and feel tired because of the accumulated waste matter from insufficient exercise.

Drinking impure water and other harmful drinks, such as tea, coffee, liquor, and all kinds of soft drinks, are other causes. These confuse the mind and cause wrong thoughts and ideas. The brain is made up of about 90 percent water and when we drink these unwholesome drinks, many of which are stimulating, the blood is made impure and the mind is very much affected.

Worry, fear, anger, unhappiness, and hate generally hinder the circulation of blood, and thus the impurities are not carried off as they should be. A stagnant condition of the skin is another cause of impure blood. Many times the blood that should be circulating near the surface of the body is in the deeper structures, overloading the various organs and causing congestion and various diseases.

Sleeping in an ill-ventilated room can be a factor in impure blood.

Symptoms The symptoms cover a large list of diseases and complaints: pimples, boils, discolorations of the skin, jaundice, headaches, drowsiness, wrinkles, premature aging, insanity, nervousness, getting angry easily, continually frowning when we should be smiling, thinking evil thoughts when we should think evil of no man, seeing darkness where there is light, gray hair, loss of hair, loss of eyesight, loss of hearing, stiff joints, and pain in various parts of the body. All of these symptoms will be helped to a greater or lesser degree when the bloodstream is purified.

Treatment To make the blood pure, the first thing to do is to eliminate all harmful articles of food and drink such as tea, coffee, all alcoholic drinks, soft drinks, all white flour products, all cane sugar products, and the liberal use of free fat or grease. The bowels must be kept open by proper diet and the use of herbal laxatives when needed. Take high herbal enemas to clean out the colon and make it active and strong. Drink plenty of fresh, pure water. Take regular outdoor exercise with deep breathing and get plenty of sleep in a well-ventilated room.

Echinacea and red clover are good blood purifiers. Both can be purchased in convenient capsule form.

Keep the skin active by cold morning baths and vigorous rubbing with a coarse Turkish towel. Take a hot bath or shower every day. Wash the body thoroughly with some good soap. A thorough salt glow is good after a hot bath. This will stimulate the skin, make it active, and open the pores.

A massage from head to foot is beneficial. Give it thoroughly on the neck and upper part of the spine and especially on the feet.

Go on a fruit diet for one week. In the absence of an abundance of fruit, eat vegetables. For example, eat the green part of leafy vegetables and carrots—either raw, grated, or baked until tender—carrot juice, and potatoes.

Reader, if you want to see wonderful results, live on the food that God originally gave to man. There is an abundance of it. Just live on fruit for a while and follow the sanitary habits previously mentioned. Make use of the herbs that God let grow for the healing of the nations and you will say with many whom the writer has heard say, "Truly the day of miracles has not passed." The fruit of the tree is for man's food, and the leaves for his medicine (Ezekiel 47:12).

Herb list to purify blood Bittersweet, blue cohosh, burdock, chickweed, dandelion, elder, fireweed, gentian root, hyssop, nettle, prickly ash, red clover, sanicle, sassafras, sorrel, spikenard, St. John's wort, turkey corn, white clover, yellow dock, borage, cleavers, echinacea, blue flag, wild Oregon grape, fringe tree, holy thistle, elecampane, sarsaparilla.

Blood Poisoning & Infection

Causes Uncleanliness, various infections, improper dressing of sores.

Symptoms The disease begins with a decided chill and a feeling of depression. Shivering sensations, followed by profuse perspiration, are frequent. The pulse rate becomes very rapid and the area around the wound looks red and angry. The breathing grows rapid and there is an anxious expression on the countenance. The temperature becomes elevated.

Treatment Echinacea is a very good herb to correct impure blood conditions, especially

Echinacea is a powerful weapon against bad blood and infection.

when there is a tendency to develop gangrene. It is useful when given internally in acute appendicitis to prevent gangrene and peritonitis, and is helpful in scarlet fever, malaria, septicemia following childbirth, tonsillitis, diphtheria, and typhoid.

Take a high enema. Take as many cups of echinacea tea a day as possible, using a teaspoonful to the cup; or if taken in powdered form in capsules, take two No. 00 capsules every two hours.

Take nothing but fruit juices for a number of days, especially grapefruit, orange, lemon, and pineapple. Do not mix the juices. Take them one at a time but drink plenty of them. Keep the temperature even and have an abundance of fresh air.

When the patient feels chilly, give a cup of hot water in which a little cayenne pepper has

A pure juice diet can be effective in fighting infection.

It is crucial to keep anyone suffering from blood poisoning warm and quiet.

been dissolved. This can be given often. One heaping teaspoonful of charcoal powder put in a cup with enough hot water added to make a paste, diluted, and drunk at once, is very good. Charcoal can also be used to advantage as a poultice. Wash the wound thoroughly with boric acid solution, and if the discharge is thin and unhealthy looking, sprinkle equal parts of powdered myrrh and golden seal directly on the sore.

Herb list for blood poisoning and infections

Chickweed, plantain, echinacea, myrrh, burdock, bloodroot, water pepper (smartweed) and charcoal (poultice), golden seal.

Herb list for gangrene

Camomile, comfrey, myrrh, willow, poplar, hemlock, echinacea.

Golden seal, smartweed, and pleurisy root are good combined and used as hot fomentations.

Herb list for lockjaw (tetanus)

Red pepper, lobelia, anti-spasmodic tincture, skullcap, fit root, cayenne pepper.

Herb list for menstruation

See women's conditions.

Herb list for hemorrhage

Bayberry bark, comfrey, fleabane (bowels and uterus), golden seal (hemorrhage from the rectum), nettle, pilewort, shepherd's purse, sorrel, St. John's wort, white oak bark, wild alum root, witch hazel, yarrow. Lemon juice, diluted and taken as cold as possible. Capsicum (red pepper), taken internally; take one No. 00 capsule and immediately drink a glass or two of water as hot as can be drunk.

Lungs (Inflammation)

Inflammation of the lungs is usually referred to as pneumonia.

Causes The direct cause of pneumonia is usually infection with some form of bacteria, virus, or fungus. Exposure to cold and dampness, with lowered resistance, is a contributing factor.

Treatment The nose and throat should be kept clean by sniffing saltwater up the nose and then blowing, holding one side shut while blowing through the other. Use one teaspoon of salt to a pint of water. Do this several times a day. Gargle and rinse out the mouth with saltwater. Take a rounded teaspoon of golden seal and one-fourth teaspoon of myrrh, steep in one pint of boiling water and use in the same way as above. Take one tablespoon of this solution six times a day.

If the lungs are not already seriously affected, take the above treatment, giving hot footbaths at the same time. The bowels must be kept open by taking enemas or herbal laxatives. Drink large quantities of water. Give the patient hot fomentations to the chest and back of the lungs, with a short cold rub between each hot fomentation.

Only liquids should be given for the first few days. The best ones to use are lemonade without sugar, grapefruit juice, orange juice, pineapple juice (unsweetened); other fruit juices may also be used. Comfrey, cudweed, elecampane, horehound, ground ivy, and ginger are lung tonics. A small amount of cayenne added to any of these herbs is beneficial.

Any one of the following herbs may also be taken. Look up the descriptions, and take the ones which are best suited for your case: plantain, lungwort, pleurisy root, slippery elm, wild alum root, coltsfoot, mustard, vervain, flaxseed, hops, hyssop, white pine, spikenard, wahoo, mullein, yerba santa, yarrow, skunk cabbage, horehound, myrrh.

Herb list for pneumonia Marshmallow, vervain, bloodroot, Peruvian bark, sage, red sage, black cohosh, willow, coltsfoot, skunk cabbage, comfrey, elecampane, wild cherry, spikenard, plantain, lungwort, pleurisy root, slippery elm, wild alum root, mustard, flaxseed, hops, hyssop, white pine bark, mullein, yerba santa, yarrow, myrrh, horehound.

Herb list for lung fever Pleurisy root, bloodroot, coltsfoot, redsage.

Pleurisy

Pleurisy occurs when the very thin, delicate lining around the outside of the lungs, called the pleura, becomes infected.

Symptoms Pleurisy frequently begins with fever, chills, and a sharp chest pain, which is made much worse by breathing. A cough is frequently present. Large amounts of fluid cause shortness of breath. In chronic pleurisy, the symptoms are slight pain, rapid pulse, dry hacking cough, shortness of breath, and increasing debility.

Treatment Strict bed rest and a highly nutritious diet are important. Apply hot fomentations to both the chest and back.

Give a hot herb tea made from equal parts of pleurisy root, yarrow, buckthorn bark, and valerian. Steep a heaping teaspoon in a cup of boiling water for 20 minutes and drink a half cupful every two hours. If the tea is not laxative enough, add more buckthorn bark. If the pain is severe and does not subside quickly, mix together equal parts of lady's slipper, skullcap, and calamus root. Steep a heaping teaspoon in a cup of boiling water for 20 minutes, and take a large swallow every hour.

A specific cure for pleurisy can be made by steeping one tablespoon of yarrow, one tablespoon of pleurisy root, and a pinch of cayenne in a quart of boiling water. Take a large warm swallow every hour. This has been known to cure many cases of pleurisy. Pleurisy root alone is very effective when taken freely.

The diet should be restricted to oatmeal water, fruits, vegetables, and grains. Positively no meat, milk, or stimulating foods such as condiments or intoxicating drinks of any kind should be given.

If these directions are faithfully followed, the pain should soon cease and any fluid that has collected will be absorbed.

Herb list for pleurisy Coral, lobelia, pleurisy root, skunk cabbage, flaxseed, cayenne, chickweed, elder, yarrow, boneset.

A tea of yarrow and pleurisy root is a powerful herbal cure.

Asthma

Causes Most, but not all, patients with asthma are found to be allergic to certain substances (antigens) that provoke an acute attack.

Symptoms Most frequently there is shortness of breath, wheezing, and coughing. This becomes so bad at times that the patient fears he may choke to death. The severest attacks frequently occur during the night or early morning. The patient feels that he must fight for air, and may have to get up and go to an open window, or some place where there is a great deal of fresh air. In severe cases, the patient may become almost black in the face or the complexion may become livid because of a lack of oxygen.

Treatment If the substance that brings on the asthmatic attack is known, it should be avoided at all costs. If the patient is a smoker, he should give up this habit immediately. An emetic is beneficial when the attack follows shortly after a meal. I have found the following emetic to be very effective: pour one pint of boiling water over one teaspoonful of lobelia; allow to steep for a few minutes, and drink several cups lukewarm. If vomiting does not occur freely, place your finger far back in the throat. If lobelia is not available, drink lukewarm water with a little salt in it, one cup after another until vomiting occurs. The addition of a little

Lobelia works as an emetic, which can relieve asthma.

mustard will be found beneficial in cleansing the stomach and lungs, a tablespoonful to a glass of water. When the stomach has been cleansed in one of these ways, there is usually immediate relief. Following this, drink a cup of hot spearmint or peppermint tea or hot lemonade (unsweetened) to settle the stomach.

Give hot fomentations over the stomach, liver, and spleen. You may also give them over the lungs. Then place the patient in a tub of hot water, just above body temperature, and have him remain in the tub for 45 minutes to an hour or longer. Do not let the water cool off, but keep adding more hot water. Finish the bath by sponging with cool water or by taking a cool shower. Cold morning baths are valuable in the treatment of asthma, applying the cold water particularly to the neck and shoulders.

It is a good practice to use some tonic herbs. A mixture that I have found excellent is the following: equal parts of lobelia, wild cherry bark, skullcap, gentian, valerian, calamus, and cubeb berries. Mix thoroughly and use a heaping teaspoonful to a cup of boiling water. Drink a cupful of this tea three or four times a day an hour before meals, and a cupful hot upon retiring.

If you do not have all of these herbs, use the two, three, or more that you do have. If you are constipated, use the herbal laxative as given on page 29, taking it at night.

Any one of the following herbs may be used as a tea in the same way as those given above: hyssop, vervain, skunk cabbage, coltsfoot, mullein, horehound, poplar, black cohosh, yerba santa, milkweed, jaborandi, boneset, chickweed, lungwort, masterwort, pleurisy root, thyme, blue cohosh, calamus, and cubeb berries. Select any one, two, or more and mix in equal parts. Take as given above. For children, the amount should be less according to age, or make the tea weaker and give it more frequently.

Antispasmodic tincture and the herbal cough preparation are valuable for treating asthma. Formulas for making them both can be found on page 18.

Diet Diet is a very important factor in helping asthma cases. A simple, nonstimulating diet is always helpful. It is better to have the heavier meal in the middle of the day and a light meal in the evening. A fruit diet for a few days is highly recommended, after which eat only sparingly of nourishing foods, with few mixtures at a meal. Either zwieback or whole wheat flakes with soybean milk are excellent. French toast may also be used with soybean milk. Vegetables may be eaten, the leafy ones being especially good. Potatoes, steamed with their jackets on, or baked and mashed, may be eaten; also natural brown rice cooked in very little water, as well as three-minute oatmeal eaten with a little honey or soybean butter.

Remember, the bowels must be kept open. Take baths daily, more often if desired, and get plenty of outdoor exercise. Practice deep breathing. Have good ventilation in your sleeping room. The water treatments and the enemas, if they are necessary, should be kept up for some time. Follow the above treatment faithfully and you will obtain splendid results.

Herb list for asthma Black cohosh, comfrey, coltsfoot, horehound, hyssop, lobelia, masterwort, milkweed, mullein, myrrh, pleurisy root, prickly ash, saw palmetto berries, skunk cabbage, thyme, vervain, wild cherry, flaxseed, balm of Gilead, red root, red sage, boneset, cubeb berries, elecampane.

Bronchitis (Acute)

Causes Changeable weather, catching cold, exposure, wet feet, chilling when not sufficiently clothed, insufficient ventilation in the house, especially in the bedrooms. Bronchitis would be uncommon if people ate the right food, kept their systems free from mucus and poisonous waste material, and dressed properly. Stomach trouble and constipation are complaints frequently associated with bronchitis.

Bronchitis is an infection by a virus or bacteria that affects the mucous membrane lining of the bronchial tubes, causing a large amount of mucus to form, which is called phlegm. It may start as a cold or as influenza and then, because of inadequate treatment, extend down the air passages into the lungs.

Symptoms Chills and fever, tightness and stuffiness in the chest, difficulty breathing.

A good cough medicine should have an immediately soothing effect.

Coltsfoot acts as a powerful expectorant and tonic.

Sometimes there is a severe cough and the attack comes on like croup. In most cases it is the larger bronchial tubes that are affected. The cough is often worse when the patient lies down and there is usually a bad coughing spell the first thing on waking in the morning. At first there may be but little mucus, but after several days it increases and turns to yellow pus, sometimes becoming frothy. Children in particular sometimes have convulsions and even become unconscious.

Treatment The same treatment as for chronic bronchitis, following. Everyone should have on hand the antispasmodic tincture and cough medicine made according to the formulas given on page 18 for use in acute and chronic bronchitis and asthma.

Bronchitis (Chronic)

Causes Acute bronchitis may become chronic if it is not properly treated; the infection may extend down into the lungs and become chronic. Occasionally, if it is not cured, it may encourage the development of tuberculosis or some other serious chronic lung disease.

Symptoms Almost continual coughing; coughing up quantities of mucus and phlegm; shortness of breath and wheezing.

Treatment If the person afflicted with this disease is a smoker, the most important thing to do is STOP SMOKING.

Take equal parts of wild cherry, mullein, coltsfoot, yarrow, horehound, and buckthorn. Mix together, using one teaspoonful to a cup of boiling water. Take a cupful four times a day.

All acid-forming foods must be eliminated. Do not drink with meals. Eat alkaline foods.

A full hot bath, steam bath, or vapor bath, followed by a short cold shower, is beneficial. Hot fomentations to the chest and spine, finishing with cold, will do much to relieve the congestion. Hot footbaths with a tablespoonful of mustard added often give great relief. A hot fomentation applied around the neck, followed by a cold compress, is also beneficial. The cold compress must be covered with a woolen cloth to heat it up.

The air in the patient's room should not be too dry. The room should be kept at an even temperature, but good ventilation is necessary.

Take an emetic using warm water. Make a weak tea of cubeb berries, using one heaping teaspoonful to a pint of hot water and a pinch of red pepper. After doing this, take a drink of the hot tea to wash out the stomach. One-fourth teaspoonful of lobelia added will relax the throat, stomach, and bronchial tubes. Take laxative herbs or high enemas if necessary.

Everyone should keep herbs on hand for colds and influenza. Chickweed, coltsfoot, cubeb berries, golden seal, lungwort, mullein, myrrh, white pine, pleurisy root, sanicle, saw palmetto berries, skunk cabbage, slippery elm, white pond lily, yerba santa, bloodroot, ginger, blue violet, bethroot, red root, red sage, and lobelia can be used singly or in any combination. Have on hand antispasmodic tincture and cough medicine made to the formulas given on page 18.

Herb list for bronchitis Chickweed, coltsfoot, cubeb berries, golden seal, lungwort, mullein, myrrh, white pine, pleurisy root, sanicle, saw palmetto berries, skunk cabbage, slippery elm, white pond lily, yerba santa, bloodroot, ginger, blue violet, bethroot, red root, red sage, elecampane, horehound, black cohosh.

Smoking-Related Illnesses
Healing by quitting

Tobacco Habit

Cigarette smoking is the main cause of lung cancer. This is the most common cancer in men in the United States, and in some states is now the most common in women also. Smoking also predisposes to cancer of the esophagus and the bladder, is one of the main contributors to heart attacks, and is implicated in some stomach diseases, such as ulcers.

Chewing tobacco is a common cause of cancer in the mouth, while pipe smoking is responsible for the development of cancer on the lips. Both weaken and debilitate the digestive organs. The loss of saliva that is caused by chewing tobacco is one of the ways

Vegetables in a broth can be a useful part of the "quitting" diet.

by which the system sustains loss and injury through the use of tobacco.

Many girls smoke to keep thin, but it is destructive to the system. The same can be said of many of the advertised reducing pills and medicines. Everyone knows that the first attempt at smoking usually makes one deathly ill and pale and causes nausea and vomiting.

I had the same experiences when first starting to use tobacco. But gradually the system becomes accustomed to it and builds up a resistance so that the evil effects are not so noticeable; however, even though they are hidden, they are still there. All the time I was using tobacco I was confident it was injuring my stomach and digestion, and while giving it up, I was extremely nervous and lonesome in the midst of pleasant surroundings. Had I known then what I know now, I could have overcome the habit in a few weeks; instead, it took me half a year to accomplish it.

The poisons in tobacco very readily find their way into the bloodstream, and anything that affects the blood affects every organ and tissue of the body. It greatly harms the blood corpuscles, has a very damaging effect on the nervous system, causing poor circulation. Smoking is not only the main cause of cancer of the lungs, it also causes other serious lung diseases such as emphysema and bronchitis.

Persons suffering from tuberculosis, palpitation of the heart, irregular pulse, cancer, inactivity of the skin, or paralysis of the nervous system who use tobacco in any form, will find that these ills may in many cases be traced directly to the use of tobacco.

Too much emphasis cannot be placed upon the fact that people who use tobacco in any form will finally find their bodies in a weakened and diseased condition.

Treatment The following treatment will be found successful in curing anyone of the habit.

Go on a diet of fruit juices and vegetable broths for a period of eight to fifteen days. Vegetable broth is very nourishing and is therefore helpful in keeping up the strength.

Take plenty of hot baths, warm enough so that you perspire freely; at least one a day. Finish with a cold towel rub or spray. Remain in the tub for 30 minutes to an hour, or longer if possible, and keep continuously adding hot water. Put cold cloths on the head and throat if you feel weak or faint. Copious drinking of water while in the tub helps one to perspire more. Poisons are given off through the skin by means of perspiration. Rub vigorously while drying off, in order to increase the circulation. Those who take Turkish baths should have one every day, with thorough rubbing.

Red clover tea is very effective in cleansing the system. Use the blossoms, one teaspoonful

Steeped red clover flowers make a cleansing, reinvigorating tea.

to a cup of boiling water. Steep, and drink from five to twelve cups a day.

Magnolia tea is specifically used for curing the tobacco habit. Also, myrtle leaves and seeds. Make the tea as you do when using other herbs.

Drinking slippery elm tea is excellent while curing the tobacco habit.

The following herbs are also good: skullcap, vervain, peppermint, catnip, nerve root, quassia chips, motherwort, angelica, burdock root (for cleansing the blood), black cohosh, blue cohosh, echinacea.

Herb list for tobacco addiction Calamus, magnolia, myrtle leaves and seeds, skullcap, vervain, peppermint, catnip, valerian, motherwort, quassia chips, angelica, black cohosh, blue cohosh, sweet flag. Use burdock or echinacea for cleansing the bloodstream.

Alcohol-Related Problems

Dealing with the effects of heavy drinking

Delirium Tremens

Causes Habitual intoxication with alcohol.

Symptoms Loss of appetite, vomiting, feeble and rapid pulse, wild expression on the face, delusions, fright because of horrible fancies. Sometimes patients have convulsions, talk incessantly, and are not able to sleep. These symptoms usually begin two to three days after the end of a drinking bout.

Treatment Place the patient in a lukewarm bath and keep him there two or three hours or more. While he is still in the bath, give him hot drinks of weak herb tea, made from the following: valerian, gentian, catnip, peppermint, spearmint, calamus root, sweet balm, skullcap. Use a small teaspoonful of herbs to a cup of water. Keep the head cool with towels wrung out of cold water. Give either a shower or sponge bath, short and cold, several times during the bath. Just before finishing, give a good brisk salt glow. Put the patient in the warm water afterwards, then give the final cold shower or rub. Dry thoroughly, rubbing vigorously and put him to bed.

To destroy the taste for liquor, give quassia chips, skullcap, and cayenne. Take a teaspoonful of hops to a cup of boiling water with a little lobelia added, steep, strain, and give this hot. It will prove very quieting.

Take a teaspoonful of golden seal steeped in a pint of boiling water, strain, and give two or three swallows four or five times a day.

Give a light nourishing diet. It is best to give a liquid diet for a while, such as oatmeal water, potassium broth, soybean milk, and fruit juices.

Select one or more of the following; take as directed: antispasmodic tincture, valerian, black cohosh, quassia chips, hyssop, lady's slipper, skullcap, lobelia, mistletoe, wood betony, vervain, motherwort, hops.

If there is a problem with elimination, give a high herbal enema or use an herbal laxative.

Herb list for delirium tremens Motherwort, vervain, wood betony, mistletoe, hops, lobelia, skullcap, lady's slipper, hyssop, quassia chips, black cohosh, valerian, antispasmodic tincture.

Even "social" drinking can lead to too great an intake.

Liquor Habit

Taking alcohol into the system always produces an unnatural condition. Habitual users of alcohol often have stomach ulcers, since alcohol injures the mucous membrane lining. Many who drink alcohol freely develop cirrhosis of the liver, which is eventually fatal.

The continual use of alcohol makes a total wreck of the person, and may lead to insanity. In order to help anyone overcome the drinking habit, he must be willing to quit. When he decides to give it up, it is very easy and simple to help him stop.

Treatment A fruit diet is very effective, followed by a light nourishing diet. Heavy sweat baths should be given every day. Take some of the laxative herbs to keep the bowels loose.

Give hot baths, with thorough rubbing, while in the tub. This helps eliminate the waste matter from the system. A massage every day is very valuable. Give the patient a vigorous cold towel rub every morning upon arising, followed by thorough brisk rubbing with a rough Turkish towel.

To help destroy the taste for liquor, quassia chips are very beneficial. Use one teaspoon to a cup of boiling water. Steep for one-half hour and keep covered. Take a swallow every two hours. In very bad cases, the patient should have a constant attendant, so he will not be able to get more liquor. Never taper off! QUIT and NEVER taste the stuff again. That is the way I did. I was a very heavy drinker when I made up my mind one day that I would give up this damnable stuff, which was ruining my health and my life. I never tasted it again, and that was about forty years ago. I was also a heavy tobacco user, both chewing and smoking. That was also given up and I have never used tobacco again either.

Herb list for alcoholism Lady's slipper (American valerian) and lobelia—equal parts; one ounce of skullcap and one-half ounce of valerian (lady's slipper) given every half hour in hot water until results are obtained, then continue taking until taste for liquor is gone.

Whatever the form in which alcohol is taken, the effects are damaging.

Weight-Related Illnesses
Herbal & dietary solutions

Obesity

Causes Obesity can be overcome to a great extent by proper living and eating. It is made worse by wrong habits of eating, excessive starch, fatty foods, and sugar in the diet; and also a lack of exercise. The basic reason for most cases of obesity is simply taking into the body more calories than are used in daily living. A small number of cases are due to a disturbance in the function of the thyroid or pituitary glands.

Symptoms Excessive fat, shortness of breath, palpitation of the heart upon slight exertion.

Treatment Reduce the calories in the diet, and eat only nourishing, nonfattening foods. Start exercising moderately, slowly increasing in vigor, and always in the open air if possible. In order to lose weight you must use up more calories than you take in. Oxygen burns up fat and waste matter in the system; therefore, deep breathing and exercise are essential. Chickweed is helpful to those suffering from obesity, as it cleanses the system and will reduce fat. Steep a heaping teaspoon to a cup of boiling water. Drink at least four cups a day, one an hour before each meal and one on retiring. If there are other troubles, clear them up with the herbs indicated. Seawrack, burdock, and nettle can be used with good results.

Great care must be exercised when using commercially prepared weight reduction formulas that are being widely promoted at the present time. Several deaths have been caused by using these preparations.

Herb list for obesity Seawrack, white ash, fennel, Irish moss, chickweed, burdock, sassafras.

See also **heart conditions.**

Correction of the diet may be a one-stop solution to a weight problem.

Gallstones

Cause The exact cause for the formation of gallstones is unknown. When the liver is overloaded it is not be able to perform its work of eliminating poisonous waste matter.

Symptoms In advanced cases there is pain in the region of the liver, which is located under the right lower ribs. The pain may extend to the right shoulder blade and violent pains may occur in the abdomen. There is often jaundice because of obstruction of the bile duct. There may be chills, fever, nausea, or vomiting.

Treatment If the pain is not too severe, give an enema, preferably of catnip tea. Apply hot fomentations of lobelia and hops over the region of the liver; but if you do not have these herbs, use plain hot water fomentations until you are able to obtain them. Give a hot footbath and a cup of hot tea as soon as possible, made of equal parts of the following: hyssop, gentian root, skullcap, and buckthorn bark. Mix thoroughly and use a heaping teaspoon to a cup of boiling water. Take a cup of this tea every hour the first day, then take one cup four times a day an hour before each meal and one upon retiring.

Continue with the fomentations. One-half hour after taking the tea, take four ounces of olive oil and four ounces of lemon juice or grapefruit juice beaten thoroughly together. After taking the lemon juice and olive oil, lie on your right side, with the hips elevated by placing two pillows beneath them. Take the lemon juice and olive oil for three days.

Fomentations of lobelia and hops will soothe the pain and dilate the bile duct so the lemon juice and oil may pass. A massage under the right ribs, rubbing towards the center of the body, will facilitate the passage of the gallstones after the fomentations have been applied. If the herbs are not available, use hot water fomentations.

When suffering from gallstones, you should go on a fruit juice diet, using oranges and grapefruit. Be sure your diet contains plenty of alkaline foods. Potassium broth is one of the best things that can be taken.

The following herbs are very valuable. Take one rounded teaspoon of either powdered wood betony or milkweed mixed in one-half glass of cold water; follow this by drinking a glass of hot water. Do this one hour before each meal and also upon retiring.

Herb list for gallstones Bitterroot, cascara sagrada, milkweed, camomile, parsley, fringe tree, cleavers, marshmallow, cherry bark, rhubarb, wood betony, goose grass, sweet weed.

Women's Health

Solutions for menstrual problems

Menstruation

Causes of tardy or suppressed menstruation Most young girls start to menstruate at about the age of thirteen or fourteen years. The menstrual periods during this time may normally be scanty and irregular and may not become well established until the age of fifteen or sixteen. Occasionally a young woman may not begin menstruating until sixteen or seventeen years of age. If the menstrual cycle has been well established and then ceases, the most common cause is some form of stress or emotional disturbance. When these problems are resolved satisfactorily, the menstrual cycle will return to normal. Occasionally undernourishment, or a lack of fresh air, sunshine, and proper exercise, results in absent or diminished menstruation. Nervousness, caused by tension at home or at school, may also affect the menstrual cycle.

Treatment The following herbs can be taken with confidence that there will be no harmful aftereffects and that they will help to reestablish normal menstrual periods. Select one, after looking up their descriptions, and take according to directions: tansy, black cohosh, wild yam, mugwort, camomile, and

Balanced, healthy nourishment is key to establishing a regular menstrual pattern in girls and young women.

gentian. Take a hot bath before retiring. Hot sitz baths are beneficial. The legs and feet must be covered and kept warm at all times. The same treatment applies to all women troubled with suppressed or scanty menstruation.

Causes of profuse menstruation There are many causes, including hormone imbalance, diseases of the womb, metabolic diseases, improper diet resulting in iron deficiency, and general debility.

Treatment Eat plain, simple food. All stimulating foods, drinks, and narcotics are harmful and should be discontinued. Keep off the feet as much as possible when menstruating. The body, including the legs and feet, must be kept well covered and warm. A warm douche of white oak bark, wild alum root or bayberry bark is very helpful; taken, of course, after the menses have ceased. Use a heaping tablespoon of one of these herbs to

Stick to a plain, simple diet and avoid anything overstimulating.

a quart of boiling water, steep covered, and use as a douche four or five times a day if needed. Also take bayberry, white oak bark, or wild alum root internally.

If the bleeding is extremely profuse, make or purchase tampons of absorbent material, immerse them in a tea made from equal parts of wild alum root and white oak bark with a little lobelia added. Tie a piece of strong string

NIGHT SWEATS

Anyone suffering from night sweats will be greatly benefited by taking a hot saltwater sponge bath before retiring. Use two tablespoons of salt to a quart of water. A hot bath followed by a salt glow is also good. Wild alum root or white oak bark tea is excellent when used in the same way. Use a tablespoon of the herb to a quart of boiling water; steep for 20 minutes.

Make a tea of golden seal by steeping one teaspoon in a pint of boiling water, and drink two cups upon retiring. This will do much to prevent night sweats. Sage, coral, or strawberry leaves may be used in the same way with good effect. The bowels must be kept open and the colon clean by using herbal laxatives or enemas, if necessary.

Menstruation (Continued)

around the middle, if one is not already present, leaving it long enough so that the end remains outside of the vagina. The tampon should be inserted far enough into the vagina so that it presses snugly against the womb. Remove the tampon every twelve hours and wash the vagina out with an herb douche.

Painful Menstruation Painful menstruation is quite common in girls around the age of 15 or 16. Perhaps as many as 50 percent of girls in this age group suffer from this problem at one time or another. In most cases, this can be considered a normal phenomenon that needs to be explained and dealt with sympathetically. Painful menstruation that develops later in life frequently has a more serious underlying cause. In a rather large percentage of adolescent girls, college students, and even older single women, one or two days of each month must be spent in bed because of the severe abdominal cramps and pain.

Treatment The girl should be reassured that she is not abnormal in any way and that the pain can usually be relieved by simple measures. She should also be made aware that this will not interfere with normal sexual function nor have any effect on childbearing.

Keep the body warm at all times, using a hot water bottle or heating pad at night, if necessary. Keep off the feet as much as possible, especially the first day.

A douche made as follows will give relief: one tablespoon of lady's slipper and one-half teaspoon of lobelia, steeped in one quart of water. Use warm. For internal use, make a tea using equal parts of black cohosh, pennyroyal, and bayberry, adding a little lobelia: take one-half cup every three hours. If you do not have all these herbs, use as many as you have. A hot sitz bath or hot fomentations to the lower spine and abdomen often afford great relief. Repeat these as often as necessary.

During the winter, never permit the feet to get cold or wet. It is also best to keep the hands out of cold water when possible. As far as possible, the patient should be urged to carry on all of her normal activities.

If, in spite of the above treatment, absent, irregular, or profuse menstruation persists, or if bleeding between menstrual cycles or following the menopause occurs, see your family doctor.

Herb list for flooding (excessive menstrual flow)
Bayberry bark tea, ginger and cinnamon tea, yarrow, shepherd's purse, wood betony, burnet, cayenne pepper, red sage, celandine, bistort.

Herb list for menstruation (to decrease flow)
Bayberry bark, pilewort, shepherd's purse, sorrel, uva-ursi, wild alum root, bistort root, plantain, red raspberry, witch hazel, sanicle, bethroot, burnet, wood betony, red sage, lungwort, celandine, cayenne pepper, yarrow.

Herb list for menstruation (to increase flow) Squaw vine, aloes, angelica, fennel, balm, bittersweet, black cohosh, camomile, catnip, coral, gentian root, ginger, horehound, marjoram, masterwort, mugwort, nettle, origanum, pennyroyal, pleurisy root, ragwort, rue, saffron, St. John's wort, summer savory, sweet balm, tansy, thyme, valerian, vervain, water pepper (smartweed), yarrow, carrot, coral with blue cohosh, squaw mint, red sage, motherwort.

Herb list for night sweats Coral, sage, strawberry leaves.

Herb list for uterus (prolapsed) Witch hazel, black cohosh, white oak bark (douche), bayberry bark (douche), slippery elm (douche). Tampons saturated in strong tea of bayberry bark, white oak bark or witch hazel bark, combined with slippery elm, make a fine medicinal support.

Herb list for ovaries Saw palmetto berries, pennyroyal, black cohosh, blue cohosh, bayberry bark, pleurisy root (for inflammation, burdock, peach leaves.

Herb list for womb (uterus) troubles Slippery elm, bayberry bark (douche), black cohosh, blue cohosh, fit root and fennel, gum arabic (inflammation), mandrake, peach leaves, rue, squaw vine, St. John's wort, witch hazel, fenugreek, bethroot, wild Oregon grape, shepherd's purse (stops excessive flow), yarrow (increases menstruation), smartweed, uva-ursi. For douches, wild alum root or white oak bark.

Camomile can be used to bring on or increase menstrual flow.

Bladder Inflammation (Cystitis)

Causes The immediate cause of most cases of cystitis is some type of bacteria. The bacteria that is the usual cause is the one that is normally found in the large bowel. Cystitis may also be caused by injury, blows or falls, infectious diseases, or the passage of catheters into the bladder. Cystitis may be found in men suffering from venereal diseases.

Symptoms Cystitis is found much more frequently in females than males. The most frequent symptoms are a burning pain on urination, frequency of urination, the passage of cloudy urine that may be tinged with blood, and a feeling of urgency to empty the bladder. There may be a fever, little or no appetite, great thirst, and a distressed countenance.

Treatment First take a high enema of catnip tea; you will find this very soothing. Make the catnip into a tea, using a tablespoon to a quart of water. Take the enema as hot as can be borne, 105° to 110°F. Then take some laxative herbs; equal parts of senna, buckthorn bark, spearmint, cubeb berries, and marshmallow are an excellent combination. After mixing these together, make the tea by using a teaspoon to a cup of boiling water. Drink one to four cups per day, more or less, to suit your case, but keep the bowels loose.

A most effective remedy is to inject an herb tea into the bladder: THIS MUST BE DONE BY A GRADUATE NURSE, OR SOMEONE WHO IS COMPETENT TO TEACH YOU.

Take one heaping teaspoon of golden seal, one of cubeb berries, and one of marshmallow. Mix these together and dissolve them in a quart of boiling water. Steep for 20 minutes, stirring well. After it has settled, strain the tea carefully. Use a small sterile soft rubber catheter and a sterile enema can. Put the herb tea, a little more than lukewarm, in the enema can and attach the catheter to the rubber tip of the enema tube; lubricate the catheter and gently insert it into the bladder. Permit the tea to flow into the bladder slowly until there is a feeling of fullness. One or two ounces will usually give this feeling, but continue until several ounces are used. Retain the liquid as long as possible. This process should be repeated two or three times a day and you will have good results. An injection of slippery elm water into the bladder in this way is also excellent, as it is very soothing and healing.

There are two herbal teas that are particularly good for inflammation of the bladder. One is flaxseed tea; use one teaspoonful of the herb to a cup of boiling water and drink three cups a day. The other is an equal mixture of buchu and uva-ursi. Make

Baby spinach leaves are nourishing and gentle on the digestion.

soybean milk with zwieback, all leafy vegetables, carrots, okra, cauliflower, and eggplant are very good.

A fruit diet is rich in alkaline salts and will help to overcome acidity.

Drink two or three quarts of water daily, so that the urine will be bland and nonirritating.

Herb list for leukorrhea (whites) Bayberry bark (douche), bistort root, comfrey, cubeb berries, golden seal and myrrh (douche and also take internally), magnolia, pilewort, plantain, ragwort, slippery elm, squaw vine, sumach berries, white oak bark (douche), white pond lily, wild alum root, wintergreen, wormwood, yarrow (increases menstrual flow), blue cohosh, tansy, ragwort (combined with white pond lily), hemlock, buchu, bethroot, cranesbill (douche), wild Oregon grape, juniper berries.

Herb list for gleet (urethritis) Cubeb berries, juniper berries, wild alum root, yarrow, bloodroot, elder, plantain, yellow dock, saw palmetto, wild Oregon grape, red clover, echinacea, prickly ash, golden seal, rock rose.

Herb list for gravel (in bladder) Broom, carrot, hyssop, marshmallow, apple tree bark, hydrangea, nettle, queen of the meadow, ragwort, sorrel, spearmint, valerian, water pepper, hops, masterwort, mugwort, parsley, squaw vine, hemlock, buchu.

a tea the same way as for flaxseed and drink one to four cups a day. These herbs may also be used in capsule form, but if you do so, be sure to drink a large amount of water.

Give fomentations over the bladder and along the length of the spine. Hot sitz baths are beneficial and can be repeated two or three times a day until relief is obtained.

Diet The diet should be light and nourishing. All irritating and stimulating foods are strictly forbidden. Avoid foods high in protein. Mashed potatoes are very good, as they are unlike the ordinary mashed potatoes because of the addition of soybean milk, which is highly alkaline, and because the potatoes are not peeled before cooking. It must be the whole potato, for when you remove the peeling, the mineral salts are lost. Also use potassium broth. In addition, soybean cottage cheese,

Pregnancy & Childbirth

Pregnancy

The first sign of pregnancy is stopping of the monthly menstrual periods. Occasionally the periods continue, but this is rare and it is usually not a normal period. An early symptom is morning sickness. Some women do not suffer from this at all, but in others it is very severe and disabling. In about six or eight weeks the breasts begin to enlarge and the nipples become prominent with a dark ring around them. Movements of the child are felt between four and five months.

Gentle herb or fruit teas are refreshing and have soothing properties.

Regular but not strenuous exercise must be taken during the entire nine months to keep the muscles in good condition, as childbirth is chiefly a muscular action. To have a beautiful baby, take plenty of gentle exercise. Brisk walking in the open air is one of the best exercises. When sleeping or resting, lie in different positions on either side, then on the stomach, then on the back. Care should be taken, however, never to exercise to the point of exhaustion.

All bad habits must be abandoned and all unnecessary medications discontinued. Due to the fact that nowadays so many women smoke and drink, it cannot be overemphasized that this will have an extremely damaging effect on the child, mentally, morally, and physically. A simple nourishing, nonstimulating diet is necessary if you would have a happy, healthy child. Meats of all kinds should be eaten very sparingly, if at all.

Inflammation of the kidneys is a frequent occurrence during pregnancy, and is greatly encouraged by the use of meat. The diet should consist largely of fresh fruits and vegetables.

Special attention must be given to the bowels. They should move every day. Use laxative herbs if necessary to keep them regular, but it is preferable to keep the bowels regular as far as possible with the diet. Figs, bran cereals, whole grain bread, raisins, and prunes are good for this.

Breastfeeding is the best method for healthy mothers who have full-term babies. There are three main advantages: nutritional, psychological, and immunological. The nutrient content of breast milk is especially suited for infants. It produces a small curd in the infant's stomach that can easily be digested. The total protein content is much lower than cow's milk, so less nitrogen has to be removed by the infant's immature kidneys and liver. The amount and type of protein in human milk are ideal for the

Prunes or figs will guard against constipation in pregnancy.

infant's growth and it is unlikely to cause any type of allergic reaction. The relatively large amount of cholesterol in human milk is needed for proper development of the nervous system and for the manufacture of steroid hormones and bile acids. Human milk contains more carbohydrate than cow's milk.

Breast milk contains immunoglobulins, lactoferrin, and bifidus factor that protect the infant from many diseases such as tetanus, whooping cough, diphtheria, shigella, salmonella, infantile paralysis, and other bacterial and viral diseases.

There is also a great psychological benefit for both mother and child. The child develops a sense of trust and closeness to the mother, and the mother is offered an excellent opportunity to develop a stable, affectionate relationship with her child.

In order to get the most benefit from breast milk, it should be the main source of food for the infant for the first 4 to 6 months of life. If it is not possible to satisfy the infant totally using only the mother's milk, some type of formula may have to be added as a supplement. The mother should continue nursing as long as possible, however, since the infant will receive benefit from any human milk it can get. Fresh cow's milk should never be used before the age of 12 months.

When the diet of the mother is nutritionally adequate, the breast milk will meet all the

Pregnancy (Continued)

growth requirements of the infant except for vitamin D, iron, and fluoride. A vitamin supplement of 400 I.U. a day of vitamin D should be started at birth. Vitamin D is necessary for the absorption of calcium and phosphorus, which are the two minerals most important in the formation of bones.

In order to prevent an iron deficiency anemia in the infant, an iron supplement should be started at 4 to 6 months of age, since at about this time the infant's store of iron is used up. Never give more than 15 mg of iron a day.

Dress Dress should be loose and suitable for the different seasons. When the abdomen becomes greatly enlarged, it will be found beneficial and comfortable to wear a wide band to support the abdomen, but do not have it tight. Tight clothing should not be worn around the breasts.

Baths Frequent sitz baths will relieve many of the local ailments that women suffer during this period. They should be taken at least two or three times a week. During the last few weeks of pregnancy they should be taken daily.

Mental attitude If you want a cheerful, happy child with a sunny disposition, that is just how you will have to be during your pregnancy.

Special effort should be made by the mother to avoid as much unpleasantness as possible. There are special herbs that will help to make childbirth less painful and save a great deal of suffering. Spearmint tea is good to take for morning sickness. Red raspberry leaves made into a tea help to relieve nausea and vomiting, is an aid to labor, and is efficacious in promoting uterine contractions. If red raspberry tea were taken continuously during pregnancy in place of ordinary tea, and a cupful taken every hour during labor, hemorrhages would seldom occur and the use of instruments would rarely be required.

Spikenard is an old Indian remedy to promote easy and painless childbirth. Indian women were noted for their painless childbirths.

Herbs can promote a healthy pregnancy and an easy labor.

Diet Tea, coffee, rich and heavy foods, fish, oysters, condiments of all kinds, and all stimulating foods and drinks should be strictly avoided in the diet of a nursing mother. Very little, if any, meat should be eaten as meat contains many bacteria that cause poisons in the intestines, and the infant as well as the mother may become poisoned by it.

To avoid constipation, eat as much bulk-containing food as possible, for example: lettuce, carrots, spinach, beets, prunes, figs, apples, apricots, zwieback, shredded wheat biscuits, wheat flakes, bran cereals, ripe olives, grapes, and berries of all kinds. Fruit juices of all kinds are excellent.

Potassium broth and mashed potatoes are both very strengthening and nutritious and will increase the milk, as will whole grain cereals, especially oatmeal and oatmeal water.

Always drink six to eight glasses of water a day. Insufficient water will always cause insufficient milk. Dill herb tea will help to increase the milk also.

The drinking of sage tea will dry up the milk. Do not take much liquid and eat dry foods.

During the entire nine months it is very helpful to massage the entire area of the abdomen with cocoa butter or some good oil every evening before retiring. This will help prevent the marks on the skin that are caused by stretching of the abdomen during pregnancy, as it makes the skin more elastic.

Herb list for antiemetics (prevent or stop vomiting) Sweet basil, colombo, red raspberry leaves, lobelia in small doses, peppermint and peach leaves in small doses, white poplar bark, clover, mint, spearmint, giant Solomon's seal. Use equal parts of white poplar bark and clover to stop vomiting in pregnancy.

Herb list for vomiting (prevention) Sweet basil, colombo, peach leaves, white poplar bark, clover, spearmint. Use equal parts of white poplar bark and clover to stop vomiting during pregnancy.

Herb list for nausea and vomiting Ginger, lavender, mint, origanum, peach leaves, pennyroyal (but should NOT be taken during pregnancy), peppermint, red raspberry, spearmint, sweet balm, wild yam, anise, giant Solomon's seal, golden seal (will allay nausea during pregnancy).

Herb list for childbirth (to help ease) Black cohosh, blue cohosh (brings on labor pains when time), shepherd's purse, spikenard, or squaw vine (taken some time before, they shorten the length of labor), red raspberry leaves—a teacupful (including the juice from one orange), three cups daily through the last month will make childbirth easier. Combine with squaw vine. Angelica to expel the afterbirth.

Infant Feeding

The natural food for infants is mother's milk. Mother's milk is richer in iron than cow's milk. If the mother is on a good diet, the baby will receive all the necessary vitamins, minerals, protein, fat, and carbohydrate. Unless the mother is in a weakened condition, or is suffering from disease, she should nurse her child. Diet recommendations for nursing mothers are given in the article on "Pregnancy."

Regularity in infant feeding is essential. The child should not stay at the breast more than 30 minutes, and if the milk supply is plentiful 10 to 15 minutes is usually adequate. Infants should be weaned by the end of the first year. Weaning should be gradual. Give a bottle once a day with the breast feeding, increasing the number of bottles each day until the child is entirely weaned.

Cane sugar in any form should never be given to infants. Malt sugar, malt honey, or honey should be used in place of cane sugar.

Diarrhea in infants can be stopped by the use of thin rice or barley water. For an older child, use oatmeal gruel.

Soybean milk is a good food for infants and children and can be given from the first day. In using soybean milk, you eliminate the danger of contaminated milk and also disease is not encountered. The flavor of soybean milk can be improved by the addition of a little powdered oatmeal, powdered wheat malt, or barley malt.

For infants, soybean milk should be diluted by using one-fourth water to three-fourths soybean milk. Discretion must be used in diluting soybean milk as in other infant food, depending upon the needs of the infant. When the infant has a weak stomach, dilute the milk more. The milk can be given full strength at the age of five or six months. When the baby is six months old, dilute four tablespoonfuls of whole wheat flakes in boiling water until completely dissolved, put through a fine sieve, and add to the baby's bottle.

Begin feeding wholesome simple foods in puree form, such as greens, vegetables, fruit juices, and gruels, when the first teeth appear. Orange juice and tomato juice may be given from the beginning, starting with a half teaspoonful at about the age of one month.

When a child is given meat, white flour products, candies, etc., he loses his taste for wholesome natural foods. Never allow children to eat between meals.

If the baby is being fed cow's milk, vitamins C and D may be lacking. A simple way to make sure the infant is getting sufficient vitamins is to use a multivitamin concentrate which contains vitamins A, C, D, and sometimes B complex. But overdosage with vitamins, particularly vitamin D, should be avoided.

Breasts (Caked or Inflamed)

Causes Infections of the breast are frequently associated with nursing and milk production. Bacteria may enter the breast through small abrasions, cracks or lacerations near the nipple.

Symptoms A hard, painful swelling occurs in the breast, accompanied by a throbbing, burning pain, restlessness, and fever. A lump may be felt beneath the skin, which is very tender and warm to the touch. The skin over the area often has a pinkish-red color.

Treatment Often just bathing an inflamed breast with alder tea will relieve the inflammation and pain. The following treatment is excellent when the breast or the nipples are sore. Use dry hot and cold applications to ease the soreness and inflammation. These should be given continuously until relieved. Then apply a solution made as follows:

Mix well together one pint of linseed oil, four ounces of spearmint and four ounces of spirit of camphor. Soak a cloth in this solution, place it on the breast, and make sure it covers all of the affected part. Apply as often as required.

When the breast is swollen, a poultice of slippery elm with a little lobelia added will give great relief. Also, a poultice made of grated poke root and cornmeal, applied warm to the breast, is very good.

Drink three or four cups of tea made of equal parts of ginger, golden seal, and black cohosh daily. If the lump does not disappear or if the redness, heat, and soreness continue after this treatment has been used, seek out competent medical help.

Herb list for breasts (to dry up milk) Sage, wild alum root (the strong tea rubbed over breasts), camphor applied to breasts.

Herb list for breasts (sore, swollen, or caked) Poke root, comfrey, parsley, and St. John's wort.

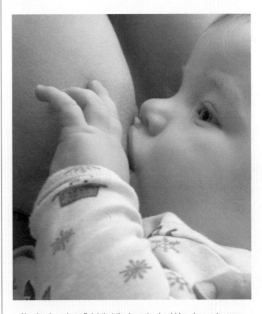

Nursing is so beneficial that the breasts should be given extra care.

Men's Health
Maintaining a healthy prostate

Prostate Gland (Inflammation)

The prostate gland may become infected by many organisms, including the one that causes gonorrhea. Infections elsewhere in the body may also be carried to the prostate gland through the bloodstream. Sometimes the prostate may become inflamed simply by enlargement of the gland, or by excessive sexual activity. Truck drivers and heavy equipment operators are very prone to develop inflammation of the prostate.

Symptoms There is usually frequency, urgency, and burning on urination, pain in the rectum, and slowness of urination with incomplete emptying of the bladder. Fever may be present.

Treatment Hot sitz baths at a temperature of 105° to 115°F may be taken with great benefit from two to four times a day. The entire pelvis should be covered with the hot water and the bath should last for at least 20 minutes. It may be necessary to put a cold pack on the forehead and back of the neck during the bath. All stimulating foods and drinks, particularly all alcoholic drinks, are strictly forbidden.

A man suffering from this disease must eat a nourishing diet consisting mainly of fruits, vegetables, and grains. Soybean milk, zwieback, potassium broth are all good, gentle inclusions for such a diet.

If the infection is acute, and fever is present, antibiotics may have to be given.

A high enema, as hot as can be borne, of either catnip or valerian gives great relief when there is much pain.

A slippery elm poultice is extremely beneficial when applied between the legs in the fork of the thighs.

Drink a tea made of equal parts of gravel root and either cleavers or peach leaves, using a teaspoon to a cup of boiling water. Drink one to four cups a day, more or less as needed. A tea made in the same way, composed of equal parts of buchu and uva-ursi is also good; or these herbs may be used in capsule form; directions on the bottle.

As an injection in any bladder trouble, take a teaspoon of golden seal, one-half teaspoon of myrrh, and one-half teaspoon of boric acid; pour on one quart of boiling water and steep for 30 minutes. This is a wonderful herbal solution to heal bladder trouble when the cause is removed. It is very powerful to remove poisonous mucus or inflammation from the bladder. Inject the solution into the bladder through a sterile catheter and let the fluid flow in freely. Everyone should learn to use a catheter correctly, but PROPER DIRECTIONS FROM A NURSE OR PHYSICIAN ARE ESSENTIAL.

Prostate Gland (Enlargement)

Causes Enlargement of the prostate gland is very common. It is usually seen in men over the age of 50. The cause of the enlargement is not definitely known, although it may be related to hormone production.

Symptoms The first thing that is noticed is a slowing down of the urine stream. This is followed by increased frequency of urination. If infection is also present there is an urgency to urinate and a burning sensation while urinating. There is occasionally blood in the urine, fever, cloudy urine, lower abdominal pain and distention, loss of appetite, and weakness. A hard lump is present in the fork of the thighs or rectum which becomes very painful when pressed.

Treatment In mild forms, no treatment may be required. Hot sitz baths taken two to four times a day are helpful. Follow the treatment given for inflammation of the prostate.

Alcohol must be eliminated. The patient should keep warm at all times. If symptoms are not relieved, and urination becomes increasingly difficult, a physician specializing in the urinary tract should be consulted.

Herb list for prostate gland Corn silk, golden seal, saw palmetto berries, white pond lily, buchu, garlic.

Buchu has a long history of use as a disinfectant of the urinary tract.

Kidney Problems
Treating kidney & urinary troubles

Kidney Stones

Causes Some of the causes for kidney stones are wrong dietary habits, drinking an insufficient amount of liquids, infection and obstruction in the urinary tract, certain diseases involving the intestinal tract, and other diseases such as gout. Many patients develop kidney stones without apparent cause. For some reason, people living in the southeastern United States are much more likely to develop kidney stones than those in other parts of the country.

Symptoms Severe pain in the back, lower abdomen, or groin is the most common symptom. If this pain is not relieved, nausea

Most nuts should be avoided if there is any tendency to kidney stones.

and vomiting will develop. The urine may turn a dark orange or reddish color. If the stones are in the urinary bladder there may be a great desire to urinate, but without success. If urination stops, a catheter must be used. The amount of discomfort ranges from a mild intermittent ache to severe unrelenting pain.

Treatment In order to prevent the formation of kidney stones, a very high fluid intake of two to four quarts a day is necessary. This will keep the urine diluted and prevent the formation of stones. Kidney stones are frequently composed of calcium oxalate, and it may help to prevent this type of stone from forming by eating a diet that is low in oxalates and dairy products. Vegetables high in oxalates are spinach, parsley, beets, beet greens, Swiss chard, asparagus, okra, collards, celery, leeks, and sweet potatoes. Many fruits are also relatively high in oxalates, particularly berries; but the highest of all is rhubarb. Several nuts are high in oxalates, particularly almonds, cashews, peanuts and peanut butter. Ovaltine and cocoa should be eliminated as should tea, coffee, and all dark cola drinks. If there is any infection in the urinary tract, this should be controlled, as it tends to promote the formation of stones. Once a stone that has formed in the kidney begins to pass down the ureter—the slender tube leading from the kidney to the urinary bladder—the pain becomes intense. When this happens, apply hot fomentations across the back in the region of the kidneys. A poultice made of hops with a little lobelia added and applied just below the waistline on the back will help relieve the pain. Make this as hot as can be borne. Herbal liniment, as given on page 28, should be freely and thoroughly applied and rubbed in well. This will also help to relieve the pain.

Give a hot bath starting with a temperature of 100°F and increasing to 112°F. Keep the head and neck cool with cold applications. If the patient becomes very weak, have him stand and sponge off with cool water, getting immediately back into the hot water. This should be continued for at least 30 minutes. Give a hot enema before the bath, using catnip tea if possible. This will give relief. It soothes the kidneys and warms up the bladder. Use a tablespoon of catnip to every quart of water. Use a one or two-quart enema for adults. Children use less in proportion to their age.

Also drink a tea of the following: equal parts of wild carrot seeds, valerian, and peppermint. Mix these together and use a teaspoon to a cup of boiling water; steep for one-half hour. Take one-half cupful every hour until relieved. Queen of the meadow, peach leaves, or cleavers may also be used with good results.

In case of hemorrhage from the kidneys or bladder, use shepherd's purse. This will help stop the bleeding. Use a heaping teaspoon to a cup of boiling water, steep for 30 minutes, strain, and drink half a cupful five or six times a day, and more if needed.

For tumors or inflammation of the bladder, use a teaspoon of golden seal, one-half teaspoon of myrrh, and one-half teaspoon of boric acid, in a pint of water. Inject through a soft catheter into the bladder. This should be done by a graduate nurse or someone with experience. I DO NOT RECOMMEND THAT PATIENTS DO THIS FOR THEMSELVES UNLESS THEY HAVE BEEN SHOWN BY A QUALIFIED PERSON HOW TO DO IT.

Follow the diet as given for treating gallstones. This diet should be used in all kidney and bladder troubles.

Parsley is an effective diuretic.

Urinary Problems

Scalding (burning) urine

Burning on urination is usually associated with pain, frequency, and urgency. The most common cause is an infection in the bladder, prostate, or urethra. The condition may be overcome by cleansing the system, and by taking the following herbs.

Mix equal parts of fennel, burdock, and slippery elm, or milkweed. Steep a teaspoonful in a cup of boiling water for 20 minutes and drink cold, one cup before each meal and on retiring. Teas made of cubeb berries, gravel root, or a combination of equal parts of buchu and uva-ursi are also excellent.

Drink plenty of pure water, as much as two or three quarts a day, if possible. Also, go on a fruit diet for a few days to rid the system of uric acid.

Inability to urinate

Retention of urine is caused by inflammation and swelling inside the bladder.

Give hot sitz baths repeatedly, followed each time by a short cold bath. Give a high enema of catnip tea; this is very necessary and may permit natural urination when other means have failed.

If possible, inject into the bladder, through a soft, sterile catheter, a tea made as follows: one heaping teaspoonful of golden seal, one-half teaspoonful myrrh, and one-half teaspoonful boric acid; steep in a quart of boiling water and strain through a fine cloth. THIS MUST BE DONE BY A GRADUATE NURSE, OR SOMEONE WHO IS COMPETENT TO TEACH YOU.

Suppression of urine

A decrease in the amount of urine is caused when the kidneys do not excrete the usual amount into the bladder.

Many urinary infections can be helped by increasing your water intake.

Symptoms If no urine has been passed for several days, there will be severe symptoms such as convulsions, extreme pain in the back and bladder, and a great desire to urinate.

Treatment The patient should have perfect quiet. A very warm high enema of catnip tea will give great relief. Hot fomentations wrung out of smartweed tea, applied to the bladder and small of the back, will afford relief. Give two or three hot sitz baths a day.

Yarrow herb is especially recommended. Steep a heaping teaspoonful in a cup of boiling water for 20 minutes. Drink a cup before each meal and upon retiring. Drink cold.

Any one of the following herbs may be used to good advantage. Prepare and use them in the same way as described above for yarrow tea: hyssop, burdock, broom, cleavers, dandelion root, wild carrot, meadow sweet, gravel root, tansy, wahoo, corn silk, parsley, St. John's wort, cubeb berries, milkweed, and buchu. If after using this treatment the urine continues to be suppressed, see your physician.

Involuntary flow of urine

When this disorder is not caused by some other disease such as gout, it can be easily remedied by using the following treatment.

Take equal parts of white pond lily, sumach berries, white poplar bark, bistort root, and valerian. Mix together. Steep a heaping teaspoonful of this mixture in a cup of boiling water; take a cup one hour before each meal and on retiring. Drink at least four cups a day. The same dose of plantain is also very good.

Herb list for scalding (burning) urine White poplar bark, burdock seed, spearmint, cubeb, queen of the meadow, peach leaves or cleavers for any inflammatory condition of the urinary organs. If there is bleeding, use shepherd's purse.

Herb list for bladder (urinary) Celandine, aloes, juniper berries, comfrey, apple tree bark, balm, beech, broom, carrot, camomile, cleavers, corn silk, cubeb berries, fleabane, golden seal, hydrangea, hyssop, nettle, peach leaves, birch, buchu and uva-ursi combined, pimpernel, queen of the meadow, sassafras, slippery elm, spearmint, sweet balm, uva-ursi, valerian, vervain, water pepper, white pond lily, wild alum root (pus in bladder), wintergreen, wood sage, yarrow, hemlock, bethroot.

Herb list for urinary problems Mugwort, squaw vine, white willow, hemlock, chicory, juniper berries, angelica, mandrake, blue cohosh, celery, comfrey, dandelion, elder, gentian root, ginseng, marshmallow, milkweed, mint, nettle, origanum, parsley, poplar bark, ragwort, sarsaparilla, St. John's wort, sweet balm, white ash, wild yam, yarrow, burdock, hops, marjoram, masterwort, tansy, fennel, uva-ursi.

Bright's Disease (Nephritis)

Causes Bright's disease is a broad term used for kidney infection. It frequently follows streptococcal infections of the throat and skin. It is sometimes associated with other diseases, such as typhoid or scarlet fever. Alcoholic drinks, tea, coffee, and spices may cause some injury to the kidneys. Patent medicines may be a cause. Food cooked in aluminum utensils is injurious and should never be eaten, especially when one is suffering from Bright's disease, either acute or chronic.

Symptoms One of the most common symptoms is loss of appetite. At other times there is a great desire for food; then, when it is set before the patient, he refuses to eat. In some cases, the skin becomes dry and there is fever, shortness of breath, and palpitation of the heart. There may be swelling of the ankles and under the eyes, which is a sign that the heart is affected. Pain in the kidneys may occur and there may be blood in the urine. The patient is usually pale. At first there may be scantiness of urine, but later the amount of urine greatly increases and contains protein, which your family physician will be able to find when he tests your urine. Often there is frequent urination at night, accompanied by a burning sensation. There may be fever, chills, headache, dizziness, nausea, and vomiting, and the patient becomes

A brisk towel rub following a cold shower helps stimulate perspiration.

very weak. This disease occurs frequently in children from three to seven years of age and should receive early adequate treatment to prevent permanent kidney damage.

Treatment Regular and adequate elimination is necessary and may be obtained by the use of enemas containing white oak bark, bayberry bark, or wild alum root bark. It is important to keep the skin clean and a daily bath, sufficiently warm to bring a glow to the skin, should be taken. While the patient is in the tub, he may be given two or three cups of pleurisy root or sage tea. This treatment will open the pores in the skin and encourage perspiration. It is good to stay in the bath at least one-half hour. Finish off with a short cold shower or a short cold towel rub and dry thoroughly. Be sure to keep away from drafts so that no chilling occurs. A salt glow will greatly stimulate the activity of the skin.

A tea of broom top and marshmallow leaves (equal parts) is very good. Be sure the patient gets plenty of rest and try to eliminate all causes for restlessness or worry. The room should be well ventilated, warm and free from drafts. Salt and water intake should be reduced at first to a minimum.

The patient should frequently change position so that bedsores do not develop.

Diet The diet should be light and nourishing. All stimulating and heavy foods should be strictly forbidden. Sprouted soybeans and lentils may be eaten.

Cauliflower, asparagus, eggplant, and vegetable broths are good. The free use of fruit juices or a fruit juice diet for a few days, before starting to partake of other foods, is excellent. Soybean milk, with whole wheat flakes dissolved in it, is extremely nourishing and very easily digested. Avoid the use of salt, and do not mix fruits and vegetables at the same meal.

Herb list for Bright's (kidney) disease
Golden seal (combined with peach leaves, queen of the meadow, clover, and corn silk), saw palmetto berries, uva-ursi, wild alum root, yarrow, peach (leaves, blossoms, or twigs), peppermint.

Herb list for kidneys
Cayenne, chicory, water pepper, white oak bark, white pond lily, wood sage, birch, black cohosh, bloodroot, buckbean, masterwort, parsley, hemlock, cayenne, wood sanicle, bethroot, wild Oregon grape, fringe tree, poke root, juniper berries, balm, beech, bitterroot, bittersweet, broom, carrot, camomile, comfrey, cleavers, corn silk, dandelion, elder, golden seal, hydrangea, hyssop, marshmallow, celandine, holy thistle, milkweed, mustard (plaster), nettle, white pine, pleurisy root, poplar, queen of the meadow, sage, sanicle, sassafras, seawrack, sorrel, spearmint, sweet balm, tansy, uva-ursi, buchu, aloes.

Children's Conditions

(This section includes some diseases that may also affect adults)

Bedwetting (Enuresis)

Causes About ten percent of young children are bothered by bedwetting at night. This is more common in boys than in girls. It is usually a functional or emotional problem and may be associated with sleepwalking. Weak and undernourished children are most likely to have this habit. Other causes may be kidney or bladder trouble, eating or drinking late at night just before going to bed, or various problems with the intestines, such as constipation, excess gas, or worms.

Treatment Do not let the child eat or drink for several hours before going to bed. No stimulating foods or drinks, such as tea, coffee, soft drinks, white bread, or cane sugar products should be allowed. No liquids or foods should be allowed after 4:00 or 5:00 p.m. If possible, the child should sleep on his side or stomach rather than on his back. It sometimes helps to elevate the foot of the bed a little. Cold morning baths with massage, if possible, and plenty of outdoor exercise, will be a great help. A special effort must be made to discover at about what time the child wets the bed. Usually, it is about an hour and a half after retiring and again at about three o'clock in the morning. The child should be awakened and taken to the bathroom just before this time until the habit is broken. Sometimes when the kidneys or bladder are very much irritated, the application of fomentations over the bladder and along the entire length of the spine will relieve the situation.

In addition, make a tea of plantain and St. John's wort, equal parts mixed together. Use a small teaspoonful to a cup of boiling water. Steep. Give the child one to two cups a day in doses of one-fourth cup at a time. The tea may be sweetened with a little honey so that the child will not object to taking it. Either one of the above herbs is effective alone, but it is well to use both.

See to it that the child is not constipated. Good elimination is very necessary. Warm herb enemas are helpful to relieve this situation when it is present.

It is of absolutely no use to scold the child, as this will only make him nervous and make it harder for him to conquer the habit. Special efforts should be made to help him overcome this distressing habit that he himself dislikes but cannot prevent unless his parents help him.

Herb list for bedwetting Plantain, St. John's wort, buchu, corn silk, cubeb berries, fennel seed, milkweed, wood betony, mullein, willow, hops, fennel.

Colic (Infants)

Causes Eating too rapidly, excessive air swallowing, indigestion, constipation.

Symptoms Sudden loud crying spells, pulling knees up on the stomach, red face, distended stomach, clenched fists.

Treatment Warm catnip tea given in a bottle, and also a catnip tea enema will be beneficial. Spells of crying come on at regular intervals, and if a very warm bath is given an hour before the expected attack, the attack can sometimes be prevented. A hot footbath or hot fomentation over the abdomen may give relief. Breast feeding is ideal; however, if the baby is fed from a bottle, dissolve wheat flakes by pouring boiling water over them, put them through a sieve, and add soybean milk to make the desired consistency. Potassium broth and oatmeal gruel are also very good for nourishment.

Herb list for colic Blue cohosh, caraway seed, carrot seed, catnip, dill, fennel, masterwort, origanum, pennyroyal, peppermint, prickly ash, rosemary, rue, sassafras, spearmint, summer savory, wintergreen, wood betony, flaxseed, valerian, fringe tree, angelica, motherwort.

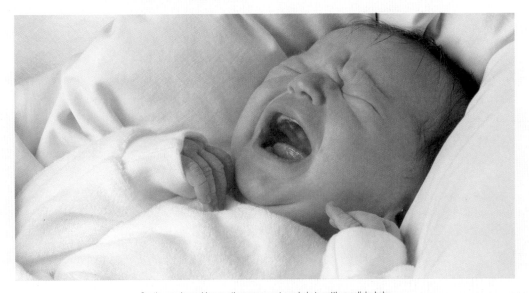

Gentle, regular rocking or other movement can help to settle a colicky baby.

Convulsions, Seizures, Or Spasms

Causes Infants and children are most frequently affected and in most of the cases the cause is not known. Sometimes the seizure will occur with the beginning of a fever. This may indicate the beginning of a severe illness, such as meningitis or encephalitis, or it may indicate the onset of an infectious disease, such as measles. Other less frequent causes include rickets, teething, indigestion, worms, brain congestion, and eating some articles of food, such as candy, ice cream, cake, pies, meat and gravy, and heavy indigestible foods. Undernourished, nervous children with emotional problems are apt to be troubled with seizures. Children of this type should be given plenty of fresh air, sunlight, nourishing food, and emotional support in the home.

Symptoms The child straightens out and becomes stiff. Many times the back is arched and there may be twitching or spasms of the extremities. Breathing seems to stop and the eyes are fixed and staring or turned upwards. The head is drawn back. Several severe attacks in succession are dangerous, and the child may never awaken. It is reassuring, however, to know that death seldom results from convulsions, unless the child is very weak. The convulsion may come on suddenly and without warning. If the child is old enough to talk, he may be able to tell when a convulsion is coming on, or if the child is very young, there may be a behavioral change. There may be difficulty in breathing, with frothing at the mouth. Often the extremities are cold and the child usually becomes unconscious. The seizure may last from a few seconds to nearly an hour.

If a child is disturbed during the night and grits his teeth and rubs his nose, it may be a sign of worms.

Children are more likely to suffer seizures at the onset of a high fever.

Treatment The first thing to do is to loosen the clothing and give plenty of fresh air.

Place a tongue blade wrapped with cloth between the teeth to prevent the child from biting the tongue. Put the child in a full bath at 100°F and increase the heat by adding hot water. Wring a towel out of cold water and put around the neck and on the head. If the gums are hot and swollen, give cold water and rub them with a cloth that has been held on ice. Keep the child in the bath from 10 to 20 minutes, as may seem best. Dry thoroughly, wrap in a warm blanket, put into bed, keep quiet, and give plenty of fresh air. If the child goes to sleep, let it sleep as long as it will.

If the child is constipated, give immediately a warm enema of catnip tea, made by putting a heaping teaspoonful of catnip in a quart of boiling water. Let it steep for 15 minutes, strain, cool to a tepid temperature, and use. Keep the bowels rather loose. If catnip is not at hand, give a warm water enema, giving as much as the child can hold.

Always have antispasmodic tincture on hand. The recipe is given on page 31. The dose for children is five to eight drops in a tablespoonful of water, according to age. Follow by drinking more water. The herbs may be sweetened with a little malt honey, honey, or malt sugar to make them more palatable.

For nourishment, give potassium broth, fruit juices of all kinds, and oatmeal gruel, to which some soybean milk has been added. After serving a liquid diet for two or three days, give vegetable puree, mashed potatoes, and baked potatoes.

A light nourishing diet is best for some time, as often a too-rich diet is to blame for the convulsions.

If there are no further convulsions after the child has had the first one; if all solid food is withheld for a few days and the child is given plenty of catnip tea and warm catnip enemas; and if the bowels are kept regular and the worm treatment is also given; there may not be a recurrence.

The same treatment applies to adults. Often, if the convulsion is very severe, the antispasmodic tincture will stop it at once. The dose for adults is 15 drops to one teaspoonful in a glass of warm water. This may be repeated as often as necessary.

If seizures continue, a serious underlying disorder may be present and appropriate medical help should be obtained.

Herb list for convulsions and spasms Black cohosh, catnip, fit root, rue, skullcap, self-heal, skunk cabbage, valerian, gentian, pennyroyal, mistletoe, antispasmodic tincture, wild yam, lady's slipper, peppermint, fennel seed, sweet balm, sweet weed, hyssop.

Croup

Causes Croup is caused by an inflammation of the larynx or "voice box." Overeating may cause symptoms that resemble croup. Overloading the system with food makes it very easy to catch cold. The fermentation in the stomach causes phlegm, which in turn causes coughing and choking spells. These same symptoms may also be caused by worms.

Symptoms Croup is most often seen in children under five years of age. Although a high fever may be present, the temperature may be normal or only slightly elevated. The child's face is flushed and the eyes may be bloodshot. The attacks are usually much worse at night. The child is awakened by a hard spasmodic barking cough and the attacks last anywhere from 15 minutes to several hours. These attacks may occur several times during the night. It is particularly difficult for the child to take in a breath, and a whistling sound may be heard. There is usually no difficulty in breathing out. In struggling to breathe, the child often sits up.

Treatment The most important part of the treatment for croup is to have the child breathe warm, moist air. This can be done by forming a croup tent, by draping a sheet and blanket over the crib and directing the moist vapor from a croup kettle into the tent. Constant attention must be given so the child is not burned by the condensation of the hot steam. Make a tea of equal parts of cubeb berries, horehound, and lobelia. Put it in the croup kettle, letting it steam so that the child will inhale the vapor. This will many times give immediate relief. If this is done before the child goes to sleep and is continued during sleep, it will sometimes prevent him from having an attack during the night. When the child is very ill, he must be kept in bed in a warm well-ventilated room.

During the day if the child is peevish, an attack can be modified or prevented by a warm

Warm steam is effective in helping a croupy child breathe easier.

Oatmeal or wheat flakes with soybean milk are gentle on the system.

bath or hot footbath. Vick's Vaporub rubbed on the chest, throat, and back is helpful. Give a catnip tea enema and then keep the bowels open with laxative herbs given in proportion to the age. Take a teaspoon of senna pods or granulated senna, coltsfoot, horehound, white cherry bark, cubeb berries, or black cohosh and mix these well together. Take one teaspoonful to a cup of boiling water, let steep for one-half hour, then give the child a tablespoonful every hour until the bowels move naturally. (If you do not have all of these herbs, use senna with cubeb berries.) This mixture will cut the phlegm and relieve throat spasm.

Give a prolonged hot bath, but be sure that the child does not go out and catch more cold afterwards. Give a thorough rubbing with oil of some kind, such as olive oil or cocoa fat, as a good preventive against catching more cold.

Hot and cold applications to the chest and neck often bring relief. Antispasmodic tincture can be applied to the throat as a liniment and will give relief. This can be taken internally: three or four drops to a teaspoonful of water for infants, and increasing the dose for older children. Give every 15 minutes if necessary.

Diet The child's diet should be regulated. Give a fruit diet for a few days consisting of baked apples, pineapple juice, grape juice, or orange juice. There is nothing that is more nourishing or better than soybean milk, either with toast or whole wheat flakes. If cow's milk is used at all, boil a little oatmeal in it and strain. For young infants about five or six months old, dissolve four tablespoonfuls of whole wheat flakes in a little hot water and add either soybean milk or cow's milk. This will keep the child from losing weight and strength. Potassium broth is excellent.

Herb list for croup Mullein, white pine, antispasmodic tincture (lobelia).

Herb list for diphtheria Golden seal, myrrh, echinacea, lemon juice, red sage, jaborandi, eucalyptus; capsicum (red pepper, make a gargle of it, very effective); lobelia.

Nerve Conditions

Herbs for a healthy nervous system

Neuralgia

Causes Neuralgia is due to irritation of a nerve from a variety of causes. Exposure to dampness and cold with resultant infection, dental decay, lack of proper diet, eye strain, and infections around the nose are some of the causes.

Symptoms Pain is usually felt in the part of the body supplied by the irritated nerve. There may or may not be accompanying muscle weakness, paralysis, or areas of decreased sensation on the skin. One side of the face may be affected or there may be pain in the temples and neck.

Treatment Hot and cold compresses to the painful area are very effective. The cold portion of the treatment must be kept very short. A hot fomentation wrung out of a tea made of mullein and lobelia and applied to the affected parts, will do much to relieve the pain. Herbal liniment (see page 28), applied freely and rubbed in thoroughly, will relieve the pain in a short time.

Placing the opposite hand and arm in extremely hot water for 20 minutes will frequently give relief.

Choose the following herbs suited to your case and follow the directions for liniment: valerian, origanum, skullcap, queen of the meadow, nettle, poplar bark, peppermint, Solomon's seal, hops, lady's slipper, twin leaf, motherwort, and wood betony.

Daily massage to the area is very helpful. Rest in bed and a nourishing diet, including adequate vitamin E, are essential.

Herb list for loss of speech Rosemary, prickly ash, red pepper, golden seal, myrrh, wild cherry, sumach.

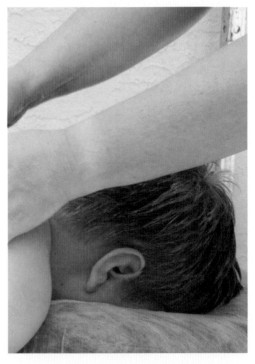

Regular massage can ease nerve pain and relax the sufferer.

Palsy

Causes Palsy is a nervous or physical condition caused by fatigue or nerve injury. The use of tea, coffee, or liquor as well as eating stimulating foods, white flour, and cane sugar are contributing factors, as they lack the properties that sustain and strengthen the nerves. Collapse, in one form or another, is frequently the result of living on a diet that is composed mainly of such foods.

Symptoms Trembling and shaking of the limbs, arms, hands, and sometimes the head: a peculiar manner of walking.

Treatment Tea, coffee, liquor, and all stimulating foods must not be used if a person wants to be helped. If the nerves have been permanently damaged, a lasting cure may be impossible.

Hot and cold applications to the affected parts, followed by vigorous massage, is very beneficial, as it increases the circulation. A warm bath and salt glow can also be given with good results. The pores of the skin must be kept open and a good circulation started. Keep the bowels open with laxative herbs or enemas.

The following herbal medicine is also good. Steep one tablespoon of prickly ash bark or berries, a pinch of cayenne, and one teaspoon of lobelia in a pint of boiling water. Take a tablespoon every two hours. Take internally any one of the following herbs. Look up their descriptions and use the one or ones best suited to your case: masterwort, skullcap, vervain, lady's slipper, and black cohosh.

Herb list for palsy Masterwort, skullcap, elder, wood betony, wood sage.

Herb list for paralysis Hydrangea, black cohosh, valerian, vervain, skullcap, ginger, prickly ash (excellent), lady's slipper, cayenne, rosemary.

Herb list for sciatica Rue, wintergreen, broom, burdock, tansy.

Herb list for spinal meningitis Black cohosh, golden seal, lobelia.

Herb list for St. Vitus's dance Black cohosh, skullcap, mistletoe (excellent).

Herb list for epilepsy Black cohosh, elder, mistletoe, Peruvian bark, vervain, valerian, skullcap, lady's slipper, antispasmodic tincture.

Herb list for hydrophobia (rabies) Lobelia, skullcap, balm, gentian, white ash, antispasmodic tincture.

Muscles & Joints
Soothing muscle & joint pain

Rheumatism & Arthritis

Osteoarthritis is the most common type and is often seen in older patients. Rheumatoid arthritis, which can be a very crippling disease, is most common in women.

Symptoms The joints become stiff and sore. Sometimes they may enlarge and become very deformed. The skin over the joints may become hot and very tender to the touch.

Treatment All unwholesome, devitaminized food must be strictly avoided. Wonderful results may be obtained from a prolonged fruit diet. Drink slippery elm tea. Solid food must be taken sparingly after the fruit diet. Take a good sweat bath every day and drink two or three cups of pleurisy tea. Mix equal parts of the following herbs: black cohosh, gentian root, angelica, columbo, skullcap, valerian, rue, and buckthorn bark. Use a heaping teaspoon to a cup of boiling water; steep and drink three or more cups per day, as the case may require. Drink a half-cupful at a time.

An excellent way to relieve the pain is to mix equal parts of oil of origanum and oil of lobelia, then add a few drops of oil of capsicum or extract of capsicum (red pepper). This can be mixed with coconut oil and used in massage. The following herbs are also very beneficial in rheumatism and arthritis: bitterroot, buckthorn bark, burdock, saw palmetto berries, black cohosh, wintergreen, yellow dock, sassafras, skullcap, and bearsfoot. Look up their descriptions and take those best suited to your case. Use singly or in combination.

Herb list for rheumatism and arthritis (see also **lumbago**) Buchu, balm of Gilead, blue flag, wild Oregon grape, cayenne, birch, bitterroot, bittersweet, black cohosh, blue cohosh, buckbean, buckthorn bark, burdock, celery, elder, hydrangea, lobelia, mugwort, nettle, Colombo, origanum, peppermint, white pine, pleurisy root, poplar, prickly ash, quassia, queen of the meadow, sarsaparilla, skullcap, skunk cabbage, twin leaf, wild yam, willow, wintergreen, wormwood, yellow dock.

Lumbago

Lumbago is a form of rheumatism that may be brought on by becoming very warm, and then suddenly cooling off or getting in a draft. Sometimes lumbago is caused by rupture of a spinal disc, which causes pressure on the spinal nerves. A back injury or strain will sometimes bring on an attack.

Symptoms Pain and tenderness in the muscles, sometimes affecting one and then another muscle. At times the pain comes on suddenly, and it feels as though there was a kink in the back. Adults are the most frequent victims, but children are also sometimes affected.

Treatment In all cases of lumbago, rest is very important. Hot fomentations followed by a thorough massage of the painful area, using herb liniment, is very helpful, and will greatly relieve the pain. The patient should be kept warm. Use the same herbs as listed for the treatment of rheumatism.

Those who suffer from lumbago should not use tea, coffee, liquor, tobacco, or any stimulating or unwholesome food. If constipated, an herbal laxative or enema may be needed.

Herb list for lumbago (lame back)
Queen of the meadow, shepherd's purse (excellent), uva-ursi, vervain, black cohosh, herbal liniment.

Herb list for backache Nettle, pennyroyal, tansy, uva-ursi, buchu, wood betony.

Tansy is an extremely powerful herb and should be used with care.

Sprains & Strains of Joints & Muscles

Sprains generally occur in the ankles, wrists, fingers, knees, or back.

Causes The cause is usually some type of injury such as a sudden or unexpected movement, missing a step in going downstairs, stumbling, falling, etc. When ligaments are torn there is extreme pain and swelling around the joint.

Treatment If the sprain is a very bad one, see a physician as soon as possible in order to prevent any possible permanent deformity of the joint.

If the injury is in the hand, wrist, elbow, or ankle, place the injured part in very hot water. Every few minutes remove it from the hot water and place it in ice water for about a minute, then back into the hot water. This can be kept up for an hour or longer. I have kept it up for two hours with gratifying results and repeated it two or three times a day. After this, gently massage the injured part for 15 or

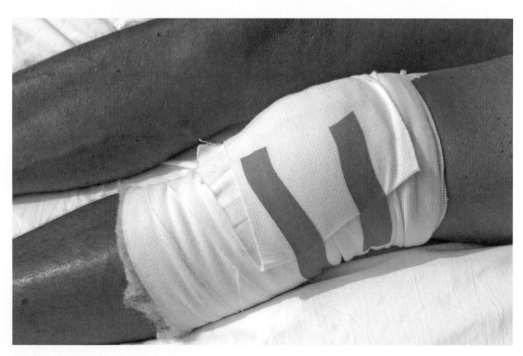

The pain of a bad sprain may be relieved by firm bandaging.

20 minutes. If it should be the ankle or foot, massage the entire foot and leg well up over the knee. If the injury is in the hand, massage the entire hand and arm to above the elbow. If using hot water makes the pain worse, use only ice water or an ice bag for 24 to 48 hours and then use the alternate hot and cold.

Keep the injured part at rest. If the ligaments are badly torn, then a fairly tight bandage (Ace bandage) may help to ease the pain and give stability to the joint. If this treatment is repeated for a few days the results will be most gratifying.

Massage the area gently at least twice a day. If swelling and fever set in before you treat the injury, use hot fomentations followed by short cold applications. Usually a total of three fomentations are applied. This will reduce the swelling and inflammation. Then use the alternate hot and cold water, as described earlier. If you do this, the soreness and swelling will soon leave. After the inflammation and soreness have abated, you can massage directly over the spot; although at first you may have to massage around it.

If the sprain or strain is in the back or shoulder, first treat the area with hot fomentations, then short applications of cold, and end with massage.

Make an herb tea of equal parts of gentian, skullcap, valerian, buckthorn bark, and a pinch of red pepper. Mix thoroughly together, using a heaping teaspoonful of the herbs to a cup of boiling water. Take a tablespoonful every hour. More may be taken if needed.

Herbal liniment, as described on page 28, will take most of the soreness out of a bad sprain in a single day. Everyone should make this liniment for himself and always keep some on hand. Apply the liniment freely and massage gently before the inflammation sets in. Keep this up for 15 to 20 minutes at a time, using it three or four times a day.

The liniment will also take the soreness out of black and blue spots. Massage the spot gently as you apply the liniment. A bad bruise on any part of the body, or a pain in the back, may be treated the same as a sprain or torn ligament. Treat with hot fomentations and short cold applications; then apply the liniment thoroughly. I have taken a bad kink out of the back in a single day with this treatment. Keep up the applications for as long as you can, giving them thoroughly.

Herb list for sprains and muscle strains Comfrey, lobelia, origanum, wormwood, bittersweet combined with camomile as an ointment.

Herb list for swellings Burdock, comfrey, elder, fenugreek, hops, mugwort, origanum, parsley, tansy, white oak bark, white lily, wintergreen, wood sage, wormwood, yellow dock, camomile, dill.

Glandular Diseases

Treatment for thyroid imbalances

Goiter

The term goiter refers to an enlargement of the thyroid gland, a rather large gland that is located in the neck on either side of the "Adam's apple."

Causes The most common cause of goiter is a lack of iodine in the diet. In North America goiter has been practically eliminated by the introduction of iodized salt in 1924. There are, however, areas in the world where goiter is still common due to a lack of iodine. In Asia alone, there are over 400 million iodine-deficient people; this is due to growing crops, which are staple foods in the Asian diet, in iodine-deficient soil.

A less common form of goiter also exists for which the cause is not known. In this form of thyroid disease, the gland becomes overactive (hyperthyroidism) and the patient complains of nervousness, rapid heart beat, increased appetite, weight loss, excessive perspiration, weakness, and diarrhea. This form of thyroid disease is much more common in females than males. There are certain vegetables that contain substances called goitrogens. When excessively large amounts of these foods are eaten, the body's normal use of iodine is interfered with and a goiter in the thyroid gland may be the result. These vegetables are: broccoli, cauliflower, brussels sprouts, turnips, raw cabbage, kale, rutabagas, and horseradish.

Treatment Build up the stomach by eating a plain nourishing alkaline diet. A good stomach remedy is composed of the following: a heaping tablespoon each of golden seal and bayberry and one teaspoon of myrrh. Mix these thoroughly and take one-half teaspoon in a cup of water an hour before each meal and one upon retiring. Use also as a mouthwash and gargle thoroughly with it. Kelp is an excellent

Using an herbal gargle can help reduce the symptoms of goiter.

Regular massage helps to increase circulation to all parts of the body.

source of iodine. If there is no diarrhea the bowels must be kept loose. Use high herb enemas to cleanse the colon thoroughly. Also take an herbal laxative. Bathe the neck thoroughly with the liniment recommended on page 28.

A bayberry poultice used at bedtime and kept on all night is excellent. It must be well covered with a woolen cloth to keep it warm. See poultices on pages 24–7. Sweat baths and massage to increase the circulation and build up the nervous system are very helpful. Take herbs for nerves.

If these simple natural remedies do not relieve the symptoms given above, and the pulse remains rapid, the blood pressure high, the skin warm and moist, the eyes prominent, and the thyroid enlarged, the aid of a physician should be sought.

Herb list for goiter Bayberry bark, white oak bark (internally and externally), echinacea, Irish moss, poke root, seawrack.

Herb list for thyroid Bayberry bark, white oak bark, skullcap, black cohosh.

Liver Conditions
Herbs to help the liver & glands

Jaundice

Causes Jaundice is caused by obstructive diseases of the liver or bile ducts that result in an increased absorption of bile into the blood.

Symptoms Yellow skin; whites of the eyes turn yellow; bitter taste in the mouth; constipation, dark urine, slight fever, headache, dizziness, and itching of the skin.

Treatment Take one-fourth teaspoon of golden seal in a glass of water one hour before meals, three times a day. At first, take nothing but fruit juices, especially lemon and grapefruit. These will help to alkalinize the system and wash out the poisonous toxins. Potassium broth may then be given. The patient should drink a glass of lemon juice every hour as long as there is fever, and continue drinking it freely after the fever has gone down. During the acute stage, fomentations to the liver and stomach will help ease the pain.

In infectious jaundice there is usually itching of the skin. Washing with very hot boric acid water will allay this. The following herbs are excellent for overcoming jaundice: dandelion, agrimony, yarrow, and self-heal. Make an herb tea according to directions given on page 19. Self-heal and dandelion are especially beneficial. Also use the herbal laxative. The bowels must be kept open.

If the jaundice does not clear, you should seek the help of a physician.

Herb list for jaundice Bayberry bark, balmony, bittersweet, buckbean, cleavers, dandelion, gentian root, horehound, mandrake, peach leaves, poplar, sorrel, St. John's wort, tansy, wormwood, origanum, bistort root, bloodroot, borage, broom, sorrel, camomile, hyssop, lungwort, marjoram, parsley, pennyroyal, plantain, wood betony, henna leaves, fringe tree, celandine, chicory, fennel.

Herb list for glandular swelling Bittersweet, yellow dock, mullein, parsley, seawrack, myrica, poke root, echinacea, slippery elm (both internally and as a poultice), queen of the meadow.

Herb list for liver Bitterroot, black cohosh, bloodroot, buckbean, fennel, parsley, plantain, wood betony, fringe tree, celandine, aloes, chicory, holy thistle, angelica, beech, bittersweet, butternut bark, carrot, cascara sagrada, celery, cleavers, dandelion, elder, golden seal, lobelia, magnolia, mandrake, milkweed, motherwort, poplar, prickly ash, rhubarb, sage, self-heal, wahoo, white oak bark, wild yam, wormwood, balm, blue flag, wild Oregon grape, red root, poke root, gentian root, red sage, hops, uva-ursi.

Spleen (Inflammation)

Causes Inflammation or enlargement of the spleen may be associated with enlargement of the liver or other organs.

It may be found with serious forms of blood disease, cancer, some infectious diseases, malaria, and various other diseases.

Symptoms There is usually some degree of pain in the left side just under the ribs. This pain may extend up to the shoulder. There may be a chill followed by fever. Constipation may be present. In some cases the urine is scanty and very dark in color. The person is very thirsty.

Treatment A light, nourishing diet must be provided. A fruit diet for a few days is excellent. Hot fomentations applied to the left side over the spleen, followed by a short cold application, will do much to relieve the inflammation and pain. This treatment should be repeated two or three times a day until the pain is relieved and then given once a day.

Herbal liniment (see page 28) should be rubbed in well over the spleen. This will do a great deal to relieve the pain. If the spleen continues to enlarge, your family doctor should be consulted.

The bowels should be kept open with laxative herbs, or by giving an enema of slippery elm tea.

Herb list for pancreas Bittersweet, dandelion, golden seal, uva-ursi, wahoo, cayenne, blueberry leaves, huckleberry leaves.

Herb list for spleen Bittersweet, dandelion, golden seal, uva-ursi, wahoo, white oak bark, balm, broom, fennel, gentian root, hyssop, marjoram, parsley, wood betony, cayenne, red root, aloes, chicory, angelica.

Dandelion leaves can help spleen inflammation.

Skin Problems

Herbal treatments to soothe & cure the skin

Skin Diseases

Many skin diseases are caused by impure blood or infection. If you have boils, carbuncles, blackheads, pimples, or a skin infection of any kind, a prolonged fruit diet would be very helpful. Stop using meats of all kinds and do not eat between meals. Use no cane sugar, white flour, or white flour products. Take plenty of exercise.

Cold towel rubs are very helpful, rubbing vigorously to increase the circulation.

Make a strong tea of red clover blossoms, using three or four tablespoons of the granulated herb to a quart of water. Steep covered for one-half hour in boiling water. Drink this tea freely in place of water. Chickweed tea may be used in the same way.

The following herbs are also beneficial in skin diseases: burdock root, yellow dock root, hyssop, sanicle, blue violet, golden seal, plantain, echinacea, beech, bittersweet, buck-thorn bark, elder, bloodroot, dandelion, sassafras, sarsaparilla, and spikenard. These can be taken singly or you may combine two or more of them in equal parts. Take one cup an hour before each meal and one on retiring.

The following is a very effective external remedy when made into a tea and applied a number of times a day to the affected parts: equal parts of golden seal, echinacea, yellow dock root, burdock root, and witch hazel bark

Red clover tea acts against skin problems such as boils and carbuncles.

mixed thoroughly. Use a heaping tablespoon of this mixture to a pint of boiling water; steep one-half hour; pour off the liquid or strain, and add a level tablespoon of boric acid; this will keep the fluid from souring.

Herb list for skin diseases Beech, bittersweet, blue violet, buckthorn bark, burdock, chickweed, cleavers, coral, dandelion, elder, golden seal, magnolia, rock rose, saffron, sarsaparilla, sassafras, sorrel, turkey corn, vervain, white clover, wintergreen, bloodroot, pennyroyal, plantain, blue flag, wild Oregon grape, poke root, prince's pine, hyssop, red root, red clover, spikenard.

Ringworm (Tinea)

There are many kinds of ringworm, and each one is caused by a fungus. Ringworm can occur on various parts of the body. When ringworm occurs on the scalp, the hair falls out, leaving a small, round, scaly area. When it involves other parts of the body, it looks like a pale round area surrounded by a zone of redness that is slightly elevated and may contain small blisters. Any form of ringworm is very contagious, and proper care should be taken so that the disease is not spread to others.

Treatment Ringworm of the scalp may be difficult to cure. The hair should be shampooed with a good quality of soap or tar soap. Every morning and evening moisten the spots with the following solution: one teaspoon of golden seal and one-half teaspoon of myrrh, steeped in a pint of boiling water. Daily application of wet dressings with boric acid is good.

For internal use, adults should take a level teaspoon of golden seal in a cup of water twice a day; make it weaker for children, according to age. Hops, boneset, and plantain may also be taken internally with good results. Bloodroot tea, made strong and applied externally, is excellent. Whitfield's ointment, available at nearly any drug store, may be used in cases of severe itching. For ringworm of the body, special ointments that will kill the fungus are readily available at nearly any pharmacy.

Herb list for ringworm Golden seal, lobelia, blood root, borage, plantain, sarsaparilla.

Blood root can also be used externally for the treatment of warts.

Eczema

Causes The exact cause of eczema is unknown; however, allergy seems to play a large part.

Symptoms Eczema may occur at any age, but is most frequently seen in infants. It causes severe itching, and stinging of the skin. Sometimes it begins in the form of small pimples that develop into larger blisters filled with water. Usually the skin dries up and forms little scales that itch intensely. There are two kinds of eczema, dry and moist (weeping) eczema. The following treatment is beneficial for either type.

Treatment Select alkaline foods. The bowels must be made to move regularly, one to three times a day. Use a weak boric acid solution for cleansing the skin. Using a salt solution of one teaspoonful to a quart of water is also helpful. Take equal parts of burdock root, yellow dock, yarrow, and marshmallow; using a heaping teaspoonful of this mixture of granulated herbs to a cup of boiling water, steep, strain, and drink one-half cupful four or five times a day. Also bathe the affected parts freely with this same tea. Herbal salve (page 23) will relieve the itching and heal the skin.

Use whichever of the following herbs is best suited to your case: golden seal, willow, poplar, yellow dock, blue violet, strawberry leaves, origanum, cleavers, plantain.

When eczema occurs in infants, gentle restraint of the hands must be used to prevent scratching. When an infant has eczema, he should not be vaccinated for smallpox, nor should he associate with others who have been recently vaccinated.

Herb list for eczema Balmony, beech, cleavers, dandelion, golden seal, nettle, strawberry, strawberry leaves, willow, bloodroot, wild Oregon grape, poke root, white poplar bark, plantain, yellow dock, blue violet, origanum.

Herb list for itching Buckthorn bark (ointment), origanum, virgin's bower, yellow dock (excellent), borage, marjoram, pennyroyal, plantain, poke root (fine), chickweed.

A gentle herbal salve will relieve the itching of eczema.

Wounds & Cuts

If the body is in a healthy condition, a wound or cut will heal readily. Tie a bandage on the cut immediately, or properly apply a tourniquet, to stop the bleeding. Wash the cut or wound with a solution of powdered golden seal and myrrh, made by steeping a heaping teaspoonful of each in a pint of boiling water for 20 minutes. If the wound bleeds freely, tie the bandage tightly over it, which will cause it to heal readily. Apply herbal liniment (see page 28) over and around the wound.

After bandaging, moisten it thoroughly with liniment five or six times a day or more often. This aids healing and will help to relieve soreness and pain.

If the cut is large and gaps open, place it in the golden seal and myrrh solution as hot as can be borne. Continue this, keeping the solution hot until the wound closes. I have kept a wound in this solution for as long as two hours. When the wound is practically closed, press it together, sprinkle a little powdered golden seal on the outside and bandage, using strips of adhesive tape to hold the skin edges together. Apply liniment all around it. This will relieve the pain and inflammation. If the wound is on the hand, wear a sling to prevent tearing the wound open again. If on the foot, it will be necessary to stay off the feet, or use crutches until healed.

I have seen many bad wounds healed in this way without stitches and without leaving a scar, and the patient does not suffer as much. Apply the liniment freely; it will work like magic. If proud flesh should develop, it can be killed by sprinkling on burnt alum. Wood sage is an excellent remedy for old wounds or anywhere where there is inflammation. Use as a poultice.

Herb list for wounds Wood sage, self-heal, chickweed, golden seal, myrrh, and slippery elm; these herbs can be effectively used as poultices and washes.

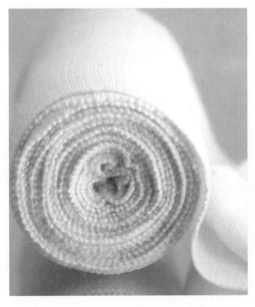

Bandages should be changed whenever you reapply liniment.

Ulcers (Skin)

Ulcers may form where the skin has been cut or broken and has failed to heal properly. When the tissue has been destroyed by a wound, bacteria produce an infection. An ulcer that forms on skin that has been exposed to the sun for a long period may be cancerous, and medical attention should be sought. Ulcers may also be caused by poor circulation, or excessive pressure on an area over a period of time.

Treatment A light diet is necessary, and the food must be well digested. The bowels must move at least once a day. Use laxative herbs and high enemas as necessary. Steep one teaspoonful of golden seal and one-half teaspoonful of myrrh in a pint of boiling water. This solution cannot be excelled for washing the ulcers, and for applying to the dressings. Also take a

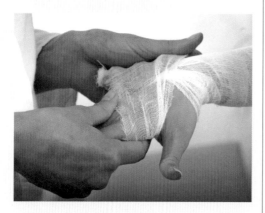

Dressings for ulcers can be soaked in golden seal and myrrh.

tablespoonful of this six times a day internally. Mix together two teaspoonfuls of powdered golden seal and one teaspoonful of myrrh, and sprinkle on the ulcer after it has been washed. Cover loosely with a bandage.

Any of the following herbs may be taken internally, or mix equal parts of two or three of these herbs: bayberry, golden seal, ragwort, lady's slipper, chickweed, sage, wood sanicle, slippery elm, bogbean, ground ivy, bittersweet, agrimony, and raspberry leaves. Use a heaping teaspoonful to a cup of boiling water, strain, and drink one cup an hour before each meal and one upon retiring.

Bedridden patients should be turned at regular intervals to prevent ulcers.

Herb list for ulcers (skin) Bistort root, borage, lungwort, pennyroyal, poplar, blue violet, hemlock, wood sanicle, chickweed, celandine, angelica, cayenne, beech, bugleweed, calamus, carrot (poultice), chickweed, comfrey, fenugreek, golden seal, gold thread, hops, mullein, myrrh, pilewort, prickly ash, psyllium, rock rose, sage, sanicle, sorrel, St. John's wort, twin leaf, valerian, virgin's bower, water pepper, white clover, white pond lily, wild alum root, wintergreen, wood sage, yarrow; use chickweed tea externally as a wash to heal ulcers and sores; take internally also.

Poison Ivy

Poison ivy and poison oak are caused by exposure to these poisonous plants. In sensitive persons, this causes a red area that may be slightly swollen and covered with small blisters. Exposed areas such as the hands, arms, and face are most frequently involved. The itching may be intense.

Treatment The following herbs are good for poison ivy or poison oak: lobelia, golden seal, myrrh, echinacea, bloodroot and Solomon's seal. A strong tea made of equal parts of white oak bark and lime water is very good for poison ivy or poison oak. Apply a bandage wet with this solution and change it as often as it becomes dry. Apply Antiphlogistine (a trademark formerly used for a poultice made of glycerin, kaolin, and aromatics) cold and renew every 12 hours for poison ivy or poison oak. Spread on one-half inch thick and cover the surrounding healthy skin to prevent it from spreading. The juice that comes from squeezing the leaves of aloe vera can also be applied directly to the rash to help stop the itching.

Herb list for poison ivy Lobelia, golden seal, myrrh, echinacea, bloodroot, Solomon's seal. Equal parts of a strong tea made of white oak bark and lime water is very good for poison ivy or poison oak. Apply a bandage wet with this solution and change as often as it becomes dry.

Poison ivy can hide unnoticed in deep grass or undergrowth.

Itch

Causes There are various kinds of itch: seven year's itch, barber's itch, bricklayer's itch, and others. The itch that went by the name of "seven year's itch" for a great many years, is caused by a very small insect called the "itch mite." These small mites bore beneath the skin where it is thin, warm, and moist, usually between the fingers, wrist, forearm, etc. When they get on children, they attack especially the feet and buttocks. The itching is greater at night when the body is warm. The irritation and scratching cause pimples and scabs to form. This type of itch is also commonly known as scabies. It is most frequent in people who do not bathe frequently. Close physical contact with an infected person is all that is needed to acquire scabies.

Treatment Before each application of the following salve, thoroughly wash the affected parts with tar soap. All clothing must be washed in boiling water. When the clothes cannot be washed or boiled, press them with a hot iron to destroy any insects that may be on them. Take one tablespoon of each of the following: burdock root, yellow dock root, and yarrow. Steep them in a pint of boiling water for a half hour. Strain through a cloth into a cooking pan (not aluminum), and add one pound of cocoa fat or Crisco. Boil this slowly,

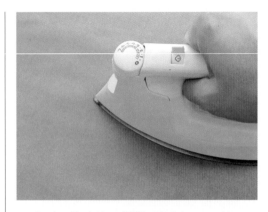
Pressing with a hot iron will kill the mite that causes scabies.

stirring frequently until it has boiled down to the consistency of a salve. This is an excellent salve for itch or eczema of any kind. If you do not wish to make the salve, bathe the affected parts with the tea as directed above. The herbal salve, described on page 23, is very useful in cases of itch and eczema, because it is both healing and soothing.

If students are found to be infected with the scabies mite, they should be kept at home until cured. Frequent washing of the body is necessary. There are now many lotions available for the treatment of scabies that are very effective. These lotions should be applied to the entire body below the neck and washed off the following day. One or two additional treatments at weekly intervals may be necessary to rid the body of all the mites.

Erysipelas

Causes Erysipelas is a disease caused by an infection from the streptococcus organism.

Symptoms Erysipelas appears as an inflammation of the skin in splotches of deep red and copper color, causing an itching and burning sensation. It is most common on the face, but may spread to other parts of the body. It sometimes starts from a slight abrasion of the skin. The involved area may contain blisters. It spreads rapidly. Even in moderate cases, the face is swollen, and the patient is feverish.

Treatment Erysipelas is very contagious and strict isolation with special nursing care should be used. Do not wash the sores with soap. Use a saturated solution of boric acid. Make a solution of the following: one-half teaspoonful golden seal, one teaspoonful lobelia, one teaspoonful burdock, one-half teaspoonful of yellow dock root, one tablespoonful of boric acid, and one-fourth teaspoonful of myrrh. Dissolve in a quart of boiling water. Dip a piece of cotton in this and touch all the affected parts. A piece of gauze may be moistened with this solution and left on the sores.

Chickweed tea, made as follows, is excellent used in the same way. Use one heaping tablespoonful of the granulated herb to a pint of boiling water.

A poultice of raw cranberries, applied cold, will allay the burning in erysipelas; also lemon juice, diluted half-and-half with boiled water.

Take internally a tea of pleurisy root, burdock root, sage, or ginger. It is good to take a heaping tablespoonful of pleurisy root, a tablespoonful of sage, and one teaspoonful of ginger steeped in a pint of boiling water. Drink one-half cup of this tea every two hours.

Herbal salve (see page 23) will give splendid results when applied to the affected parts.

Another excellent wash is the following: mix equal parts of gum myrrh, echinacea, witch hazel, and golden seal, all granulated. After thoroughly mixing, use one tablespoonful to a pint of boiling water; steep for one-half hour and strain. Apply gently with cotton.

A good remedy is as follows: cover the affected parts well with grated raw potatoes, about one-fourth inch thick. When the potatoes become dry, remove them and replace with fresh. Keep the bowels open with herbal laxatives or enemas.

Herb list for erysipelas Chickweed, coral, elder, golden seal, lobelia, magnolia, plantain, Solomon's seal, giant Solomon's seal, water pepper (smartweed), wood sanicle, echinacea, slippery elm powder (sprinkled on), cayenne pepper, myrrh, burdock.

Felons

A felon is a painful abscess, usually found on the end of a finger, thumb, or toe, near the nail.

Causes A felon is usually caused by some type of blow or injury that becomes infected.

Symptoms Pain, redness, and swelling. There is usually also some fever.

Treatment Warm some kerosene and immerse the affected part in it four or five times a day, keeping it in the kerosene from 10 to 15 minutes (or longer) each time. This alone will cure a felon or check one that has just started. This treatment is also good for painful ringworm on the end of the finger. An excellent poultice for this is made of equal parts of slippery elm, lady's slipper, and lobelia herb. Granulated herbs can be used if the powdered herbs are not obtainable.

To relieve the pain when the felon is on the end of a finger, cut a small hole in the end of

Lemon juice will relieve the pain of a felon, and can help to cure it.

a lemon and stick the finger in it. If the felon is located on some other part, slice the lemon and bandage a thick slice of it over the felon. This treatment gives excellent results and will often cure a felon.

Herb list for felons Bittersweet (poultice made of the berries), lobelia, origanum, wintergreen.

ADDENDUM

In some cases when the germs causing the infection are very resistant and the individual's general health is poor, these slower-acting natural remedies may not be successful and antibiotics may become necessary.

Bedsores

Causes Pressure on the skin from lying too long in one position. The position of a bedridden patient should be changed frequently. If good care is taken of such patients, and they are bathed and turned frequently, they will rarely get bedsores.

Treatment Hot and cold applications with thorough rubbing will produce good circulation and prevent bedsores, or will greatly relieve them. Make a tea of witch hazel and bathe the sores at least three or four times a day. Kloss's liniment, as given in this book, is also excellent to heal sores of any kind. If there is any proud flesh, sprinkle it with powdered burnt alum. The best wash for bedsores is made of one teaspoonful each of golden seal, myrrh, and boric acid added to a pint of boiling water. After washing the sore, it should be sprinkled with equal parts of powdered golden seal and myrrh. This will help neutralize the poison and heal the infection, and is very healing. Cover the sore with a bandage saturated with olive oil. Expose the sore to the open air occasionally.

Herb list for bedsores Plantain, bayberry bark, bloodroot, witch hazel, golden seal, balm of Gilead.

Bedsores only usually occur in patients who are not mobile and who remain too long in the same position.

Boils & Carbuncles

Causes The fact that one has boils or carbuncles shows that the body contains poisons and waste matter and is in a low state of resistance. Boils seldom come singly. Frequently, one is followed by several others.

Treatment When the carbuncle or boil is at the root of a hair, it is best to pull out the hair and apply a little liniment, for which the formula is given on page 28. If treated early, and if the liniment is applied repeatedly, the boil should soon disappear. In case of a pimple, it should be opened, the pus squeezed out, and liniment applied. Pimples around the face and head, however, should never be squeezed. The bowels must be kept open. Take some of the laxative herbs. Echinacea is excellent for cleansing the blood; take two capsules twice a day. A cleansing diet for a week or more with proper elimination is very effective. A hot bath followed by a vigorous salt glow is a very successful measure for preventing the spread of boils or carbuncles. Cold baths are excellent to increase the circulation and stimulate the system.

Oranges assist in restoring the body to a healthy condition so that the cause of the boils and carbuncles can be removed. Eat them freely, a dozen or more a day, either alone or combined with grapefruit. Also use plenty of fresh vegetables, especially the leafy ones. Eat canned or fresh tomatoes without seasoning. The fresh tomatoes are preferable. It is better to make a separate meal of them than to combine them with other foods.

Hot and cold fomentations applied to the boils for half an hour three times a day are very helpful. Leave the hot fomentation on for about three minutes and the cold one on for about 30 seconds. Alternating hot and cold water treatments can be used if the boils are in an accessible part of the body.

Never squeeze a pimple, boil, or carbuncle unless the area has been cleansed with alcohol or some other suitable solution, the hands and fingernails thoroughly cleaned, and any needle, knife, or other instrument that you will be using has been sterilized by boiling in water for ten minutes. This is important, as squeezing helps to force the infection into the blood which carries it to other parts of the body.

Herb list for boils and carbuncles Balm (poultice), powdered bayberry bark (poultice), burdock, chickweed, comfrey, coral, flaxseed, hops, lobelia, origanum, slippery elm, sorrel, St. John's wort, turkey corn, white clover, white water lily, wintergreen, wood sage, echinacea, birch (bark or small twigs), plantain, wild cherry (bark or small twigs).

Burns & Scalds

Treatment Immerse the burned part in cold water and keep the water cold by adding more ice or cold water. Keep the part covered with water until the heat is all drawn out and there will not be any blisters. The patient should be taken to a quiet place where the burn may be dressed. The first thing to be considered is the nature of the scald or burn, where it is, and to what degree the skin is burned. Dip a cloth in kerosene and cover the burn. This will quickly allay the pain. If there are any blisters, prick them on the edge with a sterile, clean needle and press out the water. A hot water burn should be treated in the same way.

Large burns may be bathed with the following lotion: take one teaspoonful of golden seal, one of myrrh, and one of boric acid and add them to a pint of boiling water. Let this mixture stand for one-half hour, then pour off the clear liquid and apply with absorbent cotton. This solution is an excellent remedy for deep burns. Herbal salve and liniment (see pages 23 and 28) are also very excellent for this. If the burn is deep, it will heal more quickly if just the mixture of powdered myrrh, golden seal, and boric acid is sprinkled on the sore, thus keeping the burn dry so that it will heal more readily. Cover with gauze. If there is any proud flesh, sprinkle it with burnt alum.

The following tea taken internally will stimulate the circulation and greatly aid the healing of burns: take one teaspoonful each of powdered valerian, skullcap, and peppermint. Mix these together and use one teaspoonful to a cup of boiling water. It is very quieting and soothing to the nerves.

IF THE BURN IS EXTENSIVE OR DEEP, CALL YOUR FAMILY PHYSICIAN IMMEDIATELY OR GO TO THE NEAREST HOSPITAL EMERGENCY ROOM AS SOON AS POSSIBLE.

Herb list for scalds and burns Bittersweet, chickweed, elder, onions (bruised).

Herb list for burns Aloes, bittersweet, burdock, calamus, chickweed, elder, poplar, onions (bruised), comfrey.

Bathe large burns with a solution of golden seal, myrrh, and boric acid.

Eyes, Ears & Nose

Healing strained eyes, painful earache & nose complaints

Ear Trouble

Causes Earaches are usually caused by colds, tonsillitis, or influenza; but sometimes by other less common diseases such as measles, erysipelas, smallpox, diphtheria, scarlet fever, or typhoid fever.

Symptoms When the ear becomes red or swollen on the inside, it is a sign of inflammation. There may be a sensation of fullness ringing in the ears. When an infant or young child pulls at his ears, he may have an earache.

Treatment Whatever the cause, earache can be relieved by the application of heat over the ear and around the neck. A hot footbath with a tablespoonful of mustard in it often gives relief.

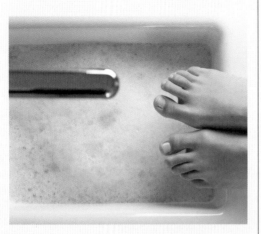

The heat of a mustard footbath can relieve earache.

Bake a large onion until it becomes soft and tie it over the ear; this will often give great relief when the pain is severe. A lobelia or slippery elm poultice is very effective in allaying the inflammation and pain. An injection of oil of lobelia or origanum, or a tea made of these herbs injected warm with a medicine dropper, will often afford relief. If the ear has abscessed and the abscess has broken, use warm peroxide to wash the ear out. Peroxide will loosen all the putrefied matter and bring it out of the ear. This should be repeated until the ear is clean. Do this before injecting any medication or applying poultices. A saturated solution of boric acid may be used for an ear wash. Never introduce objects, such as toothpicks, match sticks, etc., into the ear.

Herb list for deafness Chickweed, origanum, marjoram, angelica, oil of wintergreen, rosemary, oil of sassafras, oil of hemlock, tincture of myrrh, tincture of lobelia, mullein.

Herb list for earache Hops, origanum, pimpernel, lemon juice (pure), burnet.

Herb list for ears (running) Yellow dock, lemon juice (diluted one-half with water), oil of origanum, peroxide of hydrogen (put in ear warm), myrrh, echinacea.

Sore Eyes

Causes Eye troubles may be caused from a deficient diet. Unhealthful foods and drinks weaken the nerves and hinders the free circulation of blood to the eyes.

The all-important thing is to eat food that will give you a pure bloodstream. Inflammation of the eyes from any cause will greatly benefit by the following treatment.

Treatment For eye trouble it will be necessary to correct the diet and leave off all harmful foods and drinks. Get plenty of sleep in a well-ventilated room. Cleanse the system thoroughly with blood-purifying herbs such as echinacea, fruits and juices, and cleansing vegetables such as cucumbers, carrots, celery, and leafy greens.

Take the juice of a lemon every morning one hour before breakfast in a cup of hot water. Steep one teaspoon of red raspberry leaves and one teaspoon of witch hazel leaves in a cup of boiling water, and strain through a cloth. When using the powder, use one-half teaspoonful in a cup of water. Saturate a soft cloth with this tea and apply it as a wet pack to the eyes or bathe the eyes with it often, using an eyecup. Fennel tea is excellent when taken internally. It will benefit the eyes as it strengthens them. When used in an eyecup, dilute one-third with water.

Charcoal or slippery elm poultices, applied cold to the eyes, will relieve inflammation.

An eyewash of golden seal and boric acid will help with soreness.

An excellent eyewash for everyday use as well as when there is particular difficulty is the following: one teaspoon of golden seal and one level teaspoon of boric acid dissolved in a pint of boiling water; shake well and let settle. You may pour off the liquid, or use just as is.

Hot and cold applications to the eyes with a heavy wash cloth will relieve itching and soreness. Aloe vera gel applied to the eyelids relieves itching and burning eyes.

Herb list for eyes (inflammation) Rosemary, borage (inflamed or sore eyes), camomile (cataract), chickweed, elder, fennel, golden seal, hyssop, marshmallow, rock rose, sarsaparilla, sassafras, slippery elm, squaw vine, witch hazel, wintergreen, yellow dock, plantain, golden seal and burnt alum, tansy, white willow, angelica.

Nosebleed

Causes Injury to the nose, excessive heat, occasionally high altitude, acute congestion in the head, and abnormality of the blood.

Treatment The application of very cold water or ice over the nose and on the back of the neck will sometimes stop the bleeding. Pressure on the back of the neck hinders the free flow of blood to the head. Pinching the nostrils tightly for three to five minutes while breathing through the mouth, will usually stop the nosebleed.

A solution of golden seal and boric acid can cure colds and sinus trouble.

Take a heaping teaspoon of golden seal and steep in a pint of soft or distilled water that is boiling; add enough boric acid to make a saturated solution. Put in all the boric acid that will dissolve in the water; if some is left undissolved it will do no harm. Shake it thoroughly and let it stand until it settles, and then it is ready for use. After this solution is cold, sniff some up the nose. Do this several times a day until the bleeding stops.

Wild alum root, white oak bark, or bayberry bark are also very good. Use one heaping teaspoon to a cup of boiling water; steep for 30 minutes, then strain or let settle. Then sniff up the nose. Gargle with it also, as no harm is done if you swallow some.

The above things are all good remedies for nosebleed, as well as for colds in the head, and sinus trouble.

Another most effective herb for running nose or nosebleed is ephedra vulgaris. Use one heaping teaspoon to a cup of boiling water, and steep for 30 minutes. Let settle or strain all the sediment out. Sniff up the nose and repeat until relief is obtained. Another herb that can be used in the same way is golden seal, in powdered form.

In making any of the above solutions, use the best water obtainable, preferably soft or distilled water.

Fringe tree can help relieve nasal congestion.

Some herb solutions can be directly sniffed to stop bleeding.

Herb list for nosebleed Witch hazel, wild alum root, buckthorn, bayberry bark.

Herb list for sinus trouble Plantain, saw palmetto berries, golden seal, bayberry bark.

Herb list for mucous membranes (diseases affecting) Bitterroot, coltsfoot, golden seal, gum arabic, hyssop, myrica, red raspberry, white pond lily, wild alum root, yarrow, fireweed.

Herb list for nasal trouble Black willow (combined with palmetto berries or skullcap), witch hazel (bleeding nose), wild alum root (bleeding nose), white willow, bloodroot, fringe tree, buchu.

Mouth & Throat Problems

Using herbs for dental health

Pyorrhea

Causes Pyorrhea is infection of the gums and the most important cause is poor dental hygiene. Toxins in the system from wrong diet and poor elimination also contribute.

Symptoms Bleeding and swelling of the gums. In bad cases the gums recede and the teeth become loose.

Treatment Correct the diet by using alkaline foods. Go on a fruit diet for a time, as this is always good in overcoming an acid condition in the body. Take one teaspoon of golden seal, one teaspoon of myrrh, and steep in a pint of boiling water. Rinse out the mouth with this solution and gargle with it freely. Also brush the gums thoroughly with this solution at least three or four times a day. Herbal liniment (see page 28) is also very effective. Apply it to the gums with a small swab or rinse out the

Teeth should be brushed and flossed regularly to keep them healthy.

mouth with it. The golden seal and myrrh can be used as a powder on the toothbrush instead of making the tea. If the disease is advanced, help should be sought from a dentist.

Herb list for gums (sore) Bugleweed, myrrh, golden seal, bistort root, herbal liniment.

SORE MOUTH

In infants and children, when there is a general redness and soreness in the mouth it should be carefully sponged with the following solution: one teaspoon of powdered golden seal and one-half teaspoon of powdered myrrh steeped in a pint of boiling water, adding one tablespoon of boric acid. When this has settled, pour off the clear liquid. For adults, use this as a mouthwash and gargle several times a day, holding some in the mouth for a few minutes. White oak bark, wild alum root, and red raspberry leaf tea, used as a gargle and mouthwash, are also very beneficial.

Tonsillitis

Causes Wrong habits of eating and living lower the natural resistance, and permit these organisms to gain a foothold in the body and cause various diseases, including tonsillitis.

Symptoms The throat becomes very sore and swollen and sometimes nearly closed, so that it is almost impossible to swallow. There is usually fever and sometimes chills. The throat and mouth may become dry. Often the glands of the neck are swollen and tender.

Treatment Crush some ice and wrap it in a towel; put it around the neck. When this becomes too painful, take it off and apply a hot fomentation, keeping it on for three to five minutes. Then put the ice on again for a short time. Keep this up for an hour or more, then gargle with a solution made of one teaspoonful each of golden seal and myrrh to a pint of boiling water. Let steep one-half hour. Gargle thoroughly with this solution every half-hour, swallowing a little. Lemon juice may be used in the same way with splendid results.

Take some hot tea made of red raspberry or sage, one teaspoonful to the cup of boiling water. Slippery elm is an excellent remedy for sore throat and stomach trouble. This may be taken freely during the day, a cupful at a time. Take five or six times a day.

Diet The diet should be very light for the first few days. A fruit diet is excellent.

Another excellent gargle can be made by steeping one teaspoonful each of wild cherry bark and sumach and a small teaspoonful of powdered lobelia, in a pint of boiling water for one-half hour. Gargle or swab the tonsils with it often, and swallow a little. Do this every hour until the condition is better, and then as often as needed. A tea may also be made from red sage, wood betony, or bistort, for an excellent gargle in tonsillitis.

Herb list for tonsillitis Mullein, white pine, echinacea, red root, sage, golden seal, tansy. (Use the teas strong, gargle every few minutes, and swallow a mouthful.)

Mullein can be used to treat both bronchitis and tonsillitis.

Colds, Fevers & Viruses

Keeping viruses at bay

Catarrh (Common Cold)

Causes There are many poor health habits that lower our resistance and permit infection with the common cold virus. Among these are eating foods robbed of their life-giving properties, poor circulation, lowered vitality, lack of fresh air and exercise, eating wrong combinations of foods, poor elimination, and drinking insufficient fluids, particularly water.

Symptoms The mucous membrane lining the inside of the nose becomes swollen and makes breathing difficult. The mucous cells in this lining membrane secrete an abundant, thick mucus. Sneezing is common.

There are dryness and soreness of the throat, mouth breathing, snoring at night, frontal

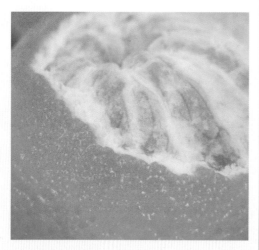

Large quantities of vitamin C have long been believed to ward off colds.

headaches, and impairment of hearing. The turbinate bones in the nose enlarge to such an extent at times that they completely obstruct one or both sides. This may be accompanied by nosebleed, and a dull aching pain between the eyes.

Treatment The mucous membranes of the nose must be kept clean, for when mucus collects around the turbinate bones, it becomes putrid and causes trouble.

The first thing to do is to wash the nose out thoroughly. A safe and effective way of doing this is as follows: take a pint of soft, lukewarm water and add one teaspoonful of salt. Bend over a wash bowl, pour your hand full of this water, and sniff it up the nose. Keep repeating this until the water comes out of the mouth. Then blow the nose, holding one passage shut and then the other.

Repeat this process until the nasal passage is entirely clean and no more mucus in expelled. To hold one side of the nose shut while blowing through the other has a tendency to suck the mucus out of the sinus cavities of the cheek and forehead.

After the nose passages are clean, gargle well with the salt solution to clean the throat.

Make a solution of one teaspoonful of powdered golden seal to a pint of boiling water.

Fruit juices, and in particular pineapple juice, are good for catarrh.

Let it steep for a few minutes and then pour the liquid carefully off. Add one-half teaspoonful of boric acid and sniff this up the nose in the same way as the salt water. Then gargle with this solution.

This is not only cleansing, but also soothing and healing. It is a very effective remedy when done along with other things that build up the body's strength, such as getting adequate rest, drinking abundant fluids (especially fruit juice), proper eating, outdoor exercise, proper elimination, and deep breathing.

If the nose is stopped up so that the water cannot be drawn through, practice for a few minutes what is called the "jumping-jack" exercise. I have seen a nose that would not open up otherwise do so when this exercise was done.

Attention must be given to the diet, which should be simple but nourishing. A fruit diet for a few days will do much to cleanse the system of mucus. Pineapple juice in particular is beneficial, but all fruit juices are good for this condition. A total of eight to twelve glasses of some form of liquid should be taken during the day; however, milk should be limited as it tends to produce mucus. When eating other foods, they should be taken dry and chewed thoroughly.

The bowels must be kept open. Take one high herb enema a day for a while. This will do much to cleanse the colon of mucus: bayberry bark would be suitable.

Take tonic cleansing herbs, such as black cohosh, calamus, and valerian. Golden seal should be taken, a teaspoonful to a pint of boiling water. Let it steep, and take two or three swallows several times during the day, or take one No. 00 capsule three times a day, drinking plenty of water with each dose.

Any one of the following herbs is good for this condition: lungwort, coltsfoot, jaborandi, skunk cabbage, buckthorn, wild cherry bark.

The faithful taking of exercise, plenty of fresh air, and following other good health habits will often prevent catarrh from progressing into something more serious such as bronchitis, pneumonia, or tuberculosis. Using the salt solution for the nose and also gargling with it will help prevent the cold from going down into the lungs.

Coughs & Colds

Causes A cough is caused by inflammation of the throat and bronchial tubes. This inflammation causes mucus to form, which the system tries to expel by coughing. The vitality of the system has been lowered by improper diet, loss of sleep, lack of exercise and fresh air, and improper elimination. If the stomach and entire body were kept in good condition, there would be but few colds.

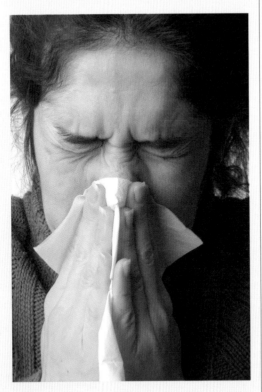

Sniffing up and blowing out a salt solution stops a cold from "taking."

Improper clothing and bedding at night are often causes of colds. The poisons and waste matter in the body make one more susceptible. If the system were kept in good health and the powers of resistance good, coughs and colds would be rare.

Treatment A cold can be treated and overcome in just one day. When the first symptoms of a cold, influenza, or cough appear, it is an indication that there is waste matter and mucus in the system. Take a pint of soft warm water and add a teaspoonful of salt. Sniff this up the nose and then blow it out. Repeat this until the nose is entirely free of mucus. Then gargle and rinse the mouth out thoroughly. After the nose is clean, take one of the good herbs such as golden seal, peppermint, hyssop, yarrow, or black cohosh, sniff it up through the nose, and then gargle, swallowing some of it. This helps to prevent the cold from developing into bronchitis, asthma, pneumonia, or maybe even tuberculosis.

Whenever there is a cold, the first precaution is to keep the nose and mouth clean. This will keep the infection from going down into the lungs and causing further trouble.

When the head is stuffed up and there is tightness in the chest, as well as an irritable, drowsy, stupid feeling, we sometimes hear people say, "My head is all stuffed up," but the fact is that they are aware of it only in their head. The whole system is involved. Anything we can do to relieve this condition in the system will help break up the cold.

Colds would not be so prevalent if the body were not filled with mucus and waste products, so one should immediately rid the body of these poisons. There is no better way to do this than to cleanse the entire colon by high enemas, continuing them until they reach the upper end of the colon and get it clean.

Keep quiet and stay in bed if possible. Take only fruit juices for nourishment. If you do not have fruit juices, drink water (hot or cold) with lemon juice, then later potassium broth, which is nourishing and alkaline. This treatment will break up the cold.

If the cough continues, an excellent help is to take one teaspoonful each of colt's foot, black cohosh, and cubeb berries, mix thoroughly and steep in a pint of boiling water. Take a glassful every hour according to age.

Occasionally there may be a feeling of severe nausea. If this is the case, take an emetic. This can be done with just lukewarm water or water with a little salt added. Drink all the water possible and run the finger down the throat to promote vomiting. This will wash the stomach out. Repeat this until the stomach is clean and then take a hot herb tea. Several cups of hot tea should be taken immediately, followed by two or three cups a few hours later. The following herbs are excellent: Sage, red sage, hyssop, yarrow, black cohosh, peppermint, and camomile. The use of one rounded teaspoonful of composition powder in a glass of water every hour for five or six hours is also excellent.

Herb list for chills Cayenne pepper, bayberry bark tea with a pinch of cayenne, myrica, peppermint, willow, peach, sage, catnip, antispasmodic tincture (lobelia).

Herb list for colds Bayberry bark with yarrow, catnip, sage, peppermint, wood betony, angelica, blue violet, butternut bark, ginseng, lungwort, nettle, white pine, pleurisy root, prickly ash, rosemary, saffron, summer savory, sweet balm, tansy, valerian, vervain, water pepper, wood sage, yarrow, bloodroot, elder, ginger, gentian, golden seal, masterwort, hyssop, pennyroyal, sarsaparilla, saw palmetto berries, spikenard, wild cherry, horehound.

Herb list for cough Blue violet, comfrey, coltsfoot, ginseng, horehound, hyssop, lungwort, myrrh, origanum, white pine, water pepper (smartweed), black cohosh, bloodroot, borage, flaxseed, marjoram, rosemary, balm of Gilead, spikenard, bethroot, red sage, tansy, wild cherry bark, mullein, golden seal, red clover blossoms, cubeb berries, skunk cabbage.

Fever

Causes A fever is usually due to an infection somewhere in the body, but many other diseases, including tumors, may cause a fever.

Treatment If there is nausea and waste matter present in the stomach, it may be necessary to take an emetic to cleanse the stomach.

Should the temperature be too high and the patient too ill for this, give a cup of golden seal and myrrh. To make a pint of this tea, steep a heaping teaspoon of golden seal and one-half teaspoon of myrrh in a pint of boiling water for 20 minutes. After taking the first cupful, take

A banana and soybean milk smoothie is ideal during convalescence.

a teaspoon every hour thereafter. More can be taken with benefit.

Cool water enemas will bring down the temperature rapidly. Have the water slightly below body temperature. If the enema contains herbs, it is even more effective. If it is used, the water should be slightly sudsy. It is the removal of the poisons from the system that brings the temperature down. Remove the clothing and then place the patient between cotton blankets. Sponge with tepid water, beginning with the face and sponging downward over the entire body. Sponge well around the head and especially around the back of the neck. Sponge the feet thoroughly, leaving the soles moist. Do this every five minutes if the fever is very high. Also give sips of cold water every five minutes. If the patient becomes chilly, stop the sponging, cover the patient well, and place hot water bottles or hot fomentations over the stomach. This will usually stop the chill. If it does not, apply a hot fomentation to the spine, or give a hot footbath and a hot drink. This should stop the chill at once.

Slippery elm tea is excellent in all cases of fever, since it is a powerful cleanser and is soothing to the stomach and intestinal tract.

Any one of the following herbs is useful in fevers. Make them into a tea and drink copiously until the fever breaks: yarrow, red sage, catnip, peppermint, wild cherry bark, valerian, black cohosh, tansy, camomile, elder, boneset, willow (bark or leaves), pleurisy root, marigold, nettle, and lobelia.

Red raspberry leaf tea is excellent for the reduction of fever in children.

Diet In all cases of fever and severely prostrating diseases, a few days of liquid diet will lessen their severity and give the stomach a much needed rest. The first point to be emphasized is to drink plenty of water, as this dilutes and carries away the toxins through the kidneys. Fruit drinks of any kind are beneficial when taken without cane sugar. The use of cane sugar will increase the fever and tend to acidify the blood. Weak lemonade, given freely, is very good. Sweeten drinks with malt honey, malt sugar, or honey, if at all. Use fresh fruits whenever possible.

When the fever subsides, special care must be taken to eat nourishing, easily digested food. The following can be used during convalescence: soybean milk, potassium broth, zwieback, baked Irish potatoes, natural brown rice, and bananas (very ripe).

Soybean milk is alkaline, very nourishing, and easy to digest. Dissolve whole wheat flakes in hot soybean milk. This is very strengthening. Well-ripened bananas made into a puree are excellent, especially for underweight patients.

The following foods are to be strictly avoided during a fever: meats of all kinds, meat broths, fish, fowl, oysters, pickles, condiments, cheese, mushrooms, and eggs. Use salt as sparingly as possible, or eliminate it entirely. This will not only allow you to taste the wonderful natural flavors in the food, but it will also help to lower your blood pressure if it is too high.

Two quarts of orange juice and an equal amount of oatmeal water is a daily ration for typhoid or any other fever. More can be taken with good results, but do not take orange juice at the same time that oatmeal water is taken: take them at least one hour apart.

Herb list for fever Catnip, sage, shepherd's purse, sumach berries, sweet balm, tansy, thyme, valerian, vervain, wahoo, wild cherry bark, willow, wintergreen, wood sage, wormwood, borage, dandelion, Peruvian bark, apple tree bark (intermittent fever), bitterroot (intermittent fever), buckbean (intermittent fever), camomile, cinchona bark, cleavers, colombo, butternut bark (all fevers), calamus (intermittent fevers), coral, elder, fenugreek, fireweed, fit root, gentian root, hyssop, masterwort, lobelia (excellent), magnolia, mandrake, nettle, parsley, pennyroyal, peppermint, pleurisy root, poplar, quassia, mugwort, cayenne, fringe tree, echinacea, angelica, yarrow (breaks up fever in 24 hours), sarsaparilla, red sage, boneset, lily of the valley, cedron (intermittent fever), black cohosh, willow (bark or leaves).

Influenza (La Grippe)

Causes Influenza is caused by three types of influenza virus—types A, B, and C. Type A causes the most severe disease. Influenza may occur worldwide involving millions of cases, or it may appear sporadically in a single community. Exposure to cold or dampness, or when the body is weakened by disease, or by following poor health habits, makes one more susceptible to the influenza virus.

It is essential to drink plenty of fluids when fighting off influenza.

Symptoms There is usually a chilly feeling, various muscular aches and pains, backache, poor appetite, ringing in the ears, dizziness, cough, sometimes a sore throat, stuffiness, and hoarseness. Headache is frequent. The fever may be more severe in the evening. Influenza starts rapidly and lasts for seven to ten days. The real danger of influenza is that if it is not checked by proper treatment, complications may set in. Pneumonia is one of the most frequent complications, and it may prove fatal unless treated vigorously. Patients who already have heart or lung disease or are pregnant are particularly prone to develop viral pneumonia with influenza. After an attack of influenza, the system should be built up with good foods.

Treatment If treatment is started when the symptoms first appear, influenza may be overcome in 24 hours.

Stop eating and go to bed. Use the following internally: one tablespoon yarrow, one teaspoon pleurisy root and a small pinch of cayenne. Steep in a pint of boiling water for 20 minutes and take a cupful every hour.

Drinking this tea will cause profuse perspiration, and when the bed clothes become wet they should be changed. If there is fever, bathe the entire body with tepid water thoroughly, one part at a time.

Alternate the herbs with fruit juices; orange and grapefruit preferably. Lemon juice is also excellent to reduce the fever. Do not use sugar in any of the juices. Orange juice is very strengthening. If you follow the treatment outlined, being sure to keep the bowels moving normally with some laxative herbs, you will find your influenza gone the next day.

If the disease progresses, take the herbs given above and also the orange juice and other fruit juices, take sweat baths and some tonic herbs such as wild cherry bark, skullcap, valerian, lady's slipper, or feverfew (*Chrysanthemum parthenium*). Plenty of fresh air in the patient's room is essential.

Dr. Zalabak gave me this formula many years ago: equal parts of cinnamon, sage, and bay leaves. Use a heaping teaspoon of this mixture to a cup of boiling water, steep, and drink as much as desired.

A very effective remedy is made by using equal parts of the following herbs: agrimony, vervain, boneset, and culver's root. Use a heaping teaspoon of this mixture to a cup of boiling water. Take a cupful every hour.

More herbs that are good for influenza are: peppermint, white pine, poplar, butternut bark, lungwort, nettle, pleurisy root, saffron, sweet balm, tansy, ginger, golden seal, saw palmetto berries, wood betony, angelica, hyssop, boneset, vervain, culver's root, agrimony, and feverfew. Use singly or in combination.

Read their description and use those best suited to your condition.

Influenza is more difficult to cure than a common cold. The symptoms may be helped, but they may not disappear with the above treatments. If so, stay in bed, drinking lots of liquids, particularly fruit juices. This disease is usually self-limited and will gradually disappear within seven to ten days, although the cough may last longer than this, sometimes for weeks or even months.

Herb list for la grippe Butternut bark, lungwort, nettle, peppermint, pleurisy root, poplar, saffron, sweet balm, tansy, ginger, golden seal, saw palmetto berries, wild cherry, wood betony, sage, angelica, hyssop.

Herb list for influenza
Peppermint, white pine, poplar, skullcap, pleurisy root.

Ripe bananas are an easy food to digest when recovering from the flu.

Measles (Rubeola)

Causes Few persons escape having measles during childhood, but adults may also catch this common disease. It is caused by a virus, and is one of the most contagious diseases.

Symptoms The symptoms appear about ten days following exposure, with fever, runny nose, cough, and sore throat. After three or four days the rash breaks out on the head or face, and after a few days it has spread over the body. Reddish white spots may be present inside the mouth before the rash appears. When the rash has developed, the fever drops.

Complications such as pneumonia and ear infections must be guarded against.

The steam from a boiling kettle can keep a room's atmosphere moist.

Treatment The patient must be kept isolated for at least five days following the appearance of the rash, and should be put to bed for as long as the fever persists or there is any sign of cough or lung infection. The eyes should be protected from bright light by darkening the room. A tea made as follows should be given: one teaspoon of pleurisy root and one-fourth teaspoon of ginger steeped in a pint of boiling water. Two tablespoons of the tea should be given every hour, more or less according to age.

In the event the patient's eyes become sore, make a solution of one-fourth teaspoon of golden seal steeped in a pint of boiling water (soft or distilled), for 30 minutes; then add enough boric acid to make a saturated solution. Strain through a cloth and bathe the eyes two or three times a day or more often.

The diet recommended for fevers is excellent after the fever has broken. Any of the following herbs are good: catnip, peppermint, camomile, vervain, yarrow, or lady's slipper. Steep a teaspoon in a cup of boiling water, covered. Give one-fourth cupful every two hours.

The air in the room should be kept moist by using a kettle of boiling water or a vaporizer.

Herb list for measles Cleavers, pleurisy root, saffron, valerian, yarrow, bistort root, red sage, raspberry leaves.

Mumps

Causes Mumps is caused by a virus. It usually occurs in children between the ages of three and 16, but is sometimes seen in adults also. When it does occur in adults, the complications can be quite serious. One attack usually affords lifetime protection.

Symptoms At first there is a slight fever and chilliness, loss of appetite, and headache. This is followed by swelling of the glands located below the ear, near the angle of the jaw. The glands on one or both sides of the face may enlarge and become very painful. The swelling begins to go down after two or three days, and it is usually gone in 10 to 14 days.

Treatment The child should be kept isolated and in bed if possible, until two or three days after the swelling has disappeared.

A light, nourishing diet should be given. Acid foods may increase the pain, and if this happens they should not be used. If there is a fever, a hot bath may be taken twice a day for about 20 minutes. If there is a high fever, sponging with tepid water will help lower the temperature. Herbal liniment (see page 28) lessens the pain of the affected part.

A poultice made of the following will give relief. Use a small handful of mullein, add one tablespoon of lobelia. Mix together, and pour enough boiling water on them to make a poultice. A little flaxseed meal or cornmeal may be mixed with these to make them stick together. Apply hot between pieces of gauze, and cover with a woolen cloth to keep the poultice warm. Nearly any form of heat will help to relieve the pain.

For internal treatment, take equal parts of ginger and skullcap and mix them together; steep a small teaspoon of this mixture in one cup of boiling water. Have the patient take a swallow of this every hour. You may sweeten it with a little honey or malt sugar.

If there is trouble with constipation, keep the bowels open with an enema of catnip tea.

Sponging with cold water can relieve the fever that comes with mumps.

Allergies

Dealing with seasonal discomfort

Hay Fever

Causes We hear all kinds of theories about the cause of hay fever, but the general belief is that it comes from the pollen of various plants, especially trees, grass, and weeds. It is most frequent in the spring and fall, but may be present all year round. I have known men to get hay fever every summer while cutting and loading hay. Ragweed and grass pollen are reported to be the most frequent causes of hay fever in the United States. This may all be true as far as I know, but it is also true that it would be a rare thing for anyone to have hay fever who had good digestive organs and whose nasal membranes were in a healthy condition. Wrong eating habits may have much to do with it.

Symptoms Hay fever usually comes on suddenly, and at about the same time every year with many people. There is a stinging, tickling or prickling sensation in the nose, with a watery discharge, sneezing, itching and watering of the eyes, and swelling of the mucous membranes in the nose and mouth. There may be coughing or difficulty breathing, with a feeling of being

Hay fever tends to arrive when the pollen count in the air rises.

smothered, much the same as in asthma. These conditions may continue until colder weather arrives.

Treatment If the offending item causing the hay fever can be discovered, it should be strictly avoided. People are frequently allergic to the hair of their pets, particularly cats or horses, and if this is true, the hay fever symptoms will continue as long as contact is made with these animals.

Warm saltwater may be used for both the throat and the nose. Dissolve one heaping teaspoonful of salt in a pint of warm water and use as a gargle. Blow the nose entirely clear of mucus, then sniff the salt water into the nose.

In addition to this, make a solution using a rounded teaspoonful of golden seal and a heaping teaspoonful of borax in a pint of boiling soft water. Shake well. Let stand an hour or two, shaking occasionally; it is then ready for use. Pour some into the hand and sniff it into the nose, one side at a time. Repeat this a number of times until the nose is entirely clean. This is very healing and soothing to the membranes and should be repeated four or five times a day.

I have had good success in treating hay fever by using ragweed and goldenrod. Use one teaspoon of each herb and also one teaspoon each of skunk cabbage and calamus root. Mix thoroughly and take a teaspoon in a

If the cause of hay fever can be identified, the solution may be to avoid it altogether.

glass of warm water an hour before each meal and upon retiring.

Another treatment is to put one tablespoon of ephedra in one pint of boiling water. Let steep one-half hour, strain through a cloth, then sniff up the nostrils, drawing it into the throat. Repeat this several times until relieved, using the same treatment three or four times a day. This treatment is also excellent for other nasal troubles.

It may be helpful to take one heaping teaspoon of powdered bayberry bark and pour over it one pint of boiling water. Steep for 20 minutes. Let settle and then sniff into the nostrils four to six times a day. This is also good when one-half glass is taken internally three or more times a day.

Herb list for hay fever Mullein, poplar, skunk cabbage, coltsfoot, black cohosh.

Glossary of Medical Properties of Herbs

Abortifacient Induces the premature expulsion (abortion) of the fetus. Same meaning as **ecbolic**. For example: pennyroyal.

Alterative Herbs that convert an unhealthy condition of an organ to a healthy one. Gradually facilitates a beneficial change in the body. For example: ginseng.

Analgesic Any substance that relieves pain.

Anaphrodisiac Herbs that decrease or allay sexual feelings or desires.

Anodyne Relieves pain and reduces nerve sensitivity.

Antacid Neutralizes the acid produced by the stomach.

Anthelmintic An agent that destroys and expels worms from the intestines. Same as **vermifuge**.

Antibilious An herb that combats biliousness, a group of symptoms consisting of nausea, abdominal discomfort, headache, constipation, and gas that is caused by an excessive secretion of bile.

Antibiotic Inhibits the growth of germs, bacteria, and harmful microbes.

Antiemetic Prevents or alleviates nausea and vomiting.

Antiepileptic An agent that combats the convulsions or seizures of epilepsy.

Antilithic Aids in preventing the formation of stones in the kidneys and bladder.

Antiperiodic Prevents the periodic recurrence of attacks of a disease; as in malaria.

Antiphlogistic An agent that counteracts inflammation.

Antipyretic An herb that reduces fever. Same as **febrifuge** or **refrigerant**.

Antirheumatic Relieves or cures rheumatism.

Antiscorbutic Effective in the prevention or treatment of scurvy.

Antiseptic Prevents decay or putrefaction. A substance that inhibits the growth and development of microorganisms without necessarily destroying them.

Antispasmodic An agent that relieves or prevents muscle spasm or cramps. For example: camomile.

Antisyphilitic Herbs that improve or cure syphilis. Also called **antiluetic**.

Antitussive Prevents or improves a cough.

Antivenomous Acts against poisonous matter from animals.

Antizymotic Destroys disease-producing organisms.

Aperient A mild laxative. Also called **aperitive**.

Aphrodisiac Restores or increases sexual power and desire.

Aromatic An herb with a pleasant, fragrant scent and a pungent taste.

Astringent Causes a local contraction of the skin, blood vessels, and other tissues, thereby arresting the discharge of blood, mucus, etc. Usually used locally as a topical application. The word topical pertains to a certain area of the skin or to a substance that affects only the area to which it is applied.

Balsam The resin of a tree that is healing and soothing. For example: myrrh.

Balsamic A healing or soothing agent.

Bitter A solution of bitter, often aromatic, plant products used as a mild tonic.

Carminative An herb that helps to prevent gas from forming in the intestines, and assists in expelling it.

Cathartic Causes evacuation of the bowels. A cathartic may be either mild (laxative) or vigorous (purgative).

Cephalic Referring to diseases affecting the head and upper part of the body.

Cholagogue An herb that stimulates the flow of bile from the liver into the intestines.

Condiment Enhances the flavor of food.

Cordial A stimulating medicine or drink.

Demulcent Soothes, protects, and relieves the irritation of inflamed mucous membranes and other surfaces.

Deobstruent Removes obstructions by opening the natural passages or pores of the body.

Depurative Tends to purify and cleanse the blood.

Detergent An agent that cleanses boils, ulcers, wounds, etc.

Diaphoretic Promotes perspiration, especially profuse perspiration. Same as **sudorific**.

Discutient An agent that dissolves or causes some thing, such as a tumor, to disappear. Also called **discussive**.

Diuretic Promotes the production and secretion of urine. For example: parsley.

Drastic A violent purgative.

Ecbolic See **abortifacient**.

Emetic Causes vomiting. For example: ipecac, lobelia.

Emmenagogue An herb that brings on menstruation. For example: camomile.

Emollient A substance that is usually used externally to soften and soothe the skin.

Esculent Edible or fit for eating.

Exanthematous Refers to any eruptive disease or fever. An herbal remedy for skin eruptions such as measles, scarlet fever, etc.

Expectorant Promotes the thinning and ejection of mucus or exudate from the lungs, bronchi, and trachea; sometimes the meaning is extended to all remedies that quiet a cough.

Farinaceous Having a mealy texture or surface.

Febrifuge Reduces body temperature and fever. Same as **antipyretic** and **refrigerant**.

Hepatic Promotes the well-being of the liver and increases bile secretion. For example: golden seal.

Herpatic A remedy for skin eruptions, ringworm, etc.

Hypnotic Tends to produce sleep.

Lithotriptic Causing the dissolution or destruction of stones in the bladder or kidneys.

Maturating An agent that promotes the maturing or bringing to a head of boils, carbuncles, etc.

Mucilaginous Herbs that have a soothing effect on inflamed mucous membranes.

Narcotic An addicting substance that reduces pain and produces sleep.

Nauseant An herb that causes nausea and vomiting. Somewhat similar to an emetic.

Nervine A substance that calms and soothes the nerves and reduces tension and anxiety.

Opthalmicum A remedy for diseases of the eye.

Parturient A substance that promotes labor.

Pectoral Relieves disorders of the chest and lungs, such as an expectorant.

Poultice Plant material that is prepared in a special way and applied to the surface of the body as a remedy for certain disorders.

Pungent Irritating or sharply painful. Producing a sharp sensation of taste or smell.

Purgative A substance that promotes the vigorous evacuation of the bowels.

Refrigerant Relieves fever and thirst. A cooling remedy. Lowers body temperature.

Relaxant Tends to relax and relieve muscular tension.

Resolvent Promotes the resolving and removing of abnormal growths, such as a tumor.

Rubefacient An agent that reddens the skin by increasing the circulation when rubbed on the surface.

Sedative Allays excitement, induces relaxation, and is conducive to sleep.

Sialagogue Promotes the flow of saliva.

Soporific Herbs that help to produce sleep.

Stimulant Herb that increases the activity or efficiency of a system or organ; acts more rapidly than a tonic.

Stomachic Herbs that give strength and tone to the stomach, stimulate digestion, and improve appetite.

Styptic Astringent: arrests hemorrhage and bleeding.

Sudorific Herbs that cause heavy perspiration.

Tincture A solution of the active principal of an herb in alcohol.

Tonic Herbs that restore and strengthen the entire system. A general tonic would be one that braces up the whole system, such as a cold bath.

Vermifuge An agent that expels intestinal worms or parasites. Same as **anthelmintic**.

Vesicant An agent that causes blistering, such as poison ivy.

Vulnerary Used in treating fresh cuts and wounds, usually used as a poultice. A healing substance.

Index

Acknowledgments

PICTURE CREDITS
The publisher would like to thank the following for their permission to reproduce the images in this book. Every effort has been made to acknowledge the images, however we apologize if there are any unintentional omissions.

Alamy/Arco Images GmbH: 94TL; Niall Benvie: 63L, 90R, 116L; Frank Blackburn: 46L, 53R, 58L, 62L, 64, 66L, 70L, 72R, 102, 107R; Daniel Borzynski: 88R; Cleuna (Medicinal Plants): 43R, 122L; Florraly: 118L; John T. Fowler: 79L; Geoffrey Kidd: 47TR, 52R, 66R, 101L, 109L, 122R; Melba Photo Agency: 101R; Kevin Schafer: 54R; TH Foto: 65R, 85L; Maximilian Weinzierl: 52L; Wildlife GmBH: 95R. **Brousseau Collection:** 100R © 1995 Saint Mary's College of California. **DK Images**/Neil Fletcher: 43L, 111; Steve Gorton : 39L, 97; Dave King: 81L. **Getty Images:** 53L, 57L, 59L, 79R. **George Hartwell:** 42R. **Louis M. Landry:** 105R. **Photolibrary**/Michael Davis: 78L. **Alex Popovkin:** 115R. **David Tharp:** 64R.